Russian Plays for Young Audiences

Five Contemporary
Selections

Translated and
edited with
an introduction
by Miriam Morton

Foreword by
Natalya Sats

New Plays Books, Rowayton, Connecticut

The translations of all the plays in this collection are fully-protected under international copyright laws, and New Plays for Children is the exclusive, authorized agency to handle all rights in the United States, Canada, Great Britain, and all other English-speaking countries.

Performances of all of the plays are subject to a royalty. All rights, including professional and amateur production, motion pictures, recitation, radio and television broadcasting, reprinting of scripts, and the rights of translation into other languages, are strictly reserved. Arrangements for production must be made in writing with:

> **New Plays Incorporated**
> **Box 273**
> **Rowayton, CT. 06853**

CONTENTS

Introduction   i

THE TWO MAPLES   by Evgeny Shwartz   1

THE CITY WITHOUT LOVE   by Lev Ustinov   65

HEY, THERE—HELLO!   by Gennadi Mamlin   125

THE YOUNG GRADUATES   by Victor Rozov   203

THE YOUNG GUARD   by Anatoly Aleksin   315

Afterword:
A Note to the Director by Pavel Khomsky   398
The play's director for the Central Moscow Children's Theatre.

FOREWORD

The publication in English translation of a collection of Soviet plays for young audiences is indeed a welcome event for us and for the world of children's theatre. I heartily congratulate Miriam Morton, who selected and translated these works, for her diligent efforts in making the philosophy and objectives, the history and scope of the Soviet stage for children and youth—and now some of our outstanding plays—known in the United States and in other English-speaking countries. And I share with the playwrights the deep gratification of having their works introduced where they have been hitherto inaccessible because of the language barrier.

Evgeny Shwartz, Lev Ustinov, Gennadi Mamlin, Victor Rozov, and Anatoly Aleksin, whose plays are included in this volume, are five of our prized dramatists. Their plays have been enjoyed by millions of young Soviet theatregoers and by many thousands of young people in other lands. May they give equal pleasure to young audiences whose language is English.

Those of us who labor in children's theatre are guided and inspired by the conviction that educating young hearts to feel is our most important and honorable task. Like blooming gardens, the theatres for the young have become part of the lives of Soviet school children, and more and more such gardens are being planted all over the world. But gardens need gardeners who love and respect nature, who know clearly how and why they cultivate them, who know the right time for tying a broken branch, when to throw another handful of fresh seeds into the soil. Those who come to work in theatres for the young cannot afford to forget for a moment that they are a special breed of gardeners, helping to raise a most precious crop—the children who will shape our future.

Contemporary times render compelling many new themes for the stage—themes vital to proper emotional and intellectual growth of children of all ages, and particularly of adolescents and youth. But the tendency to want to "mature" the theatre for young audiences, to have it increasingly approximate adult theatre because today's children are more informed, more skeptical, and generally more aware, is a grievously mistaken one. For nothing is more vital to the well-being of children than the preservation of their childhood, the gradual and timely maturing of their psyches.

Praiseworthy is the effort to have the theatre meet the special needs of today's adolescent and youth, but this effort must remain intelligent and wise; it must not seek superficial solutions to the problem.

Plays like the five offered in this volume splendidly succeed in addressing contemporary young theatregoers with all the power and sorcery of the stage. What meaningful thoughts, what deep feelings they arouse in the impressionable young spectator! And how the humor and satire delight him!

Those of us whose professional lives are centered in theatre for the young reap great rewards when we do our work responsibly. What good fortune it is to be able to make a contribution to a fine art which is so effective in molding young boys and girls into genuine human beings.

Natalya Sats

First Artistic Director of the Central Children's Theatre of Moscow

President of the U.S.S.R. Center of ASSITEJ

Honored Artist of the U.S.S.R.

INTRODUCTION

The five plays for young people this sampling offers are inevitably only partially representative. The dramatic literature in the Russian language for the Soviet youth theatre—there is also a developing literature in the languages of other Soviet republics—is exceptionally extensive, reflecting an exceptional variety of genres and themes. The four to five hundred plays staged every year for young theatregoers include traditional and modern fairy tales, contemporary psychological melodramas and comedies, revolutionary and other historical dramas, musicals, Russian and foreign classics, ethnic epics and modern plays, dramatizations of poetry and biography.

Nevertheless this modest collection is a valuable beginning, inasmuch as it is a pioneering effort to bring to the young English-speaking theatregoer, and the theatre practitioner and reader, at least five notable works. These were written by five leading contemporary Russian playwrights, and each is of a different genre. Every one of the plays has been a great favorite with young audiences in the U.S.S.R., and each is currently in the repertories of numerous theatres for young spectators throughout the country. The plays reflect the wide age-range (from seven to eighteen) and the main qualities and currents of the world's leading professional children's theatre.

The history of the founding, development, philosophy and goals of the Soviet theatre for young audiences, which can be outlined here in only the briefest form, speaks for its seriousness of purpose and outstanding artistic and educational achievements. The establishment of children's theatres by the Soviet state, in Moscow and Leningrad, in the early post-revolutionary years (1918-23) has had an importance beyond the borders of the Soviet Union.

It marked the beginning of a new chapter in the history of theatrical culture, for these were the very first professional children's theatres in the world.

Dynamic individuals, mostly intellectuals, exhilarated by the new opportunities to bring the joys and wisdom of the stage to the masses of deprived Russian children, were the pioneers in this movement. The names of Natalya Sats, who started the first children's theatre in Moscow in 1918, and of Alexander Briantsev, who similarly pioneered in Petrograd (Leningrad), deservedly occupy first places in the Hall of Fame of Russian children's theatre history. Despite the post-Revolutionary chaos brought on by the civil war, foreign intervention, famine, and total economic disruption, the new Soviet government continuously allocated funds—though meager at first—and personnel for children's theatres.

Although playwrights, actors, and directors in the new children's theatres had no tradition to follow, no current examples outside of Russia to study and emulate, they had the tradition of high professionalism, high standards, and almost messianic dedication of the Russian adult theatre to follow.

From the time when the first adult drama was staged in Russia in 1747, and from the year when the first adult theatre was opened in St. Petersburg in 1756, to this day, when there are several hundred repertory theatres in the Soviet Union, the Russian public has avidly supported its theatre.

i

The founders of the children's theatre benefited from this ardor. They also gained from the teachings of several brilliantly creative mentors, foremost among them Stanislavsky. From 1898 to 1938—a period of forty years—Stanislavsky developed a meticulous naturalism in Russian stage technique and virtually sanctified the call of the actor. Early on, he spoke often about the need for a separate children's theatre, as leaders in public education also clamored for one. He said unequivocally, with the mesmerism of an oracle, that children's theatre had to be even better than that for adults, for the young are the future adult spectators and must be educated to become exacting audiences if the Russian theatre is to continue to flourish. This pronouncement by the great Stanislavsky has remained the guiding principle for the leaders of the professional children's theatre.

In the relatively short period between 1918 and 1940 a total of seventy-one state professional children's theatres (as distinct from the one hundred and twenty puppet theatres) opened their doors to Soviet children and adolescents from seven to eighteen years of age. These troupes gradually acquired their own buildings, their own permanent creative personnel. The major ones also had their own actors' training schools, libraries and museums. These were repertory theatres. The word "repertory" as it describes the Russian situation is only an approximate equivalent of the way it is used in America. The Soviet repertory theatre is more complex and tightly knit. The term infers greater permanance, longer-term directorial leadership, a longer list of diversified productions, a more lasting following. And, most importantly, there is constant, generous financial support from the government.

By 1940, before the war with the Nazis began, the seventy-one theatres drew a young audience of five million yearly. The Germans destroyed all but twenty of these theatres. Since the end of the war, twenty-one of them have been rebuilt and several more erected in cities that never before had a children's theatre. The now existing forty-nine TIUZ's (Theatres for Young Spectators) are located in almost as many different cities over the breadth and length of the country.

Since the pace of establishing additional theatres for the young has not kept up with the audience growth, adult companies are required by law to include children's productions in their repertories or lose their government subsidies. The attendance of five million young theatregoers in 1940 increased to twenty-three million by 1974.

As for the growth of children's theatre literature, in the period between 1920 and 1970 four children's theatres alone (two in Moscow, one in Leningrad, and one in Saratov) staged four hundred and twelve plays by Russian authors. Another one hundred or so works by non-Russian Soviet authors were staged in the various national republics by their local youth theatres in their own languages.

In exploring Soviet writings on theatre for young spectators, one inevitably comes upon the following quotation of Mark Twain, whom Soviet intellectuals, and readers generally, greatly admire:

Theatre is the only teacher of morality, conduct, ideals which never bores the schoolchild—on the contrary, he always regrets that the lesson comes to an end so soon. . . .

The Russian pioneers in children's theatre were in total agreement with the American author. But they saw still other lofty goals that the stage could aspire to for its young audiences: it could not only "shape souls" but also cultivate a sense of the beautiful in the natural world, in human relationships, in the achievements of mankind.

In the context of these objectives, special emphasis is given to the children's stage as a school for the emotions. Nikolai Putintsev, who has been for thirty years the man in charge of choosing plays for the Central Children's Theatre of Moscow, reminds us that the French philosopher of the Enlightenment, Diderot, once despairingly exclaimed, "But where, oh where, is there a school of feelings?" And, as though calming the lamenting Diderot, he joyfully contends that the professional Soviet theatre for young audiences has been just such a school.

It is held that to teach the young to feel will help them to be good friends and good citizens, in the deepest and broadest sense of those words; it will lead them to adopt values which will help them in self-esteem; it will stimulate them to want to make the most of their capabilities and to make some positive contribution to their society and even to the world. Consequently, the theatre is regarded as a shaper of souls, by reason of its special power to educate the mind and the heart. And it is a foregone conclusion that only a theatre of high aesthetic standards can achieve these objectives.

The professional theatres for young spectators serve three distinct groups: seven to ten, eleven to fourteen, and older teenagers, fifteen to eighteen. The youngest groups attend performances on weekend and holiday mornings; the middle groups on weekday and weekend afternoons; the oldest groups from seven to nine in the evenings. The productions are classified for the different groups on the basis of the play's content and length, the nature of the incidental music, the style of acting, the stagecraft. The aim is to assure the maximum enjoyment and responsiveness, which, in turn, depend on the child's physical, mental and psychological readiness to benefit from the play's intellectual and aesthetic elements.

At times the theatre gives preference to plays dealing with historical periods currently being studied in the schools, but far more often than not the selection is determined by the artistic preference of the theatre's directorial staff. Some theatres prefer the psychological play, others the play with up-to-the-minute youth problems, still others plays which lend themselves to stylized staging, such as the living newspaper type of presentation.

Russian stage plays by playwrights such as Chekhov, Gogol, Ostrovsky, and Gorky are a very important part of the repertory for adolescents.

Plays in the present sampling:

The Two Maples, *(Dva klyona)* for children from about seven to ten years of age, is a fairy-tale play by Evgeny Shwartz. He is a dramatist of distinguished talent, whose plays have for many years now enjoyed recognition in his own country and abroad, both on the children's stage and in theatres for adults. A master of the dramatic fairy tale, Shwartz ingeniously shapes characters and situations with just enough realistic touches to bring them closer to the experiences of the modern child.

Among his several noted fairy-tale adaptations, *The Two Maples,* is the only one with distinctly Russian folk and legendary characters. It abounds in lovely satirical comment on meanness, greed, deviousness, and smug ignorance. It is affecting in its celebration of love, kindness, courage, skill at work, and resourcefulness. The play speaks to the young theatregoer with wit, humor, and poetic eloquence about the eternal contest between good and evil.

The City Without Love, *(Gorod bez liubvi)* is an allegorical play suitable both for young and older children. Lev Ustinov, the playwright, has been tremendously imaginative and successful with allegorical fantasy. Here he posits a city where the sentiment of love in all its forms is forbidden by law, and violators are subject to severest punishment. This seemingly far-fetched hypothesis is not irrelevant for our times, in which values are in such disarray and violence is so ubiquitous. It is dramatized with inspired imagination and clarity, in terms and situations well within the emotional and mental reach of the child. The younger child will enjoy the plot and characterizations. The older one will find ideas that are disturbing, exciting, and thought-provoking.

Lev Ustinov's parable plays have had successful runs in numerous Soviet cities as well as in Stockholm, Vienna, Halle, Munich, and other western European cities, and in Tokyo. *The City Without Love,* for instance, was recently given eighty-one performances in Stockholm.

Hey There—Hello! *(Hey, ty-zdrastvuy!)* is a comedy with serious overtones for playgoers in their early teens. First produced by the Moscow Theatre for Young Spectators (TIUZ) in 1969, it was staged by one of its most gifted directors, Pavel Khomsky. It has since played in close to a hundred theatres in the U.S.S.R. Although the play has only two characters, a boy and a girl of fourteen, the conflict of attitudes and personalities, played against the love-hate charade typical of young teenagers, builds an exciting, diverting, yet thought-provoking theatrical experience for their peers in the audience. Four mimes act out the boy's memories of dramatic events and his Walter Mitty type of fantasies. With brisk pace, with a skillful and forthright mingling of humor and pathos, with deep dramatic overtones relieved by hilarious turns of dialogue, the playwright deftly shapes his two young characters out of the resistant clay of the adolescent psyche. In the meantime he gives significant insights into value conflicts that today beset Soviet people—conflicts which young theatregoers in American can easily identify within themselves.

iv

The Young Graduates, *(V dobryi chas!)* is by Victor Rozov, a noted contemporary playwright for both youth and adult theatres, whose works have been published and produced abroad as well. (He also wrote the screenplay for the classic film, *The Cranes are Flying*). His seven plays for and about teenagers, of which this is one, have had a profound effect on the development of Soviet dramaturgy for this age group. He has brought to the stage plays of greater candor, dealing with questions that particularly trouble contemporary youth. Rozov is a staunch partisan of the teenager. In his plays, he passionately defends the young person's rights to assert his individuality, to follow his own bent in choosing his life's work, to voice his disapproval of shoddy behavior on the part of parents and other adults, to criticize his society's shortcomings, to fall "prematurely" in love. At the same time Rozov stands guard, indefatigably, over those life values by which the individual and society survive spiritually and move forward. He exposes petty or gross hypocrisies and self-seeking with bitter irony. *The Young Graduates* deals with such matters at a time in the lives of its young characters when they are expected, whether ready or not, to choose their future professions, while the pressures of parents and societal norms bear down heavily upon them.

The Young Guard, *(Molodaya gvardia),* for teenage audiences, is based on the documentary novel of the same title by Alexander Fadeev. Anatoly Aleksin, a major author of stories, novels, and plays for young people, adapted it for the stage. It memorializes a tragic event in which a large number of young partisans —boys and girls of sixteen and seventeen—were put to death by the Gestapo during the Nazi occupation of their coal-mining town in the Donets Basin. The executions took place only days before the Soviet victory at Stalingrad and the liberation of the occupied town.

In addition to its tensely dramatic action scenes, *The Young Guard* provides an uncommonly absorbing battle-of-ideas between a clever Gestapo general and the young prisoners he interrogates. The action and the interrogation, in counterpoint, build to a powerful climax, intensified by the seven lyric poems written for the play by the celebrated young contemporary poet, Robert Rozhdestvensky and set to music by Oscar Feltzman, a greatly admired composer for the youth theatre.

Dramatist, composer, lyricist, and the play's director, Pavel Khomsky (who provides an afterword giving the background of the events which the play documents, and advice to directors) have all earned high honors for their work as artists. The Central Children's Theatre of Moscow, where the play was first produced, received the highest national award, the Lenin Prize, on the occasion of its 50th anniversary.

The translator and editor of the present sampling has attended performances of all the five plays in the U.S.S.R. Some she saw more than once. She fully shared with the young Soviet audiences the pleasure, the excitement, and the enchantment of their theatre as a mirror of human imagination and experience. In selecting and translating these plays, the hope was ever present that American and other English-speaking young theatregoers, reading or seeing them, would be similarly delighted and moved.

Meeting and speaking with four of the five playwrights here represented (Evgeny Shwartz, unfortunately died in 1968) convinced the editor-translator that the youth theatre in the Soviet Union is in excellent hands. The four writers are utterly devoted to their craft and to the young people to whom they are addressing their works. These talented men are inspired by their deep faith in the power of the word and the stage to help boys and girls understand themselves, the world around them, and to want to improve both. At the same time, the playwrights are fully aware that young people in the theatre need diversion and laughter as well as to think and to feel. . .as this sampling shows.

Miriam Morton

THE TWO MAPLES

A Fairy-Tale Play in Three Acts

By Evgeny Shwartz (Eugene Schwartz)

Translated from the Russian
by Miriam Morton

CHARACTERS:

Vasilisa-the-Hardworker

Fedya (or Feden'ka), her oldest son

Egorushka, her second son

Ivanushka, her youngest son

Baba-Yaga

The Bear

The Cat

Sharik, the Dog

Mice

Pronunciation of the names:

Vasilísa	Both *a*'s are pronounced as in Mama, both *i*'s as in n*ea*t. The accent is on the 2nd i.
Fédya	The *e* is pronounced as the *a* in f*a*te; the *ya* as *ia* with the *a* as in Mama. The accent is on the *e*. In Feden'ka the *n* is pronounced as in *n*ew.
Egórushka	The *e* is pronounced as *ye* in yes; the *o* as in d*o*g, the u as *oo* in b*oo*k, the *a* as in Mama. The accent is on the *o*.
Ivanushka	The *I* is pronounced as in n*ea*t, the *a* as in Mama, the *u* as *oo* in b*oo*k, the *a* as in Mama. The accent is on the first *a*.
Bába-Yagá	All the *a*'s as in Mama. The first *a* in Baba and the last *a* in Yaga as accented.
Shárik	The *a* is pronounced as in Mama, the *i* as in n*ea*t. The accent is on the *a*.

ACT I

Two young maple trees stand side by side in a birch forest clearing. It is a bright, sunny day. A soft breeze makes one of the maples stir, as though waking from slumber. The crown of this tree sways slightly toward the other. There is a rustling, a whispering, and the maple speaks in a human voice.

THE FIRST MAPLE

Brother Fedya! There's a nice breeze! Wake up!

THE SECOND MAPLE

Sh-h-h . . . don't talk, Egorushka, I'm dreaming. I'm seeing Mother in my dream.

EGORUSHKA

Lucky you! Ask her if she's looking for us.

FEDYA

She says she is.

EGORUSHKA

Ask her if she's forgiven us for running away.

FEDYA

She says, yes.

EGORUSHKA

Now ask her if she knows that Baba-Yaga turned us into maples.

FEDYA

She says, "You know, all kinds of things can happen in life."

EGORUSHKA

Ask her if she knows how much longer we'll have to stay in this awful prison.

FEDYA

Mama! Mama! Will we stay prisoners here much longer? Mama! Oh, she's gone! Shucks, I'm awake! Hello, Egorushka.
He whimpers.

EGORUSHKA

Don't cry, Feden'ka—after all, you're not a baby any more.

FEDYA

I'm not crying. It's the dew. It dropped into my eyes.

EGORUSHKA

How can you cry on a day like this! Every blade of grass is happy, every twig! Try to be happy, too.

FEDYA

I'm happy. I keep hoping that any minute now Mother will come, and we'll hear her call to us: "Fe-den'-ka! E-go-rush-ka!"

VOICE

Fe-den'-ka! E-go-rush-ka!

EGORUSHKA

Is that an echo?

FEDYA

How can you ask such a question? Have you forgotten how tricky Baba-Yaga is? No one can hear us—not people, nor birds or beasts, nor wind or water, nor the other trees. Not even the echo can hear us.

VOICE

E-go-rush-ka! Fe-den'-ka!

FEDYA

Sh-h-h. . .don't answer. It's Baba-Yaga taunting us—trying to make us cry. She can imitate any voice, even Mother's.

VOICE

(*Quite near now, calling out desperately*)
Egorushka, my son! Feden'ka, my boy! It's your mother! All over the world she's been looking for you, and can't find you!

FEDYA

It is Mother! Baba-Yaga is very smart, but even she can't imitate a tender voice like Mother's. Mama! Mama! Here we are! Look, we're waving our branches!

EGORUSHKA

We're rustling our leaves.

FEDYA

Mama! Mama!

EGORUSHKA

She's going away!

FEDYA

No, she's standing still, looking about. She won't go away and leave us!

EGORUSHKA

Look, she's turned around. She's hurrying over to us.

Vasilisa, a sturdy-looking woman, about forty, appears in the clearing. She is carrying a full sack on her back, and a sword is stuck in her belt. She's known in her native region as "Vasilisa-the-Hardworker."

FEDYA

Mama! How unhappy you look!

EGORUSHKA

Your hair's gotten gray.

FEDYA

But her eyes are as gentle as ever.

EGORUSHKA

She's wearing Father's sword.

VASILISA

Oh, dear children, where can you be? For two years now I've been wandering, without rest, searching for you. But somehow I feel so much like stopping and resting here, as though I've already found you.

FEDYA

Here we are!

EGORUSHKA

Mama! Don't go away!

VASILISA

The maples are making such a sweet and soothing sound. I think I'll just rest here a while.

She lowers her sack, sits down on a rock.

Who is that in the forest, wearing fur in midsummer? What creature are you? Speak! Hey there, good soul! Come over here.

The Bear runs into the clearing with a roar.

BEAR

Who summons this Fierce Beast?! Wait, I'll show him how dangerous I can be. What trouble I can cause! It will set the sky on fire!

BEAR (Cont.)

He sees Vasilisa and is so startled that he stands stock still as if turned to stone.

Oh, you poor woman! What brought you here? My life is bearable only because no one ever wanders into this accursed place, so that I haven't had to hurt anyone, or take a bite out of him. I don't like to do that sort of thing, for I have a heart of gold!

VASILISA

All right, if you are so kind, then don't touch me.

BEAR

Impossible! Baba-Yaga hired me as her watchman.

VASILISA

How did such a terrible fate befall you?

BEAR

To make the story short and simple: The dog and the cat lived like friends at my former master's. With the years they got old. That's life, you know. It happens to everyone. But my master got rid of them, drove them away. I saw those homeless oldsters begging for their food and being given mighty little. What could I do? I couldn't stand to see them starve, and my rations weren't enough to feed the three of us. So I "borrowed" a bushel of grain from Baba-Yaga. She caught me, and for this she made me her slave for a year, chained me, and ordered me to be her watchman.

VASILISA

Then where is your chain?

BEAR

I keep breaking it. I am incredibly strong.

VASILISA

Must you serve her much longer?

BEAR

It's been nearly three years now, not one, but she won't let me go. When we start figuring the time I've already served her, she mixes me up and forces me to go on with my servitude. What rotten luck!

VASILISA

Poor Mishka!

BEAR

Don't pity me, my good woman. Feel sorry for yourself, oh, you unlucky one!

He cries.

Your life isn't worth a penny now! I won't harm you, but that Baba-Yaga will surely ruin you!

VASILISA

Don't cry, Mishka! Here, have a treat—here is some honey.

BEAR

Don't trouble yourself. Nothing calms me when I get this miserable. On second thought—what kind of honey is it?

VASILISA

Taking a pot of honey from her bag

There, see for yourself.

BEAR

Smelling the honey

Lime-blossom honey! All right, let me have some. Maybe it will lighten my grief. Come, let me have all of it, since poor you will soon perish anyway.

VASILISA

No, you can't have it all. I brought it for my boys.

BEAR

Boys? What boys? Where are they?

VASILISA

I've lost them, Mishka.

BEAR

What a misfortune! How? Why? When did it happen?

VASILISA

Here, eat and listen while I tell you the whole story, from beginning to end. My husband was a warrior—Danila-the-Warrior they called him. Have you heard of the Snake Dragon?

BEAR

Who hasn't? He kidnapped my Grandfather in a trice, and set him on fire—just for fun.

VASILISA

Well, my strong and brave Danila killed this Snake-Dragon, but, alas, he himself perished in the battle. The four of us continued to live together—I and my three sons—Feden'ka, Egorushka, and Ivanushka. When Feden'ka reached the age of thirteen, he came to me and said, "Mama, I'm a Valiant Knight now!" I said to him: "Come to your senses, son! What kind of a Knight would you make? You have no strength, no skill, and mighty little learning. When you come to a crossroads, how will you read what it says? A Valiant Knight must be able to read what's written on a milestone as he passes it at a full gallop. How else will he know which road to take? Wait. At the right time, I'll let you go." Feden'ka said nothing. That very night he ran away.

BEAR

Oh! Where to?

VASILISA

To give battle to Villains! To defend their victims!

BEAR

That's good, isn't it?

VASILISA

Couldn't be nobler. Only next morning a stranger brought me Feden'ka's sword. The boy didn't notice that his sword strap had torn. Three days later this "Knight's" steed came home, without his rider. His master didn't take care of him—didn't curry him, clean him, or feed him.

FEDYA

Mother, I thought of only one thing—whom I could fight.
They can't hear him.

VASILISA

My Feden'ka never returned.

BEAR

Oh!!

VASILISA

Three years passed. Egorushka was now thirteen. A bull attacked him one day. Egorushka grabbed him by the nose and chained him up. He comes to me, tells me all about it, and says *he* is a Valiant Knight now. That night he, too, ran away. Forty days later his horse returned. But the saddle was empty. The horse looked at me, whinnied mournfully, and fell to the ground, dead.

EGORUSHKA

It was because he had seen what had happened to me.
They can't hear him.

VASILISA

What was I to do? I left the farm in Ivanushka's care, though he was
only ten at the time, and went in search of the other two boys.

BEAR

Have you been looking for your cubs for a long time now?

VASILISA

Nearly three years.

BEAR

Too bad! Too bad! When you find them, they'll be so grown that
you won't recognize them.

VASILISA

I'll recognize them all right. A person who runs away from home
without good reason doesn't get wiser and therefore doesn't grow
older. They are still only thirteen.

FEDYA

That's true, Mother.

EGORUSHKA

Feden'ka and I are now the same age.

VASILISA

My search has brought me to this brooding forest. Mishka, maybe
you know where my children are?

BEAR

Don't ask me—or I'll throw myself to the ground and die of grief, like
that horse. I feel so sorry for you and so useless because I can't be of any help.

VASILISA

Then I'll have to question Baba-Yaga. Take me to her.

BEAR

You mean to her house? It's a hut on chicken legs—here today, there
tomorrow. That's the way with hens, you know. All they ever do is run
about, pecking at the ground.

VASILISA

Come, let's find that hut. Is it there that my boys are hidden?

BEAR

We needn't bother looking for that hut. It will come by itself if we call to it. Chick-chick-chick. . .

There's a noise, a crackling in the brush, and a small hut comes out of the woods. At each corner are two chicken legs. Vasilisa approaches the hut.

VASILISA

She lives boldly—that Baba-Yaga. She has no lock on her door.

BEAR

She depends on the chicken legs for protection. They strike out at strangers.

VASILISA

Are they mean?

She comes closer to the hut.

What if I talked to them kindly, and stroked them?

BEAR

Try it. Who knows? They've never been shown affection before. . .

VASILISA

Chicks, my darling chicks, how you adorn the barnyard, what pleasure you are to the farmwife! Listen to the song I just made up about you.

She sings.

> My lovely little chicks,
> May I stroke your speckled feathers,
> Admire your busy little ways,
> Sing a song in honest praise
> Of your pretty round eyes,
> Strong wings and perky tails,
> Your soft little walk,
> Your tuneful little talk?

As she sings, the chicken legs shift from one foot to another, then they start to dance. Vasilisa comes closer to them. They stand peacefully.

That's better!

The door springs open. Baba-Yaga appears behind the doorway.

BEAR

Baba-Yaga!. . .how did you get here, you evil one?

BABA-YAGA

Silence! or I'll swallow you! A tamed bear is supposed to be glad to see his mistress, and you call me ugly names!

BABA-YAGA (Cont.)

She jumps to the ground and orders the hut away.

Go on, move away from here!

The hut walks away.

Hello, Vasilisa-the-Hardworker. I've been waiting for you a long time!

VASILISA

Waiting?. . .for *me?*

BABA-YAGA

Yes. For very long. I do have great skill in finally catching you miserable mortals. I, Baba-Yaga, am about the cleverest thing in the world, smart as a whip, and cute as a button, too, and as swift as a swallow—in short, I am a sweetheart, and altogether a dear little old lady!

VASILISA

You certainly are in love with yourself.

BABA-YAGA

Oh, it's more than love. I simply dote on myself. And that's what gives me power. You, little mortals, love one another, whereas I love only myself. You have thousands of cares about your friends, your kin, but I worry only about little me. That's how I come out on top.

She admires herself in her hand-mirror.

My treasure! What would you like, my spry little oldster—a bit of tea? some water? I think from the marsh—it has a special smell. Vasilisa, run to the marsh and bring me a little pail of water.

VASILISA

I'm not your servant.

BABA-YAGA

You'll serve me yet. I'm very cunning about setting traps for you helpless mortals. I snare one of you poor creatures and soon others are caught in the same trap. A brother comes to free his brother, a mother her sons. . .Say, Vasilisa, they tell me you are a master of all trades.

VASILISA

While raising three sons, I had to learn how to do many things.

BABA-YAGA

That's just the kind of servant I need. If you want to save your boys, become my servant. Work for me until I have reason to praise you. When I *praise you,* take your youngsters and go wherever you please.

BEAR

Don't agree to this! You'll never hear a good word from her. She praises no one but herself.

BABA-YAGA

You be quiet! You don't understand me.

BEAR

I understand you only too well.

BABA-YAGA

Wrong! Only those understand me who are enchanted with me. Well, what do you say, Vasilisa? Do you agree? Do what I tell you. Try your best, and if I praise your work one single time. . .ha! ha!. . .then your sons will be free again.

(aside)

That's a clever trick I thought of!

VASILISA

Work has saved me from all kinds of troubles. I'll try it. And you will praise me! You won't be able to help yourself. But first show me my sons. Are they really here? You're not deceiving me?

BABA-YAGA

No, I'll not show them to you. They're too well hidden. But I'll let you hear their voices. It is my wish that you speak to your mother.
She takes a deep breath and blows mightily toward the maples.
Boys, speak up!
The maples rustle their leaves but Vasilisa doesn't notice it.

FEDYA

Mama! Mama! Don't leave us!

EGORUSHKA

Mama! We are big boys, but we feel awful—we feel frightened.

VASILISA

Feden'ka! Egorushka! Where are you?

BABA-YAGA

Silence! Don't answer! You've had a chat now, and that'll do.
She stops blowing out her breath. The maples fall silent.
Well, have you made up your mind? Are you staying?

VASILISA

I'm staying.

BABA-YAGA

That's just what I need. Goodbye, servant. I have no time to stay around and gossip with the likes of you. I'm awaited in a thousand places. To rob this one, beat up that one, punish another for no reason at all. Everyone is waiting for me. So long. . .

VASILISA

Goodbye, Baba-Yaga.

Baba-Yaga disappears with a clatter and a swish, flying up and across the stage between the trees, and immediately reappears as if from underground.

BABA-YAGA

While I'm gone, clean the hut so that it glistens.

VASILISA

Don't worry, I'll clean it well.

BABA-YAGA

Goodbye, Vasilisa.

With a clatter and a swish, she disappears, but instantly reappears.

I haven't given you enough work to do. I don't want to spoil you. In the last 300 years I've buried 300 treasures in 300 places. But I no longer remember where. You are to find every one of them, count them, but see that not a penny is missing. Goodbye. . .

VASILISA

Goodbye, Baba-Yaga.

Baba-Yaga disappears and reappears in the same way as above.

BABA-YAGA

I think I've still given you too little work. You'll get lazy that way. I stored 300 bushels of rye and 300 bushels of corn in my granary. The mice gnawed at the bags—the rye and the corn got mixed together. You are to separate them and grind them into flour. When this little dove returns, she will be wealthy with gold and rich with grain. Then I will praise you. So long.

VASILISA

Goodbye. When will you be back?

BABA-YAGA

Tomorrow, by sunset. Ha-ha-ha!

BEAR

How can she finish all that work so soon? You have no heart, Baba-Yaga!

BABA-YAGA

Right you are, Mishka. I don't have one, and never had. Ha-ha-ha!
*With a shout and a swish, with fire and smoke, she disappears over
the trees.*

BEAR

Off she flies. Look, the tops of the trees are bent over. What are we
to do now? Let's have a good cry.

VASILISA

That cat and dog you've befriended will help us. Let's go talk to them.

BEAR

We don't have to go to them, they'll come here willingly.
He calls to them.
Sharik, Sharik!—here, Sharik! Hurry, Sharik! There's work to be
done. . .And you, Mrs. Cat, please be good enough to come here. You
have to talk politely to a cat, or it will get stubborn. This one doesn't
even know what "psst" means.

VASILISA

How formal she must be.

BEAR

Sharik, where are you?! Mrs. Cat, please come.
*Sharik comes running. He's a middle-aged dog, large and still strong.
He now races around the clearing in circles.*

SHARIK

Who's making that noise behind the bush? Don't you dare make that
noise around here! Hey, you titmouse, don't you dare stare that way at
Master Bear! He's my boss! And who's that behind the stump? Don't
you dare crawl into our glade!

BEAR

Come over here, Sharik. We have work to do.

SHARIK

I can't, Master Bear. At least I have to make a show of being a watchdog.
That's required of me, you know.
He barks indifferently.
I guess that will do for today. Hello, Master! How handsome you are. . .
I can hardly take my eyes off you. How gracefully you carry yourself—
I can't admire you enough. . .Gr-r-r! And who is she? Gr-r-r!

BEAR

A good woman, Vasilisa-the-Hardworker.

SHARIK

Gr-r-r-r! Forgive me, good woman, for growling. But I must do it—it's required of me. Gr-r-r-r! All right, that'll do for now. Hello, Vasilisa-the-Hardworker!

VASILISA

Hello, Sharik.

BEAR

You are to do whatever Vasilisa tells you.

SHARIK

I'll obey her, Master.

VASILISA

Baba-Yaga buried 300 treasures in 300 different places. If I find them, she'll free my two sons. Sharik, will you help?—you have a stronger sense of smell then we people.

SHARIK

That's very nice to know! In that case, I'll take my nose for a walk through the forest.
He barks cheerfully.

VASILISA

No, let's wait. We'll make the search at night. Until then, you'd better stay here and guard the place. Give me a warning when Baba-Yaga approaches—very likely to interfere with my work.

SHARIK

That's nice too—I don't mind doing guard duty.

VASILISA

And where is the cat?

VOICE

I've been standing here, at the maple tree, for a long time.

VASILISA

Why don't you join us?

VOICE

A proper cat looks around three times before entering.
A large, fluffy cat comes out slowly from behind the bushes.

VOICE (Cont.)

A shortish boy, about thirteen, comes into the glade. He continues to sing.

> I'm Ivanushka
> Velikanushka *(diminutive for giant)*.
> I go on my way
> Doing no wrong all day.
> I don't brawl or bother,
> I'm looking for my mother.
> I'm Ivan-the-Giant!
> Ivan the Great-Great-Giant!

EGORUSHKA

In a half whisper

Ivanushka, run from here, or you'll be turned into a tree!

FEDYA

Half whisper

He can't hear you. Even if he could, he wouldn't understand what you are warning him about.

IVANUSHKA

Who's there, in the bushes? Come on out!

SHARIK

From the bushes

Gr-r-r-r. . .

IVANUSHKA

Delighted

A dog! What luck! Come here, puppy! What's your name!

SHARIK

Softer

Gr-r-r—Sharik.

IVANUSHKA

Come out of there. Don't be afraid. I'm so glad to see you—you won't believe it. I've been wandering through the forest a whole month now and haven't met anyone but wolves. And with wolves you can't have a good talk. When they see you, they slink off.

CAT

In the winter they'd surely "talk" to you. . .

CAT

Some guardian you are! You were about to leave everything and go with them.

SHARIK

But I didn't. Did I? I stayed. Oh, let's stop arguing. Don't be so cross with me. I hate it when my friends are cross with me. Let's shake paws.

CAT

Don't come so near, my dear. You reek of dog.

SHARIK

That's because it's going to rain.

CAT

Rain has nothing whatever to do with it. You should lick yourself clean once in a while.

SHARIK

We dogs don't have that odd habit—to wash ourselves with our tongues a hundred times a day. I. . .

CAT

Sh. . .someone is coming.

SHARIK

From which direction?

CAT

From the forest.

SHARIK

(Sniffing the air)
It's a human. And he is furious.

CAT

He's shouting and stamping his feet.

SHARIK

I'll have to bite him.

CAT

First, let's see what kind of monster it is. Come, let's hide in the bushes. *They hide. A voice sings out merrily with all its might.*

VOICE

I'm Ivan-the-Giant! I'm Ivan-the-Great-Great-Giant!

VASILISA

And as they are separating the rye from the corn, you will tell them fairy tales until they have finished. Funny ones, so that they are too busy laughing to eat the grain.

CAT

Tell fairy tales to mice?! No, I must draw the line there! That I certainly won't do! I won't do it! On third thought, I'll do it, I'll let you have your way.

VASILISA

We'll do all this at night. In the meantime, listen carefully and warn us if you hear Baba-Yaga sneaking around.

CAT

Listen, I can. We cats never refuse to listen.

VASILISA

I'm leaving both of you here in full charge. Bear and I will go to chop down some trees for the windmill furnace. Chick-chick-chick.
The hut on chicken legs enters.
Off we go.
The hut trots off into the forest with Vasilisa and the Bear inside.

SHARIK

Bow-wow-wow! Wait for me, take me with you!

CAT

Don't move an inch from here!

SHARIK

How I hate it when my Master doesn't take me along. It makes me fee' that life isn't worth living!

CAT

Don't you dare move an inch.

SHARIK

Don't shout at me! You are not a person.

CAT

Didn't you hear your Master's order? He left *me* in charge.

SHARIK

Me too, me too.

VASILISA

How handsome you are! You are not by any chance a Siberian cat?

CAT

Well, you might say. . .

VASILISA

Bayoon—the giant storyteller cat—is he a relative of yours?

CAT

What makes you ask?

VASILISA

Nothing. I'm just curious.

CAT

My great-grandfather.

VASILISA

Then you are a master at both catching mice and telling tales—right?

CAT

What makes you ask?

VASILISA

Nothing. I'm just curious.

CAT

Yes, a master.

VASILISA

If so, can you chase all the mice in the forest into Baba-Yaga's granary?

CAT

No, I cannot.

BEAR

Koshka Ivanovna, is it nice to refuse a favor to a good person?

CAT

A wise cat agrees only after having been asked three times. I'll not chase the mice into the granary, I'll not. But, on third thought, have it your way.

VASILISA

Thank you! As soon as you get them in there, tell them to separate the rye from the corn. Agreed?

CAT

No, not yet, not yet. All right, have it your way. I agree.

IVANUSHKA

It's too long to wait till winter. Kitty! Come out of there! I can see your gleaming eyes. Sharik! Sharik! Here Sharik!

SHARIK

Comes out

Oh, Ivanushka, Ivanushka! Why did you follow your mother without permission? What a beating you will get!

IVANUSHKA

Nonsense! Valiant Knights are never spanked, and I am a Valiant Knight.

CAT

Who, pray tell, knighted you?

IVANUSHKA

I did it myself.

CAT

Normally knights come a lot taller than you.

IVANUSHKA

It's not the size that matters—it's *courage*! After living a long time, I suddenly realized that I was no longer afraid—not of anything. That meant that I had grown into a Valiant Knight.
Cat comes out from the bushes.
Oh, what a beauty you are!

SHARIK

And me? And me?

IVANUSHKA

You too. The kitty is more beautiful. Sharik is very clever. Did you two by any chance see my mother? They call her Vasilisa-the-Hardworker. Kitty, why did you stop purring all of a sudden?

CAT

My name is Koshka Ivanovna.*

IVANUSHKA

Why do you look at me that way, Koshka Ivanovna?

CAT

Should I reveal the truth to him?

*Mrs. Cat. If the role is played by a male, it would be Kotofei Ivanovich (Mr. Cat).

IVANUSHKA

Tell me, my dears, tell me my friends! You don't know how much I've missed her! Is my mother here? Is she?!

SHARIK

To cat
We'll have to tell him.

CAT

Your mother is here, Ivanushka.

IVANUSHKA

Yipes!
He rushes into the bushes.

CAT

There's a Valiant Knight for you! Afraid of his own mother. . .

SHARIK

Well, didn't you hear him say how much he missed her? Didn't you!

IVANUSHKA

Peeking from the bushes.
Of course I missed her. But she told me to say at home. And I disobeyed. When she sees me she'll be so upset. No, no. I won't let her see me.

CAT

Then, pray tell, why did you bother to come?

IVANUSHKA

I was dying to get a glimpse of her, to hear her voice. I'll just stay here quietly. I'll do something really heroic—to help her. Then, maybe she'll forgive me for everything. But where is she?

SHARIK

She went with our dear master, Mikhail Potapych to chop some wood for the windmill furnace. I have a feeling they're going to be back soon.
We hear a racket.

CAT

They're bringing the wood now.

IVANUSHKA

I'm not here!
He hides in the bushes. Vasilisa and Bear enter the glade.

BEAR

Eh, brothers, this is real work! Not like wasting time being chained up and growling at intruders. This kind of work is mighty nice. It's fun! Go and look at how much wood we brought.

VASILISA

We have no time for that. Run, Mishka, to the blacksmith—at the third crossroad. You know the place and the blacksmith, don't you?

BEAR

He's a famous person. He shoes the warrior's horses, repairs their armor and helmets. . .

VASILISA

Hurry there and ask him to give us 36 pounds of nails, two saws, four planes, and four hammers. Tell him why we need them. He won't refuse us.

BEAR

Off I go!
He disappears.

VASILISA

I think I'll stretch out for a while. We'll have to work all night without a wink of sleep.

CAT

Sleep peacefully. We'll keep watch over you.
She goes into the thicket.

VASILISA

The maples rustle so gently, so sweetly—it makes your eyes heavy.
She closes her eyes. It grows dark gradually. From a distance we hear the voices of watchmen in field and forest exchanging calls.

SHARIK

Softly
Bow-wow-wow.

CAT

Miauw, miauw, keep your eyes peeled.

IVANUSHKA

Sings

Sleep, dear Mama—
Bayou-bayoushki-bayou!
You sang to us long ago —
Bayou-shki-bayou.

FEDEN'KA AND EGORUSHKA

Continue the song.

Now your three sons
Sing the same lullaby to you.

IVANUSHKA, FEDEN'KA, EGORUSHKA

In unison

Get your strength back,
Rest your hands,
Your loving heart.
Sleep, sleep, sleep.
Bayoushki-bayou—
We sing a lullaby to you.

END OF ACT ONE

ACT II

The Two Maples   Same as Act I. The clearing has changed
to the point of being unrecognizable.
Paths have been laid out and covered with
sand. A windmill has been built, and its
blades turn merrily. Near it an open shed
has been constructed. Sacks of grain and
flour are piled up in the shed. There is a
second shed sheltering bags of gold.

The Cat paces near the grain sacks.

CAT

Keep on sorting out the grain, my good little mice. There's only half
a sack left.

SQUEAKING LITTLE VOICES

We're doing it, we're doing it. We're trying. But you, Mistress Cat, go on
telling us your stories. Our mouths are watering—we can hardly keep
from nibbling the grain.

CAT

Then listen, little mice, the cat's true friends, so sweet and nice. . .

A squeaking laughter

Once upon a time there were three mice. One was red, another white,
and the third striped.

Shrill giggling

They were such good, good neighbors and protected one another so
cleverly that even the cat was afraid of them. He'd get ready to pounce
on the white one, when the red mouse would scratch his paw, the
striped mouse would pull his whiskers.

Laughter

When he went after the striped one, the white mouse pulled his tail,
the red one his ear. What was he to do? He thought hard, then called
two of his brothers for advice. He called them. . .why aren't you laughing?

SQUEAKING LITTLE VOICES

We don't feel like laughing now.

CAT

You'd better laugh, or you'll be in trouble!

Forced laughter

So the cat called his two brothers for advice and said to them: "The mice
keep making a fool of me. Help me get even with them. I think I have a
good idea. I myself am red, so I will catch the red mouse. You, brother,
who are white, catch the white one, and you who are striped, the striped
one. We'll show these insolent mice. . ." Go on, laugh!

CAT (Cont.)

Forced laughter.

The three mice overheard the cats and were very frightened. How were they to outsmart the cats and save themselves. They soon thought of a way. They scampered into the fireplace, rolled in the ashes, and all three came out looking gray.

Mice laugh happily.

They came out of the fireplace and ran straight into the three brother cats. The cats stood with their mouths open, not knowing which one of the mice each of them was to catch.

Happy laughter.

Ever since then all mice have been gray.

Happy laughter.

But cats continue to catch mice, not caring about their color.

Laughter stops.

Go on, laugh!

MICE

There, Mistress, we've finished all the work. Let us go now. Permit us to go back to our holes. Our children are alone and they miss us.

CAT

Wait a minute. Let me check your work. Don't be afraid. I won't touch you. Stop your squeaking!

She examines the sacks.

You've done your work well. Everything is as it should be. You may go. Your reward shall be that I shall stop eating mice for a whole year.

MICE

Thank you, Mistress! Thank you, Koshka Ivanovna!

CAT

Off with you now.

MICE

Goodbye, Koshka Ivanovna. Ha-ha-ha! The striped one caught him by the tail, the red one scratched his paw—ha-ha-ha! The white one pulled his ear, the striped one his nose—ha-ha-ha!

Laughter fades away.

CAT

Sighs

I've told them three hundred and thirty three stories. I'm worn out!

CAT (Cont.)

She sits down under a tree to rest, starts licking herself diligently. The Bear comes running out of the mill. He's covered with flour, like a miller. Sharik is at his heels.

BEAR

How about the last sacks? Are they done?

Cat doesn't answer.

SHARIK

Don't ask her any questions now. When she is washing herself she's deaf.

Runs over to the sacks

They're ready. Let's take them in.

He helps the Bear lift two of the sacks onto his back.

BEAR

The sun is still high above the horizon but we've already finished most of the work. That's pretty good!

He runs off, Sharik after him. Then the dog changes his mind, turns around and goes toward the Cat. He changes his mind again and runs to the mill. At last he stops because of his indecision.

SHARIK

To the Cat

Let's go inside the mill.

CAT

I don't want to.

SHARIK

Why are you so stubborn? Why do you cause me so much trouble? You're a scoundrel! Don't you understand that when I'm in the mill, guarding it, I worry about you. When I'm out here keeping an eye on you, I worry about my Master. Take pity on my poor heart! Please, please me for once, and do as I tell you. Stay with us in the mill and I'll guard both of you well.

CAT

Right now that's impossible.

SHARIK

Why is it impossible?

CAT

I may be sitting here licking my paws, but my ears are pricked up. I am hearing strange sounds.

SHARIK

Bow-wow-wow! Is it she?—is it Baba-Yaga?

CAT

Whoever it is, it's sneaking up.

SHARIK

Bow-wow-wow! Watch out! I warn you. . .whoever you are!

CAT

Oh, quiet! Don't interfere with my work. Go ahead to the mill. In case of danger I'll meow a warning.

SHARIK

Gr-r-r-r! Let her dare steal up on us! I'll bite her bony legs through and through. I'm good at chewing bones.

He goes off. The Cat stops licking herself and freezes with one paw in the air. She listens carefully. There's a rustle in the bushes as they stir. Cat hides behind the tree. With his back to the audience, Ivanushka steps from the bushes pulling a table set with a meal.

CAT

Is that you, Ivanushka, by any chance?

IVANUSHKA

Yes, it's me, the Valiant Knight.

CAT

What are you dragging out there?

IVANUSHKA

I caught some fish, gathered some mushrooms, built a stove, and cooked a meal.

CAT

For this you deserve praise!

IVANUSHKA

I guess I deserve it. They've worked all night. They're probably starving by now. I thought I'd surprise them.

CAT

If only your mother doesn't guess who did it.

IVANUSHKA

She'll never guess. How can she? When she left home I couldn't even cook an ordinary cabbage soup. Now you can order anything and I'll cook it right.

CAT

Well, let's take a look at what you've cooked up.

IVANUSHKA

Go ahead and look.

He turns his face to the Cat as he speaks and the Cat, uttering a piercing scream, jumps about seven feet away from him—and for good reason. Ivanushka's hair is like a disheveled mop. His face is covered with soot and dirt. He looks more like a monster than a boy.

Why are you staring at me like that?

CAT

Take a look at yourself!

IVANUSHKA

I haven't got the time.

CAT

You have dirt all over you, from head to toe. Lick yourself clean.

IVANUSHKA

You can't keep clean doing the kind of work I've just done. The stove smokes, the wood doesn't want to burn. I blew on it so hard that my cheeks nearly burst.

CAT

Looking at the food on the table.

What did you catch the fish with—your paws?

IVANUSHKA

What do you mean—paws? With a fishing line, of course. We Valiant Knights never leave home with empty pockets. Look at all the things I have in mine. Here's the fishing line. A fishhook. A whistle. Some nuts. Flint and steel. A slingshot.

CAT

Put that thing away! I can't bear to look at slingshots. Boys are forever shooting with them at us cats.

IVANUSHKA

Boys may do it, but I'm no ordinary boy. I am a Valiant Knight!

CAT

Just the same. . .

IVANUSHKA

Don't be afraid, I never did that even when I was little. By the way, be

IVANUSHKA (Cont.)

careful, don't drop any hint to Mother that I was the one who prepared the meal.

CAT

Who should I say did It?

IVANUSHKA

Think of some magic tale to explain it all. You are good at it.

CAT

I presume that will be unavoidable. Now you go to the river and scrub that filth off you.

IVANUSHKA

Later, later. I want to see how glad Mother will be that I cooked this dinner.

CAT

Then hide yourself. The millstones are silent. They're through at the mill. I hear them coming.

IVANUSHKA

I'm vanishing.

He hides. The Bear appears instantly, carrying sacks of flour, accompanied by the happily cavorting Sharik.

BEAR

All done! No one can beat us! Now all that's left is cleaning Baba-Yaga's hut, and there are still hours before sunset. I feel happy all over! My legs won't stand still—they dance by themselves.

He dances and sings.

>My dainty little paws,
>My cutest bandy legs,
>You carry me as I dance and sing—
>As lightly as a bird on the wing.
>Then, how come I do not fly?
>Because I do not care to try.
>I do not hop, but love to swim,
>Pretend I am a peacock if I have the whim.
>Oh, my dainty little paws,
>My cutest bandy legs,
>With you I'm graceful as a faun—
>Dancing airily from early dawn.

BEAR (Cont.)

> I soar in the air like a feather,
> In every possible kind of weather,
> My dainty little paws,
> My cutest bandy legs.

He tries to jump into the air and bumps into the table.

Heaven's above! What miracle is this?

SHARIK

A ready meal.

BEAR

White mushrooms! Fried fish! Whoever fried it wasted his time. It is so delicious when raw! Mistress, mistress, come and see—we've been blessed with a miracle!

Vasilisa appears.

Mistress, just look! The table is set and dinner is served!

Vasilisa goes to the table.

VASILISA

A real miracle! And just in time. Koshka Ivanovna, what kindhearted person was so thoughtful? Why don't you say something? You were on guard duty—you must know. Or did you fall asleep?

CAT

Sit down and eat, Mistress. I did see the one who showed such concern for us. In fact, he is near us at this moment, no doubt—glad to see how pleased we are.

SHARIK

That means it is Iva. . .

The Cat secretly kicks Sharik. Ivanushka, in the bushes, holds his head in dismay.

VASILISA

To Sharik

Who did you say it was? Iva?

SHARIK

I. . .

CAT

He is right. The kind sorcerer, Ivamur Murmuraevich—it was he who prepared our dinner.

VASILISA

I never heard of a sorcerer by that name.

BEAR

His mouth full

Go on and eat, Little Mother, eat. Hurry, or there won't be anything
left. Eat in peace, my friends.

SHARIK

From the table? May I really eat from the table?

BEAR

Just eat and don't ask questions.

SHARIK

I won't get a beating if I eat from the table?

BEAR

Today is a special day—no one will get punished.

VASILISA

What kind of a sorcerer is Ivamur Murmuraevich? I wonder why I
never heard of him.

CAT

Mur. . .mur. . .Little Mistress, there are old wizards about whom
everyone has heard, and there are young ones. Ivan Murmuraevich is
still a mere kitten.

VASILISA

What does he look like?

CAT

Frightful. One of his cheeks is coal black, the other white. His nose is the
color of smoke. His paws are greasy. He does not know how to walk. . .

BEAR

He doesn't? How does he move?

CAT

He can only run or jump. And what energy he has! A fence might have
been standing there for a hundred years, but he could knock it down
with one blow.

BEAR

Does he have claws?

CAT

Yes he has, but he carries them separately—in his pocket. He uses them to catch fish.

BEAR

Can he fly?

CAT

When necessary. He takes a fast run, somersaults, and up he flies. But he hates to wash, though he loves to swim. You can't drag him out of the water with a pair of pincers even when he is blue with cold. Yes, he is a strange one! But when he loves someone, there is nothing he won't do for her. You ought to have seen, Mistress, how he admired your work, to have heard how many questions he asked about you. Yes, he is the *kindest* of wizards.

VASILISA

He's not much of a cook for a sorcerer. Some of the fish is overcooked, some almost raw.

CAT

That is because he is still a kitten.

VASILISA

Getting up from the table
Well, Ivamur Murmuraevich, if you can hear me, accept my thanks for the meal. I'll say this—if you are a kitten don't go away far from your mother, my dear little friend, and if you get into trouble, call her and she'll come running. My dear children, can you hear me?

FEDYA

We hear you, Mama!

EGORUSHKA

We've been quiet so that every little breeze helped you in your work.

VASILISA

My dear children! I've been working from the minute I woke. Haven't had a chance to talk with you. I run from one task to another—that's the life of all mothers. I would like to cheer you up, and tell you funny stories, or sing you a song, but I don't have the time—that's the way it is with all mothers. But when I have earned your freedom, we'll all go home together, holding hands, and we'll talk to our hearts' content.

EGORUSHKA

Mama! Mama!

FEDYA

How can we ever feel hurt by you?

EGORUSHKA

We love you. . .

VASILISA

To the Bear, Sharik, and Cat

We've done everything, my friends. There is only Baba-Yaga's hut to be scrubbed. We'll do that quickly. Koshka Ivanovna! Sharik! Let's go to the river and get the hut there.

BEAR

What about me?

VASILISA

You stay here and watch over everything. Be sure not to fall asleep.

BEAR

How can you say such a thing! After all, it isn't wintertime.

VASILISA

Friends, fetch some soap, wash-rags, brushes, brooms, and follow me.

BEAR

To himself

How can I sleep in the daytime? Hamsters can do it. Also owls—they sleep away the day. But bears—
He yawns.
never! It's true, I worked all of last night
Yawns.
then I had a nice full meal—nice and full—so, naturally, I feel drowsy. I think I'll keep myself awake with a song.
He sings.
Sing, my Mishka, my bandy-legged babe, my shaggy little one, my dearest darling. . .No, that's the wrong song—it's a lullaby. I just imagined for a moment that I was with my Mommie in our cave and she. . .she. . .hum. . .
He falls asleep. Ivanushka runs out from the bushes.

IVANUSHKA

I knew this would happen. I just felt it! I was going to wash up at the river, stay around near Mother, then I remembered that the table had to be cleared. I come back here and find the watchman asleep. Mikhail Potapych! Wake up!

IVANUSHKA (Cont.)

The Bear doesn't move.

Robbers! Help, Robbers!

The Bear snores.

How can I wake him? Should I tickle him?

He tickles the Bear. The Bear giggles in a thin voice, but doesn't wake.

He's still asleep. I guess I'll have to get some water and pout it over him.

He is about to run into the forest.

No, I mustn't leave. Some one is sneaking up here.

Baba-Yaga, walking on her tip-toes, comes out from the forest.

Baba-Yaga!

Ivanushka hides in the bushes.

BABA-YAGA

Oh, poor little me! Poor baby! What am I to do? What rotten luck—
I found a good servant. She's clever, that Vasilisa, a real worker.
What a misfortune! Now whom am I going to scold, or begrudge a
piece of bread? Is it possible that this unlucky little dove —me—will
have to praise her own servant? Never! That's unhealthy for vipers
like me. It's a good thing I was cunning enough to get back here ahead
of time. I'll change everything my way. At once. The Bear is asleep
now and even a cannon-shot won't wake him. I'll steal a bag of
gold—from myself—then demand it from her later.

*She goes toward the sacks. Ivanushka dashes out from the bushes
and confronts her. She backs off in terror.*

What kind of monster is this? I've lived here three hundred years
and never have I seen the likes of him. Who the devil are you?

IVANUSHKA

I am a sorcerer: Pussy Ivan Murmuraevich.

BABA-YAGA

A sorcerer!

IVANUSHKA

Yes.

*Baba-Yaga takes a step toward Ivanushka. He quickly takes the
whistle from his pocket.*

Don't dare to touch me!

He blows a deafening blast.

BABA-YAGA

Stop, you are deafening me.

IVANUSHKA

Don't come any nearer. We sorcerers can't stand that.

BABA-YAGA

What a monster! He looks like an ordinary boy, but he's not afraid
of Baba-Yaga! He looks like a midget, but whistles like a giant. He's
terrifying! Look here, Ivamur, how can you prove that you are
a sorcerer?

IVANUSHKA

Just try to leave me and I will pull you back.

BABA-YAGA

You? Pull me? Never!

IVANUSHKA

Turn around and walk away. Don't look back.
*Baba-Yaga does this. Ivanushka gets the fishing-line with the hook
and sinker and swings it in the air, then "casts" it in Baba'Yaga's
direction. The hook catches on the bottom of her skirt. He pulls her
toward him. She struggles. She wiggles.*
You won't get away! Even a catfish couldn't get loose, so how could
you, Baba-Yaga?
*He allows her to pull away, then jerks her back, forcing her to come
near him. He removes the hook from her skirt and jumps away
from her.*
Now are you convinced that I'm a sorcerer?

BABA-YAGA

But can you do this?
She snaps her fingers making sparks fly.

IVANUSHKA

With sarcasm
I'll do it as a favor to you.
*He takes the flint-and-steel from his pocket, strikes them, making
brighter sparks than Baba-Yaga.*

BABA-YAGA

Do you see those cones on the pine tree? Do you see that one?

IVANUSHKA

Yes.

Baba-Yaga in the Leningrad TIUZ production.

Mishka, Vasilisa and the Cat in the Moscow TIUZ production.

BABA-YAGA

Ph-ph-ph—oo!
She blows at the tree and the cone she pointed to drops to the ground.
Did you see that?

IVANUSHKA

Now you look at that cone—that one over there. Higher. Still higher.
He points. He takes the slingshot from his pocket and aims at the tree. The pine cone he pointed to drops to the ground.
Did you see *that*?

BABA-YAGA

You'd better not make me mad or I'll chew you in two!

IVANUSHKA

I dare you! You'll break your teeth.

BABA-YAGA

Not I. Just watch!
She picks up a stone from the ground.
You see this stone?
She bites it in two.
You see, I bit the stone in half so I can certainly do the same to you.

IVANUSHKA

Now watch what I can do!
He picks up a stone from the ground, palms it, replaces it with a nut. He bites the nut and eats it up.
Did you see? I bit the stone in half and swallowed it. So I can certainly do the same to you.

BABA-YAGA

What *is* all this? Nothing like this has ever happened to me! For so many years everyone has trembled before me, and this Ivamur only makes fun of me. Is it possible that I'm no longer mistress of my own domain? Fiddlesticks! You will not outsmart me! Goodbye for now, Ivamur. You may have come out on top this time, but you just wait!

IVANUSHKA

Doubled with laughter
Did I scare her! "Wash your face," they say. "You must wash your face"—who needs it?! If my face had been washed, would I have scared Baba-Yaga? "Don't stick everything into your pockets"—and why not stick everything into my pockets? How else would I have fooled her—without my hooks, flint, and whistle?

SHARIK

Poor puppy!

CAT

No, lucky kitten. I can still remember how good it felt when my mother licked me clean and bit me gently.

VASILISA

There. Now you are clean.
She leads Ivanushka from behind the bushes. He gleams with cleanliness.
Now I recognize you. Stand still—your shirt is torn—I'll mend it.

IVANUSHKA

Baba-Yaga did it—she tore it.

VASILISA

With needle and thread in hand
Don't fidget or I'll stick you.

IVANUSHKA

I'm fidgeting with happiness, Mama. Just think—for three whole years nobody took care of me, and now, suddenly, you are mending my shirt on me. Your stitches are so tiny.
He looks at his shoulder.

VASILISA

Don't squint—you'll get cross-eyed.

IVANUSHKA

I'm not squinting—I'm just looking. My seams are as crooked as a snake. Yours are always so nice and straight. Mama, are you still mad at me?

VASILISA

I ought to be, but I am glad you are here.

IVANUSHKA

Then why do you look angry?

VASILISA

That's the mistake you children always make. I'm not angry, I'm worried. Your brothers are Baba-Yaga's prisoners. I had hoped she'd praise me—but look what happened instead.

IVANUSHKA (Cont.)

every day—even when I wasn't dirty. And I cleaned our house—all of it. . .I swept it the way you showed me. I didn't sweep any of the dust under the furniture and trunks or anything like that. And before leaving I tidied up and washed the floor.

VASILISA

Did you say you were lonely?

IVANUSHKA

Yes, especially toward evening. And on my birthday. On my birthday I'd get up in the morning, wish myself a happy birthday, but that wasn't enough for a person, isn't that true Mama? I'd bake myself a strawberry pie, but I'd still be lonely.

VASILISA

Were you ever sick?

IVANUSHKA

Once. The pie I so carefully tried to bake somehow remained raw. I ate it anyway—I was that unhappy. That was the only time I was sick. *The Cat and Sharik return with a bucket of hot water and a brush.*

VASILISA

Put them there—behind the bushes. Come, child, I'll give you a bath.

IVANUSHKA

No! No! Let me do it myself.

VASILISA

Come on, now!

IVANUSHKA

From behind the bushes
Ouch! Mama, it's too hot! Never mind, I'll suffer bravely, like a Valiant Knight. Ouch! I can stand anything. . .Ouch! The soap got into my ears!

VASILISA

You're just imagining it, my boy.

IVANUSHKA

Mamochka, my neck is still clean!

VASILISA

That's what you think.

VASILISA

How can you not praise me, since I've done everything you ordered me to do?

BABA-YAGA

No, there's no law that says one must praise an insolent servant. So you ground some flour—what's so marvelous about that? Any miller can do as much. Go, flour sacks, get you to the granary!
The sacks of flour run off as though alive.
So you dug up the treasures. Any ditch-digger could have done that. Go, gold, get underground again.
The sacks of gold sink into the ground.
No, you haven't earned any praise—not any. I'll assign other work to you. If you do it—I'll praise you.

VASILISA

Then tell me what I am to do.

BABA-YAGA

I'll have to think about it. Get ready for a hard task. I'll return soon to give you my orders.
She disappears.

IVANUSHKA

Mamochka! Dear Mama!

VASILISA

Ivanushka!
They embrace. The Cat and Sharik appear from the forest.

SHARIK

Go on and enjoy your reunion. We'll stand guard.

IVANUSHKA

Mama! Mamochka! I stood it for as long as I could—for three years! Then I got so lonesome for you—I couldn't bear it any longer. So I set off to find you. Are you very angry with me?

VASILISA

Koshka Ivanovna, Sharik, fetch a bucket of hot water and a brush, a stiff one. . .
The Cat and Sharik run off.

IVANUSHKA

It's only today that I got so dirty—before, I washed myself almost

IVANUSHKA (Cont.)

Baba-Yaga appears soundlessly behind Ivanushka.

And they call me "little boy, little boy." Me who proved himself even stronger than the Bear. He fell asleep, while I handled Baba-Yaga all by myself.

BABA-YAGA

And she, the little pigeon, here she is again.
She grabs Ivanushka.

IVANUSHKA

Mama! Mama! Mama!
Vasilisa comes running.

VASILISA

I'm here my child! Let go of my boy, Baba-Yaga!

BABA-YAGA

What next! Did you ever know me to let my prey out of my hands?

VASILISA

Let him go, I tell you!
She raises her sword and swings it over Baba-Yaga's head.

Do you recognize this sword? It cut off the head of the Snake Dragon and it will soon put an end to you!

BABA-YAGA

She lets go of Ivanushka and gets her own sword from between the folds of her skirt—it is black and crooked.

My clever one, I prefer to hit from the back, but when necessary I can fight face to face as well.
They fight so hard that sparks fly. Vasilisa knocks the sword from Baba-Yaga's hand.

Don't kill me, don't kill me, or you'll never find your other sons.

VASILISA

Tell me this instant where they are!

BABA-YAGA

I'd rather die first! I'm stubborn enough not to spare little me.
Vasilisa lowers her sword.

That's better. When I have reason to praise you, then and only then will I tell you where your children are. Judge for yourself—is it possible to praise a servant who has raised her hand against her mistress?

IVANUSHKA

Mama!

VASILISA

But we'll win out over the wicked one if we work together. You are a brave boy and a pretty sensible one.

BEAR

Wakes with a start.

Help! Robbers! The flour is gone! And the gold! Help! How come? Who did it? I didn't close my eyes for a second, and look what happened!

VASILISA

You dozed a while.

BEAR

Then I must have dreamed that I was awake. . .

CAT

Careful—Baba-Yaga is coming.

She enters.

BABA-YAGA

I've thought of a task for you.

VASILISA

What is it?

BABA-YAGA

Find out where your boys are hidden. Find them and I'll praise you. If you fail, you'll have yourself to blame. I might punish you into the bargain. You have been a heap of trouble to me. I, a prominent woman, had to cross swords with the likes of you, a mere servant. Just think how that degraded me.

To Ivanushka

Why do you laugh, urchin? Watch out, or I'll turn you into a stone. What do you say, Vasilisa, will you undertake to find your sons?

VASILISA

I'll find them.

BABA-YAGA

You have until sunset.

BEAR

How can you be so mean! The sun is already about to set.

BABA-YAGA

That suits me just fine. Well, Vasilisa, one, two, three, begin your search. When you find them—call me.
She disappears.

VASILISA

Let us all start looking. No, all of you begin now. I'll think awhile. . . Was it really the boys I seemed to hear, or did I imagine it?
The others disperse and start looking for Feden'ka and Egorushka. Vasilisa stands still, deep in thought.

EGORUSHKA

Ivanushka, we are here!

FEDEN'KA

Here, kitty, ps-tt-t. . .Sharik, Sharik, here' we are. Here! Here!
Bear looks down into the bushes.
No, no, Mishka, look up, look up!
Suddenly a voice is heard—Baba-Yaga imitating boys' voices— the voice sounds from a distance.

BABA-YAGA'S VOICE

Mama, mama, come, quick, we are here—near the muddy swamp!

BEAR

We are coming!

EGORUSHKA

Don't believe it, Mama!

FEDEN'KA

It's Baba-Yaga calling.

EGORUSHKA

She can imitate any voice.

BEAR

Why are you waiting, little Mother? The sun will set soon. Let's hurry to the swamp.

VASILISA

Wait a minute, Mishka, let's listen once more.

BABA-YAGA'S VOICE

From a distance

BABA-YAGA'S VOICE (Cont.)

Dear Mother, we are here, in the deep gully, under the old birch tree.

SHARIK

Bow-wow-wow! That's right—there is such a gully.

BABA-YAGA'S VOICE

From a distance, desperately

Mama, hurry! Baba-Yaga is sneaking up to us. She has a sword in her hand!

VASILISA

We're coming!

She walks quickly toward the thicket. She turns around.

I knew it! Here is where they are!

Calls

Baba-Yaga! I found my children.

Baba-Yaga appears as if from out of the ground.

BABA-YAGA

Where? Where are they?

VASILISA

Pointing to the two maples

Look: what is that?

She points to the drops on the maple leaves, which are covered with tears; they glisten in the setting sun.

I am asking you: what is that? Answer!

BABA-YAGA

Why do you ask? That's nothing but a couple of maples.

VASILISA

Then why are they crying?

BABA-YAGA

It's the evening dew. . .Oh, all right! You've guessed. They are your boys.

BEAR

Oh you! How many times have I passed them! How many times have I scratched my back against their bark, without even suspecting that they were people. Forgive me boys, forgive a silly Bear.

VASILISA

Well, Baba-Yaga—I'm waiting.

BABA-YAGA

What are you waiting for?

VASILISA

Release my sons.

BABA-YAGA

What an idea! Turn them into boys again?! They are much less nuisance when they are wooden—obedient, never taking a step away from home, never saying a fresh word.

IVANUSHKA

Oh, you cheat!

BABA-YAGA

Thank you for the kind word—of course I'm a cheat. No, Vasilisa, your joy is premature. Did you ever know good people to triumph over us, evil ones? I'm like a snake—I always get around people. No, Vasilisa, you do one more task for me—maybe then I'll free your boys.

VASILISA

Name it!

BABA-YAGA

Don't be in such a hurry. Morning is wiser than evening. I'll tell you tomorrow.
She disappears.

VASILISA

Come, my friends, let's make a bonfire. We'll guard the boys through the night. No one is to fall asleep. We'll make sure Baba-Yaga doesn't harm them.

BEAR

No, no sleep. Who would think of such a thing?

VASILISA

We'll sing songs.

CAT

And tell stories.

VASILISA

Summer nights are short. They pass quickly.

They gather kindling and wood and make a fire, as Vasilisa sings.

VASILISA

> Fedya, Feden'ka, don't you cry,
> Egorushka, my child, don't you sigh.
> I've brought you a treat,
> Good things to eat,
> Clean shirts to wear,
> New boots to tear.
>
> I'll scrub you clean, my boys
> So your faces shine.
> I'll feed you, my sons,
> So your strength is fine.
>
> Fedya, Feden'ka, don't you cry,
> Egorushka, my child, don't you sigh.
> Your mother has come for you, my boys,
> She's brought you happiness and joys.

END OF ACT II

The Two Maples   Same as Act I. It is near dawn. The fire is
                          still burning. Vasilisa stands near the
                          Maples, looking at them worriedly.

VASILISA

Children, children, why are you trembling so? Are you feeling that
there's more trouble coming? Or has the wind chilled you? Answer
me, answer me—don't hesitate. I might understand you.

EGORUSHKA

Mother, do you hear the forest noise?

FEDYA

All the trees are saying the same thing. . .

EGORUSHKA

They're saying: "Brother Maples, poor kids!"

FEDYA

They're saying: "Watch out! Watch out!"

EGORUSHKA

"Baba-Yaga has left her hut! Watch out! Watch out!"

FEDYA

"Watch out, she's holding things in her hand that mean death to a tree."

EGORUSHKA

"A hatchet and an axe, a hatchet and an axe!"

VASILISA

I didn't get the words you said, but I know you are frightened, my
children. Don't worry, my poor ones—before dawn I, too, often feel
uneasy. It is dark, chilly, fog creeps over the swamp. Be patient, in a
while the sun will rise. It will surely rise—the sun always remembers
its work. In the meantime we are watching out for Baba-Yaga. We'll
know it if she is plotting some evil deed.

The Bear comes running.

BEAR

Baba-Yaga is no more.

VASILISA

What do you mean—she's no more?

BEAR

She came out of her hut carrying in her hand. . .I better not mention what—Feden'ka and Egorushka might hear me. She came out, and we followed her. She rose in the air and suddenly melted away, like a cloud, together with her hatchet and her axe. Not a trace left of her. I hurried here, in case you needed my help. Sharik went after her. For a dog it makes no difference whether he can see her or not—whether or not she's melted away. Sharik will follow her footsteps. He will not lose her. He—
Sharik runs in.

SHARIK

Mistress, Mistress, give me a good beating. Here, I brought the switch. . .

BEAR

What did you do wrong?

SHARIK

I lost her scent. Baba-Yaga led me into the swamp. She appeared in one spot, then in another, then she disappeared altogether. But don't worry, the Cat is sitting nearby, still as a corpse. She's watching out for her. Stalking her as if she were a mouse. I hurried here so that you can punish me.

VASILISA

I'm not angry with you. Baba-Yaga has a magic hat that makes her invisible.

BEAR

Yes, she's got one. It's old and tattered, but she's too stingy to buy a new one. It still works well in half-light—at dawn and when the sun has set. But don't worry, good woman, magic hat or no magic hat, she'll not get away from the Cat!
The Cat appears noiselessly at Vasilisa's feet.

CAT

Baba-Yaga went off somewhere.

BEAR

She's gone?

CAT

I couldn't prevent it. She's gone.

BEAR

What are we going to do now? Should we all have a good cry?

CAT

What good will that do?

BEAR

What else is there left for us to do?

CAT

Tell stories.

BEAR

No story can help us!

CAT

Anyone who says that doesn't understand. Vasilisa-the-Hardworker, dear Mistress, be good enough to tell them to sit down in a circle, with me in the middle.

VASILISA

Do what she tells you.

CAT

And you sit down, too, Mistress.
They all sit in a circle around the Maples, the Cat in the middle.
Listen to me carefully, my tale is not a simple one. Once upon a time there lived a wood cutter.

BEAR

Here? In our forest?

CAT

In the next one.

BEAR

That one I never saw. I only heard of it. Is it the one that's sort of dark?...

CAT

Don't keep interrupting me! Why do you ask so many questions?

BEAR

Since I let Baba-Yaga get away, everyone is mad at me. I want to know—are you on speaking terms with me or not?

CAT

I also let her get away.

BEAR

But no one will grumble at you. But me, poor little orphan that I am...

SHARIK

Jumping up
Bow-wow-wow!

CAT

Go after her! Go, go, hurry!

SHARIK

Baba-Yaga is sneaking up.

CAT

Move, go after her. Go, go!

SHARIK

No, I was mistaken.

BABA-YAGA

She's invisible.
Aha! I've fooled you!
Ivanushka appears at the spot from where the voice came, jumps up and grabs something in the air. Baba-Yaga becomes visible at once. Ivanushka dances about with Baba-Yaga's magic hat in his hand. Baba-Yaga chases after him.

VASILISA

Put on the magic hat, Ivanushka! Quick!
Ivanushka tries to put it on, but Baba-Yaga manages to grab hold of it. The two pull at the hat. The worn hat tears in halves, and Ivanushka and Baba-Yaga fall to the ground. Rushing to the place where the two had fought, Vasilisa manages to grab the hatchet and axe, which Baba-Yaga had dropped to reclaim her hat.

BABA-YAGA

What an outrage! Instead of going to sleep, my servant sits around all night, bringing nothing but trouble to her mistress. All of you soft-hearted ninnies are in for a lot of trouble. My patience has come to an end.
She goes away.

IVANUSHKA

Mama, see what a good plan Cat and I thought of! We came away from the swamp and Baba-Yaga followed us here. Cat began to tell her story while I hid in the bushes—not even breathing. Baba-Yaga sneaked up to listen—then I pounced on her. Everything happened the way we planned it. It's only too bad that I didn't think of putting on the magic hat Shucks! But I did help you more today than yesterday, didn't I, Mama?

VASILISA

Yes, you did, my boy.

The sun rises. Its first rays fall on the clearing.

You see, Feden'ka, do you see Egorushka? As I told you, the sun has risen, the fog has lifted, and it is bright. Cheerful. Why are you so quiet, my children. Say something.

FEDYA

Mama, if you only knew how hard it is for a boy to stand still on a morning like this.

EGORUSHKA

If you only knew, Mama, how hard it is for a boy to be still as a stone while everybody else tries to help him, works for him. . .

VASILISA

Don't be sad, cheer up, children, you'll not have to wait much longer.

Baba-Yaga's angry voice is heard from the wings.

BABA-YAGA

Kish! Kish! Just you wait. I'll cook a stew out of all of you.

Baba-Yaga's hut comes running out on its chicken legs. Baba-Yaga sits inside, in her armchair, in the doorway.

Step lively, chicken legs—don't crawl like snails.

The hut stands still—the chicken legs don't move.

Oh! I'm exhausted.

BEAR

What are you tired from—other people's hard work?

BABA-YAGA

What rot he's talking. Do you think it's so easy to live by another's labor? Do you think it's sweet as sugar to do nothing? When I was still a wee girl-Yaga, I went to school and never had an hour to myself. The goody-goodies at school crammed their lessons, then slept peacefully. But I, little tyke of a Yaga, I lay awake all night thinking how I could get away with knowing nothing at the same time getting good grades. And that's the way it's been all my life—getting something for nothing. You folks are just common workers, you work and sing songs, while I strain myself trying to live like a Queen, without earning a thing through work. So I have to scurry about, dash here and there, fly hither and yonder, using my wits and my sword all the time—that way forcing others to labor for me. So Vasilisa, what task do I give you now?

VASILISA

You'll decide that, Baba-Yaga.

BABA-YAGA

I thought and thought and finally I thought of something. I'll give you a simpler task so that I may scold you the harder when you don't do it right. Look at my hut—the windows have strong grills, which no one can break, not even I. But my door has no lock. You make a strong lock for it, and maybe I'll praise you. Are you willing?

VASILISA

I'll do it.

BABA-YAGA

While you make the lock, I'll take a look at myself in the mirror. I haven't admired myself all day.
She looks in her hand-mirror, and talks to herself.
You, lazy one, you dear little mischief. Oo-tiu-tiu. . .

VASILISA

To the Bear
Step lively, Mishka—break this iron rod in half.

BEAR

It's as good as done.

VASILISA

And you, Ivanushka, smooth a piece of board for me.

IVANUSHKA

Right away, Mama.

VASILISA

You, Mrs. Cat, wet this ring.

CAT

Let's have it, Mistress.

VASILISA

And you, Sharik, you keep an eye on Baba-Yaga. Let me know when she's about to disappear.

BABA-YAGA

I'm not planning to go anywhere right now. I'm comfortable enough at home. My, how hard they're all working! Just look at them. I've never seen anything like it! Usually I come home when everything is already

BABA-YAGA (Cont.)

done for me. Ivanushka, what do you call that little box you have in your hand?

IVANUSHKA

A carpenter's plane.

BABA-YAGA

Why does it make those white ribbons for you?

IVANUSHKA

Those are shavings.

BEAR

Don't pretend not to know. I saw how well you handle a hatchet and an axe.

BABA-YAGA

Meaningfully

Of course I know how to bring down a tree and chop it. This is an ordinary kind of work—but to build something, that's not easy. This someone else can do for me. And what kind of stick do you have in your hands, Vasilisa?

VASILISA

A file.

BABA-YAGA

Come to think of it—why do all of you little creatures work so hard?

VASILISA

You'll soon see why.

BABA-YAGA

Do you hope to save your children?

VASILISA

Yes, I do.

BABA-YAGA

Do you love your boys?

VASILISA

Of course I love them.

BABA-YAGA

And which one do you love the most?

VASILISA

The one who needs me most. When Feden'ka falls ill—he is
that day my most beloved son, and until he gets well. When Ivanushka
gets into trouble, he's more precious to me than the other two—until
I help him get out of it. Do you understand?

BEAR

How could she understand anything about love?

BABA-YAGA

No, I do understand. It's not all that difficult. What I can't understand
is how you didn't get sick and tired of the kids when they were small
and whined from morning till night without reason. I would have
gotten rid of such pests—thrown them out the window!

VASILISA

That just proves that you are a witch, not a human being. Do little
children ever cry without reason? This is the way they call to their
mother. This is the only way they can say; "Mama, help me!" And as
soon as the mother comforts them, they smile, don't they? And that's
the mother's reward.

BABA-YAGA

And when your whiners grew up and got some sense in their heads—
didn't they wear you out with their stubbornness—upset you with
their disobedience? You give them affection, and they pay you back
with insolence. I'd chase them right out of my house.

VASILISA

Again you prove that you are Baba-Yaga and not a human being. Do
you think that they are fresh on purpose? It's only that when they are
upset, their kind words sometimes sink to the bottom and the
unpleasant ones rise to the very top. There, I fixed a lock on your door.

BABA-YAGA

You've done it too fast. It's probably not strong enough.

VASILISA

Don't find fault with it before you test it.
Vasilisa bangs the door shut, locking Baba-Yaga inside the hut.
Well, does the lock make a nice sound?

BABA-YAGA

No, not nice. Did you think you'd catch me unawares—that I'd forget
and praise you, like a little fool?

VASILISA

You'll praise me yet. You won't be able to help it.

BABA-YAGA

Ha-ha-ha!

VASILISA

There's nothing to laugh about—just try and open that door.

BABA-YAGA

Rattles the door
You hussy! Did you lock me up?

VASILISA

Yes I did, Baba-Yaga. Is my lock strong enough?

BABA-YAGA

It's not! It doesn't work.

VASILISA

If it doesn't, then try to come out.
Baba-Yaga shakes the hut, trying to open the door. She howls. Then she sticks her head out of the window.

BABA-YAGA

Vasilisa! Open up. I order you!

VASILISA

Did I fix a good lock for you?

BABA-YAGA

Just the same, I won't praise you.

VASILISA

In that case, stay inside. Don't shout, don't bang on the door.

BABA-YAGA

Chicken legs! Stamp on her!
They shift from one foot to another but don't move.
Forward, march!
They don't move.

BEAR

They won't obey you.

BABA-YAGA

And why is that?

BEAR

All the years that they've been serving you, they never heard a kind word. Vasilisa-the-Hardworker talked to them as she does to people. She even sang them a song.

BABA-YAGA

Vasilisa, if you don't let me out of here, I'll bring such misfortune upon you as no tale ever told or pen ever described. '

VASILISA

And what kind of misfortune would that be?

BABA-YAGA

Exasperated
Oh! This trouble will be the death of me!

BEAR

Don't believe her—she won't die.

BABA-YAGA

Vasilisa, no matter what you do, I'll ruin you in the end. No one can defeat me, the Evil One. I'll always come out on top.

VASILISA

Not once in your whole life did you build a box, or weave a basket, or grow a vegetable, or think up a story, or make up a song. All you ever did was break things, do harm, and steal. How do you think that you who have no skill at any work can get the better of us?

BABA-YAGA

Hey, Cannibal Cannibalovich! Hurry over here! They are insulting us Villians! Help!

BEAR

What makes you think he'll come? You quarreled with him over two cents, and drove him away. The only cannibals left around here are the mosquitos, and they are not that terrifying.

BABA-YAGA

Witch! Witch! Hurry, my friend! Save me!

BEAR

You've quarreled with her as well—over one penny.

BABA-YAGA

Tell me, Vasilisa, what do you want of me?

VASILISA

Free my boys.

BABA-YAGA

Not for anything. You won't get me to do that. They will remain as they are to the end of time. I'll not grant you your request.

VASILISA

You will. Just wait!

BABA-YAGA

Not under any circumstances.

VASILISA

Chicken legs! Take her into the swamp—where it's deepest!
They obey Vasilisa.

BABA-YAGA

Stop! Stop! You, too, will drown there.

CHICKEN LEGS

We'll manage to scramble out of it. We're famous scratchers.

BABA-YAGA

Vasilisa, make them come back.

VASILISA

Calling to the chicken legs
Tsip, tsip, tsip. . .
The hut returns.

BABA-YAGA

Vasilisa, let's make up.

VASILISA

Free my children.

BABA-YAGA

Come closer, I'll tell you something.

VASILISA

Say it so that all can hear.

BABA-YAGA

I'm ashamed. . .

VASILISA

Never mind, say it.

BABA-YAGA

I don't know how to free them.

VASILISA

Don't lie!

BABA-YAGA

May I lose my precious health if I'm not telling the truth. It wasn't I who turned them into Maples—it was my friend, the Evil Witch. I paid her half a ruble for each one of your boys.

FEDYA

Mama, that's true.

EGORUSHKA

Some little old woman *was* with her—she did something with a nut-tree twig.

VASILISA

Chicken Legs, take her off to the swamp!

BABA-YAGA

Wait! Wait! I myself can't free them, but I know how it can be done.

VASILISA

Then tell me.

BABA-YAGA

Walk all the time to the East—don't ever change your course—straight on and on—do you understand? You'll come to a marsh—don't stop, walk right over it. You'll come to the sea—swim across it, only be sure not to change your direction or you'll lose your way. And when you get to the opposite shore, you'll see to your right a forest whose trees are three times as tall as the ones in ours—and their leaves won't be green but white and gray—the forest is that ancient. In the middle of it you'll see a mound overgrown with white grass. Inside the mound is a cave. In the middle of the cave is a white rock. Push aside the rock, under it you'll find a well. The water in this well is hot. It bubbles like boiling water and is luminous. Bring back a jug of that water, pour it at the foot of the Maples and they will come to life at once. That is all. Phew! I'm tired out.

BABA-YAGA (Cont.)

Never in my life have I talked so much about something else than myself. Usually I like to talk about me, little treasure that I am. . .

VASILISA

And how long will it take me to reach that well?

BABA-YAGA

Not less than a year.

Fedya and Egorushka cry out sorrowfully.

VASILISA

You are lying!

BEAR

No, this time she isn't. How lucky!

He laughs.

Woe! Woe!

He weeps.

VASILISA

What is the matter with you?

BEAR

When I calm down, I'll tell you.

BABA-YAGA

Get started, Vasilisa, don't waste time.

VASILISA

We'll take you along.

BABA-YAGA

The hut will not be able to get through the thick of the forest. No, you'll have to go by yourself. One year one way, another year back, and in two years a great deal can happen. Maybe things will happen my way yet. Go, go, what are you waiting for?

VASILISA

I'll first ask my friends' advice.

Vasilisa and the rest move to the side.

What's wrong with you, Mishka? Why do you laugh, then cry?

BEAR

Ha-ha-ha! Oh! Oh! Oh! The thing that will save us is right here, but we can't get to it.

VASILISA

Why?

BEAR

Vasilisa my dear, listen: I'll tell you right now, ha-ha, I'll tell you, oh! oh! just how it happened. Do you remember what I told you about my grandfather, how the Snake-Dragon stole him just for fun and set him on fire?

VASILISA

I remember, Mishka.

BEAR

When this awful thing happened, my father rolled all the way down to that cave, to get some of that magic water. He hurried back home with it as fast as his legs could carry him. At that time we lived not far from the cave. Ha-ha-ha! Oh! Oh! Oh!

IVANUSHKA

Go on, go on, don't torture us with the suspense!

BEAR

He comes back with a pailful of the magic water. Oh, my! The old man lies there, not breathing any more. The family stands around him, sobbing. Father sprinkled him with the magic water—what a miracle! His singed fur curled again, like new. His old heart beat again, like a young one. Grandfather rose and sneezed, and the whole forest said: "God Bless You!" Ha-ha-ha! Oh! Oh! Oh!

SHARIK

Stop crying, Master, or I'll have to start howling.

VASILISA

Go on with your story.

BEAR

I have a whole pitcher of that magic water. Ha-ha-ha!

VASILISA

Where is it?

BEAR

In my little trunk, ha-ha-ha!

VASILISA

And where is the trunk?

BEAR

In Baba-Yaga's hut. She keeps it under the stove in order to keep me from leaving without her permission, oh-oh-oh!

VASILISA

Then we'll have to undo the lock.

CAT

You mustn't. The old "mouse" will escape from her mousetrap. We'll get that pitcher in a different way. I'll climb in through the chimney.

BEAR

She'll hear you.

SHARIK

Don't worry. I'll annoy her somehow so that she won't notice what Cat is doing.
The Cat disappears. Sharik runs to the hut.
Baba-Yaga, you once boasted that you understood dog language.

BABA-YAGA

Of course I understand it. It's the best language for quarreling. And I adore quarreling!

SHARIK

Bow-wow! What did I just say?

BABA-YAGA

You said: "This way, hunter, the squirrel is in the pine tree."

SHARIK

What do you know?—she really understands. And this?
He barks.

BABA-YAGA

"You get closer and I'll tear your tail off."

SHARIK

And this?
Barks.

BABA-YAGA

You nasty dog!

SHARIK

Did you understand that?

BABA-YAGA

Do you dare to say to me that any pigeon is kinder than I! Then this is what I have to say to you!

She barks. Sharik answers her in kind. They bark vociferously at each other for a while, like angry dogs who are about to pounce on each other. Suddenly Baba-Yaga stops barking.

Help! Robbers!

She disappears into the hut. There is meowing, hissing and screeching from the hut, then total silence.

SHARIK

Bow-wow-wow! Our kitten is done for. Wow!

IVANUSHKA

I must get inside the hut somehow.

BEAR

Could *you* go down the chimney? Oh, it's all my fault—the devil take me! Why did I leave the magic water in my trunk!

VASILISA

Wait, maybe our Cat is still alive and well. Pst, pst, pst.
No sound.

IVANUSHKA

Poor kitty!

VASILISA

Wait—I forgot that she doesn't understand what pst, pst means. She is a serious cat that Koshka Ivanovna.
There is a sound of purring from the roof.

BEAR

She's alive!

SHARIK

Why don't you come down—why do you always give me heart failure?

CAT

From the rooftop
I'm licking the ashes off myself.

BEAR

We thought you were dead.

CAT

No, she caught me by the tail, but I got away.
She jumps to the ground holding a large pitcher in her paws.
Is this the pitcher, Mishka?

BEAR

The very one.

BABA-YAGA

In the window
The water has lost its magic power—it's lost its magic.

EGORUSHKA

Mama!

VASILISA

Get out of the way, my friends.
They all move to the side. Vasilisa walks over to the Maples. The pitcher is carefully sealed with a round oak wood stopper. When she removes the stopper, a blue flame escapes from the pitcher. Vasilisa sprinkles the water on the Maples. They disappear instantly in a bluish mist. The sound of music is heard as though from the depths of the earth. Gradually the music becomes louder and gayer. The mist lifts. Where the Maples stood now two boys are seen. They are the same height; they resemble each other and Ivanushka. They look around dazedly, as if they had just wakened, and suddenly notice Vasilisa. They cry out.

FEDYA AND EGORUSHKA

Mama!

VASILISA

Embracing them
My dear boys, my boys!

CAT

Rejoice, rejoice. Now no one will dare touch you!

FEDYA

Little brother!
He hugs Ivanushka.

VASILISA

My children! You look just the way you did the day you were lost to me. You don't look a day older.

FEDYA

Mama, we'll never run away again.

EGORUSHKA

Now we'll start growing, not by the day, but by the hour.

FEDYA

Mama, let's go, let's go! We've been standing still for so long!

EGORUSHKA

So long that our feet will no longer stand still.
To the trees.
Good-bye, trees, good-bye, friends. Don't feel bad that we're in such a hurry to leave, to get home.
The trees rustle softly but fervently

BABA-YAGA

Will this outrage never end! They stand there and rejoice before my very eyes. Don't you know that I can't bear to see people happy? Let me out of here this minute!

ALL

Never!

VASILISA

Ignoring Baba-Yaga
Come, let's start, my friends. Let's walk hand-in-hand. We're on our way!
They join hands and, dancing in a circle, leave the stage.

THE END

Anna, the Hollow Man and the Mayor in the production of the Junge Garde Theatre in Halle, East Germany.

THE CITY WITHOUT LOVE

A Fantasy in Two Acts

by Lev Ustinov

CHARACTERS:

Commentator

A Clown

The Mayor

Anna, his daughter

The Hollow Man, also the Executioner

Queen of the Swallows

Guard of the city's gate

An Urchin—from nowhere?

Two Soldiers—"Tarabars"

COMMENTATOR

He addresses the audience directly, as he does throughout the play.

Have you ever seen a city painted entirely in gray? No?. . . Well, here is one right in front of you. The houses, sidewalks, pavement, doors, window-frames, roofs, prison towers, the city gate—they are all gray. Dark gray, light gray, almost black-gray, almost white-gray, speckled gray, but gray just the same. Isn't this a strange city? You don't like it?. . . I don't either.

GUARD

Chasing a fly

Get away! Disappear! Only gray flies are allowed to buzz in this city. You are green. If you don't get away from here I'll. . .

He trips and falls

Damn fly! (*To the audience*) Don't laugh, there's nothing funny about it. When I was a boy and stupid I, too, laughed a lot. Laughing without a good reason is the sign of foolishness. Twenty years ago our Mayor outlawed laughter. I didn't much mind—by then there wasn't much to laugh about. And when he outlawed love, it was a happy day for me. At the time I was madly in love with two girls and didn't know what to do. The three of us would always go around together and we would always quarrel. Then the no-love order was given and everything became simpler. Love forsook our city. It seems that love doesn't like to be outlawed.

COMMENTATOR

And here comes Anna, the Mayor's daughter. You notice, there's nothing unusual about her. She has hair like many other girls and her eyes are ordinary eyes. Only, her nose is short and cute and a little bit turned up. Girls with a cute nose like that usually giggle or laugh a lot. But all that was forbidden when she was barely a year old, and she simply doesn't know how to laugh. She sighs instead.

ANNA

A curse on your head, Old Man!

GUARD

And on yours, Anna!

COMMENTATOR

That is how people greet each other in this city. Here they avoid every expression of friendliness. . . .since friendliness softens the soul and a tender soul is so prone to love.

ANNA

What's new, Mr. Guard? Has any stranger come into our city?

GUARD

No, no one has come. (*Sighs*)

ANNA

And why do you sigh?

GUARD

From joy, I guess. Before I would have laughed with joy. Now I sigh.
When you're near me, Anna, I feel somehow warmed by your
presence. . .
He hesitates and looks around uneasily
No, I mean. . .I mean. . .don't mean "warmed". . . I meant to say
I feel "mean". . .

ANNA

Is it because you're afraid of me? Only the Hollow Man doesn't fear
me, but I really despise him.

GUARD

Now don't you take it into your head to tell him so.

ANNA

I know. . .

GUARD

No, I'm not afraid of you, for I know that you have a gentle. . .
Catching himself
I mean. . .a hard heart. (*In a whisper*) And in our city this can be
very dangerous. A person with a gentle heart is the first to
get into trouble.

ANNA

Show me that you're not afraid of me.

GUARD

How?

ANNA

Laugh! I want to know how it sounds.

GUARD

That's not fair. You know that it's against the law, and you know
that I can't refuse you anything.

ANNA

Come on, laugh! I won't breathe a word about it to anyone.

GUARD

Makes an attempt to laugh but only a hoarse growl comes out
I can't do it. I've forgotten how.

ANNA

Oh, try to remember! You used to laugh before.

GUARD

Makes another unsuccessful attempt
It's nò use! Laughter can live only when it's nourished by laughter.
Otherwise it starves to death. Speaking of nourishment, wait
here while I go and take my soup off the stove.
He exits.
Anna whistles quietly and the SWALLOW appears and runs to her.

ANNA

I came here yesterday but you were gone. Where did you fly to?

SWALLOW

There's much to do. You see how near we are to spring.

ANNA

I see no signs of it.

SWALLOW

No, you wouldn't see it from here. But high up in the sky you'd
see how spring is moving over the earth. I have to build my nest
and teach the young ones. They frolic about too much. They must be
taught how to take care of themselves. Believe me, it's not easy to be
the Queen of Swallows.

ANNA

And are you a strict queen?

SWALLOW

I try. But they don't really believe I'm strict.

ANNA

Why?

SWALLOW

They know that I'm really kind.

ANNA

Then how do you make them obey?

SWALLOW

I just keep explaining things to them, patiently. . .

ANNA

Come, Swallow, let's have a little dance.

SWALLOW

What if someone sees us?

ANNA

We'll watch out as we dance.

ANNA AND SWALLOW

They dance and sing

> In my new shoes I walk,
> To the friendly birds I talk,
> I run from the sharp-eyed hawk.
> Along the way I'll find—
> What? What?
> Somewhere, someone a song will sing,
> Somewhere, someone a gift will bring,
> What? What?
> Maybe a big box of sweets,
> Or a big bag of other treats.
> This will be our secret—
> Ours! Ours!
> If you sing a little song,
> If you try, if you wait,
> Happiness will come along.
> When? When?

We hear heavy footsteps

SWALLOW

Watch out! The Hollow Man is coming!

ANNA

Oh, hurry! Fly away!

SWALLOW

It's too late! He saw us!

ANNA

Frightened
What are you going to do?

SWALLOW

I'll fly up, not high, and you look very angry and throw a
stone at me.

ANNA

What if I hit you?!

SWALLOW

Don't worry, I'll manage to dodge it. I'm good at that.
*The SWALLOW flies away. ANNA pretends anger and throws
a stone at her. ANNA shudders as she hears a sharp cry
from the SWALLOW.*
*The HOLLOW MAN enters, leaning on a large gnarled staff.
He looks around suspiciously, his long pointed beard pointing
this way and that.*

HOLLOW MAN

Don't try to lie to me. I saw everything!

ANNA

I'm not! Didn't you see me throw a stone at her?

HOLLOW MAN

You pretended to want to hit her. Before that you danced with
her. I'll report it to your father and you'll be punished. And the
bird—I'll order it to be destroyed.

ANNA

Father won't believe you.

HOLLOW MAN

He'll believe me all right. He knows that I see everything. I can
even look through walls.

ANNA

Oh, go ahead and look! Look all you want! I despise you
just the same.

HOLLOW MAN

Aha! You've just declared your hate for me. Now you will become
my wife! Yes, yes! Now you'll have to marry me! According to the
70th Paragraph of the 71st Statute of the 72nd Law, that marriage is
considered ideal when the groom and the bride despise each other. I've
now said everything there is to be said, and I'm going.
He exits.
*SWALLOW appears. She's limping and leaning on one wing and
leg. Her other leg is broken.*

ANNA

Running to SWALLOW
What happened to you?

SWALLOW

Nothing — it's all my fault.

ANNA

The stone hit your leg! Didn't it?!

SWALLOW

I know you didn't mean to hurt me.

ANNA

Of course I didn't! Oh, what will happen to you now?

SWALLOW

Nothing so terrible. . . They'll just choose another swallow to be queen. You know that the queen has to be perfect.

ANNA

And now they can't take you along when they fly south before Winter sets in here.

SWALLOW

I wouldn't want to fly away with them, anyhow.

ANNA

Why?

SWALLOW

Well, because I'd rather die here, at home.

ANNA

We're both unlucky! I'm also in deep trouble—I declared my hate for the Hollow Man.

SWALLOW

Oh, why did you do that?!

ANNA

I couldn't stand it any more! I'm so tired of pretending!
In the distance we hear the thud of marching feet. The sound gets closer.
Hide! It's the soldiers, the Tarabars!
She crouches with SWALLOW in a niche in the wall.
Two soldiers enter goose-stepping.

COMMENTATOR

Now you understand why Anna and the Swallow are so frightened.
The Tarabars have a very menacing look, don't they? Look at
their rifles with their long bayonets. The Tarabars' whiskers
are longer than any cat's, and the spurs on their boots would make
any rooster simply die of envy. And as to the song they sing, let's
say right off that it doesn't resemble a lullaby!

SOLDIERS

They sing as they exit

> Love is the cause of all evil!
> It must pay a price, which must be met!
> Or it is death, death by bayonet!
> Te-rem, te-ret!
> Te-rum, te-ret!

ANNA and the SWALLOW come out from their hiding place

ANNA

I'll bandage your leg right away.
Without hesitation, she pulls at her sleeve, tearing off a piece of it.

SWALLOW

What are you doing! This is your favorite dress!

ANNA

The life of a friend is more precious that the most favorite dress!
She bandages the injured bird's leg with tender care.

SWALLOW

Watch out! The Guard is coming!

ANNA

Don't be afraid of him. He's an old grump, but he'll never betray me.
Guard enters.

GUARD

Damn it! I hurried with that soup and burned my tongue! It feels
like a swollen potato. I can hardly speak.

ANNA

That's not so terrible — it just means you won't grumble as much.

GUARD

Alarmed

What are you doing? Have you gone mad?!

ANNA

Poor Swallow has a broken leg.

GUARD

In a whisper

If anyone sees you show pity and finds out that I saw it and didn't
report you, we'll both get it! Stop this at once!

ANNA

You'd better be sure that no one sees us.

GUARD

You're not being fair! You know that I can't refuse
you anything.

CLOWN

Appearing above the city wall

Greetings!

*The GUARD is so startled that he staggers and falls to the ground.
SWALLOW and ANNA freeze on the spot.*

*This is a Wandering Clown, who follows the custom of wearing
his make-up and his costume when entering a strange city. He now
peers over the wall of the Gray City wearing his two-colored,
black-and-white hat with little bells on its sharp point.*

GUARD

Who are you?

CLOWN

Open the gate my good old man and I'll tell you who I am.

GUARD

Jumping up with indignation

What are you, an informer? Are you going to denounce me as being
kind? Don't make that mistake! I'm fierce! I'm the most nasty
man in this city! And don't ask me for anything, Stranger.
Neither food nor water will you get from me.

CLOWN

First, I do not intend to beg for bread or water—I earn them.
Secondly, I see that your Swallow has only one good leg and to make
two out of one—for me this is the simplest of tricks.

ANNA

Come, Guard, let him in—let him in quickly.

GUARD

He's lying. It's all idle talk. I know of ways to make one leg out of two, but two out of one. . . It's all lies, idle talk.

CLOWN

So you don't believe me? Then watch this: do you see this finger? . . .

He moves his right hand over the index finger of the left and this finger disappears. After a brief pause and a triumphant glance at the old GUARD, he passes the right hand with a flourish over the hand with the missing finger and it is back in place.

GUARD

All right, I'll let him in. But mind you, Anna, this is the last time I grant your wish.

He opens the gate. The CLOWN enters the city. His costume matches his half-white, half-black hat. He goes over to SWALLOW, makes a wide gesture with his hand.

CLOWN

P-paz!

SWALLOW

Screams and squats, legless
Oh, where is my good leg?

CLOWN

A moment's patience, please! P-paz!
SWALLOW jumps up and stands on two whole legs.

ANNA

Look! You have two good legs again. You'll go on being Queen of the Swallows!
To CLOWN
A curse on your head!

CLOWN

Surprised
What for?

ANNA

You don't know our ways yet. In our city this is the way we greet people.

CLOWN

How incredibly pleasant! . . . In that case, a curse on your heads.

ANNA

Tell us who you are.

CLOWN

I am a Wandering Clown, an Illusionist, Conjuror, Improvisator.
And who are you?

ANNA

I am the daughter of the Mayor. My name is Anna.

CLOWN

Bowing
It's a pleasure. . .

ANNA

Don't say that word! You're expected to say "I'm disgusted."

CLOWN

I understand. . . I've been to many strange cities but this is the strangest.
Taking the guitar hanging from his back, he plays and sings
> I met a girl in this strange town,
> I bowed and said, "It's my pleasure!"
> Her answer was only a shrug and a frown. . .

URCHIN

Appearing above the wall and singing in the same melody
. . .It's better such a new friend to treasure!

CLOWN

Annoyed
Not you again! (To GUARD) Don't let him in! Three weeks now he's
been at my heels. He wants to learn the secrets of my trade. My
head is spinning from his endless questions about my tricks!

URCHIN

They don't let me in anywhere, but I get in everywhere. . .

CLOWN

Chase him away!

URCHIN

Calm down! No one can get rid of me.

GUARD

Swinging his cudgel
And why is that?

URCHIN

Jumping down off the wall
There's no place to chase me to.

GUARD

Go! Get back where you came from!

URCHIN

I came from nowhere. I have no home, no father, no mother—
not even a sister or brother.

ANNA

Then who feeds you?

URCHIN

I breakfast on Curiosity, for lunch I have what I discovered at breakfast,
and for supper I have the hope of the next day's breakfast. And if
now and then I find a crust of bread, I eat it between meals.

ANNA

Here is a candy for you.

URCHIN

Thanks. I happen to have a free minute and will devour it mercilessly.
He takes the candy, makes the face of a ferocious beast and swallows it

ANNA

I permit him to remain in our city.

URCHIN

Thanks, but I don't need your permission. It's much more fun to do
things without permission!. . . A curse on your heads!
He runs off, disappearing around the corner of the nearest house.

GUARD

To Anna
You've been showing pity for others too often. Watch out or
you'll have reason to pity yourself. . .

SWALLOW

The birds are waiting for me. I have to fly away now. Thank you,
Clown. My subjects will be very happy if you stay.
She flies away.

CLOWN

Has love been forbidden in your city for a long time now?

GUARD

Yes, a long time. I forget—maybe as long as twenty years.

CLOWN

Is it possible that for twenty years no one here has fallen in love?

GUARD

There were cases. . .

CLOWN

And what happened to those people?

GUARD

Those who fell in love were put to death, and the ones they fell in love with were imprisoned for life.

CLOWN

But there is such a thing as a secret love. . .when one loves but can't get himself to declare his love, not to the last day of his life.

GUARD

There were such cases, too.

CLOWN

And were they spared?

ANNA

Here we have a way of finding out even a secret love. Father's deputy, the Hollow Man, has devised an awful invention. Once a day a signal is given and every citizen of the city must put a special stethoscope to his heart.

CLOWN

A stethoscope?!

ANNA

Yes. . . It's a kind of disk at the end of a rubber tube. . . When a person has a sore throat, or a bad cough, the doctor always listens to his chest with that kind of thing.

CLOWN

Please forgive my ignorance, but I've never been sick.

ANNA

So the Hollow Man invented this special stethoscope that at once betrays the one who has dared fall in love, and in the Central Control Room, on an electric panel, a small red light appears among the green ones.

CLOWN

What if a citizen of your city refuses to apply this devilish stethoscope?

ANNA

He will be discovered anyway—up there on Lover's Mountain.
Look, there it is, towering over the city. It's enchanted. Anyone
who hides his love will be drawn irresistibly to this Mountain.
A telescope with a camera automatically photographs the victim
up there. Then the picture is used as evidence. Don't you think
that's pretty clever?

CLOWN

It would be even cleverer of me to get out of here! Goodbye. Good luck!

ANNA

Are you leaving? Don't. . .

CLOWN

There's no work for a clown in a city where no one knows how to laugh.

ANNA

Can *you* laugh?

CLOWN

Of course.

ANNA

Pleadingly
Show me how you do it.

CLOWN

Just like that? Without a reason? It's not easy to do, but a clown
knows how.
He laughs hard.

ANNA

That's strange. I thought laughter sounded quite different. Did
it hurt you to laugh?

CLOWN

Certainly not? Why would it hurt?

ANNA

You seemed to be scowling and your teeth were bared like an angry dog's.

CLOWN

Laughs at the remark

Poor girl! You have never laughed and you've never seen others laugh. What you've missed!

ANNA

What?

CLOWN

Everything—and then some!

He extends his hand to ANNA

Goodbye! I wish that you may feel what you fear most of all—love.

GUARD

Here, let go of her hand! That looks too much like affection. A curse on your head, and get going!

We hear the sound of singing. It gets nearer.

VOICES

> The color of gray! The color of gray!
> It's the greatest color—Hooray! Hooray!

ANNA

That's my father coming.

GUARD

And the Hollow Man is with him.

COMMENTATOR

And here they are. Did you hear that song? It's the Mayor's theme song. Look at him—he wears gray shoes, a gray polka-dotted suit, a gray derby. And on the derby is his light gray crown. He walks through the town with a defiant hop-skip-and-jump, sticking his nose into everything, making himself a general nuisance. Everyone is sick and tired of him. At one of the city ceremonies he declared that he felt young and vigorous, that he had no intention of ever dying, and therefore ordered that he be called Immortal. He's convinced that everything is in order in his city, that everything is going according to his rules. And when one is that satisfied with himself, why not sing a song?

MAYOR

Sings

> The color of gray! The color of gray!
> It's the greatest color—Hooray! Hooray!

MAYOR (Cont.)

> So if we spare not the gray paint,
> Lovers will not kiss or faint.
> To gray will turn the blood in their veins,
> And thoughts of loving will vanish from their brains.

> The color of gray! The color of gray!
> It's the greatest color—Hooray! Hooray!
> The dark gray cloud over hill and plain,
> Will pour from the sky its good gray rain,
> Wrapping the world in a wet gray sheet,
> Or covering the earth with squishy sleet.
> The color of gray! The color of gray!
> It's the greatest color—Hooray! Hooray!

Noticing the CLOWN, the MAYOR falls silent and gazes at him in surprise

MAYOR

A curse on your head, Stranger. Who might you be?

CLOWN

A wandering conjuror, Your Gray Highness.

MAYOR

With false modesty

Now, now, you needn't address me with such fancy titles. Address me the way everyone does, simply as "Your Immortal Municipalship!"

CLOWN

An extraordinary title! I will address you that way on every appropriate occasion. (*He bows*)

MAYOR

To show proper respect to a ruler, any occasion is appropriate. Address me thus as long as you are in our city. Are you staying long?

CLOWN

No, I'm just passing through.

GUARD

Permit me to make a report to you, Your Immortal Municipalship.

MAYOR

Go ahead.

GUARD

The regulations for entering the city have been fully observed. This stranger swore that he had never loved, does not love now, and will never love.

CLOWN

He is about to contradict the GUARD, but changes his mind
Don't worry. I won't remain here long. I'll earn a few coins, buy myself some food, have a good meal, then I'll be on my way.

MAYOR

So you intend to buy food. And do you know when a man should eat—do you know the rules for eating?

CLOWN

A rich man eats whenever he wants to, a poor man, when he can afford it.

MAYOR

Not at all, not at all. Everyone must breakfast at breakfast time, dine at dinner time, and sup at supper time. And if anyone should dare to breakfast at supper time, or sup at dinner time, he would be severely punished.
He does a slight knee-bend, as though doing part of an exercise drill.

COMMENTATOR

The Mayor always does this when he's especially impressed with what he has just said, and everyone around him does likewise as a sign of agreement. Now watch, the Mayor will shout as if speaking to the whole world from a platform. He will then begin not to make sense, and on such occasions the Hollow Man tugs at his sleeve, and he falls silent, like a broken toy. Then he begins to talk more normally.

MAYOR

Still addressing the CLOWN
If you fail to answer the next two questions correctly, I will instantly run you out of town.
He pauses dramatically, then throws each question as he would a sharp dagger at a target.
Into what does the Volga River empty?. . . No one is to prompt him! Anyone who does will be severely punished!

CLOWN

The Volga empties into the Caspian Sea.

MAYOR

Correct! And what do the horses of this world eat?

CLOWN

Horses eat oats.

MAYOR

Very clever. The earth is round, water is wet. Feathers are soft, rocks are hard. What is useful is not harmful and what is harmful is not useful. The ruler is useful. . .

MAYOR (Cont.)

The HOLLOW MAN tugs at his sleeve, and the MAYOR is
silent, then. . .
Very well. Now show us one of your tricks.

CLOWN

Observe!
He takes a flask from his pocket and takes one swallow from it,
then walks over to the MAYOR, takes one of the large gray buttons
of his uniform between two of his fingers and tears it off.
No one has ever dared do such a thing to the MAYOR. His mouth
has dropped open and he is choking with rage and hardly able to
utter a word. Finally finding his voice. . .

MAYOR

What—what—have you done? You spoilt. . . You seized
public property! What belongs to me belongs to the city. And
vice versa.

HOLLOW MAN

Will you order him to be hanged, burnt alive, or merely beheaded?

MAYOR

Here we have to account for every button! Here we count. . .

CLOWN

Splendid! Since you love to count, watch this. I have in my hand just
one button. I swallow it.
He puts the button in his mouth and makes a big show of
swallowing something so big
Now, give me your full attention. Concentrate. Look at my ears.
He makes several gestures with his hands and takes a button
like the one he tore off the MAYOR's jacket from each of his ears
Let me congratulate you, Your Immortal Municipalship.
Now your city is richer by one button. A spare one will always
come in handy.

MAYOR

Again getting wound up, shouts as from a tribune
We need nothing superfluous. Too much muchness gives rise to
indulgence. And indulging breeds love. Happy is he who lives
only by the rules. But love does not obey *any* rules. People
love whomever they want to, in whichever way pleases them, and
most often any old way. Taking the aforementioned into account,
we have determined with absolute finality that love is an evil!

MAYOR (Cont.)

In our city only one kind of love is permitted—rulers must
love to rule and the governed must love to be ruled!

He does his knee-bend with enormous satisfaction.

*Everyone does likewise, including the Hollow Man who at the
same time tugs at his sleeve.*

However, it is very interesting how you do this trick.

ANNA

It's fascinating.

CLOWN

Smiling at ANNA and pleased at her praise

It's a trade secret.

ANNA

Poutingly

Daddy, I want to know his secret.

CLOWN

Telling the secret spoils the trick.

HOLLOW MAN

If I were you I'd prefer to spoil the trick and save my life.

MAYOR

Tell us how you do it and be quick about it!

CLOWN

Once I unintentionally swallowed a plum pit and suddenly I
felt a tickle in my ears. I put my fingers into them and found
a plum pit in each. It was then that the happy thought came to
me to become a magician.

MAYOR

Very interesting! When I was young I liked to drink beer, and
everything doubled—only not in my ears but in my eyes. . .

HOLLOW MAN

Your Immortal Municipalship!

MAYOR

Hm-m-m. I was only joking. That never happened. Never! Didn't.
Never didn't! . . .

The HOLLOW MAN tugs at his sleeve

Very well. What are you going to do with him—let him stay or
throw him out?

ANNA

Let him stay.

MAYOR

Sternly
How dare you answer for me?!

ANNA

Frightened
No. . . I only wanted to. . .

MAYOR

Only I can answer my own questions.

HOLLOW MAN

Permit me, Your Immortal Municipalship, to pose a certain
question to this so-called magician.

MAYOR

I permit it.

HOLLOW MAN

Can you swallow a gold piece and take two out of your ears?

CLOWN

I can.

HOLLOW MAN

Then swallow one.

CLOWN

Such a profitable trick demands a good price.

HOLLOW MAN

How much?

CLOWN

A gold piece.

HOLLOW MAN

Addressing the MAYOR
Should we agree to that?

MAYOR

Agree. Hurry up and agree! Let him make us some money! Hurry!

HOLLOW MAN

Here, take it.
Gives the CLOWN a gold coin

CLOWN

Putting it in his pocket as payment for the trick
Now give me your gold piece.
The HOLLOW MAN gives the CLOWN a gold coin. He quickly swallows it and produces two gold pieces from his ears

MAYOR

Hurrah! All rules have been honored, all problems solved!
Tomorrow, from early morning on, you'll start swallowing gold
pieces without a stop! You're the person I need! I issue a
Proclamation to the entire population that we are embarking
on an era of great wealth! The magic formula that we've been
searching for so long has been found! An economic miracle!
At last I—we—I shall become rich! Rich! At last! I command
that the magician be rewarded with a ham!
*HOLLOW MAN tugs at his sleeve. Then he shouts an order
in unintelligible words. The TARABARS carry in a ham, place it at
The CLOWN's feet, and march off with goose-step.*
Yes, yes. . . And you, my loyal Hollow Man, for your excellent
idea I award you this medal, "For Outstanding Severity in Service"
and in addition you may ask me for anything you desire.

HOLLOW MAN

Your Municipalship! Your Immortal Municipalship!. . . This
morning your Anna declared her hatred for me. So, according
to this rule and custom of our great city, she should marry me.

ANNA

Daddy, I don't want to marry him!

MAYOR

Please, she's too young for you. . .

ANNA

Daddy, look at him—he's so old! I'll be so miserable!

HOLLOW MAN

Being miserable hardens the soul, and makes one more severe.
And severity is exactly what Anna lacks.

MAYOR

You are right. But, perhaps we can wait a while with the wedding. . .

HOLLOW MAN

Your Municipalship, if you yourself violate the rules. . .

MAYOR

Never! Little daughter. . . Annushka. . . Don't cause me to lose you! If you refuse to obey the rules. . .

ANNA

Damned city! Damned rules!

To HOLLOW MAN

If I could, I'd strangle you with my own hands!

HOLLOW MAN

Delighted

Your Municipalship! Did you hear her? She's becoming tough and merciless!

ANNA

You're mean and heartless!

HOLLOW MAN

Aha! This time you've spoken the truth. *I* have no heart! You don't believe it? Hey, Clown, listen to my chest, and tell her!

CLOWN

Puts his ear to the HOLLOW MAN's chest

There's a grave-like silence there.

HOLLOW MAN

Yes! And in this grave are buried the hopes of those who tried to make a softy out of me.

CLOWN

What did you do with your heart?

HOLLOW MAN

I was smart! When I learned that every human being is born with a kind heart, I plucked mine out of my breast. Even as a youth I decided to become powerful, and merciless! Even as a mere boy I killed frogs, then birds. . .

He freezes. The scream of a siren is heard over the city and a bell rings ominously. there is general panic.

CLOWN

To the GUARD

What happened—a fire?

GUARD

Someone has probably fallen in love.

The TARABARS goose-step in. Stamping their feet in place and speaking in the peculiar language* in which the HOLLOW MAN always addresses them, they announce:

TARABARS

A-ka *flow*-kow-*er*-ker *has*-kas *bloo*-koo-*med*-ked *i*-ki-*n the*-ke *de*-ke-*sert*-kert!

HOLLOW MAN

(*Translating*) A flower has bloomed in the desert!

MAYOR

Horrors!

HOLLOW MAN

What are your orders?

MAYOR

Destroy it and its roots! Follow me!

CLOWN

Addressing ANNA
What language did the TARABARS speak?

ANNA

The Hollow Man has taught them a secret language and they obey only him.
The MAYOR, the HOLLOW MAN, the GUARD and the TARABARS run off stage.

URCHIN

Coming down from a roof like a drift of sun-warmed snow
What a panic in the city! A regular show! Everybody scurried home, locked their doors and shutters, put out their fires! No one is cooking or baking anything. . . And I love the smell of food! By the way, do you know that if you breathe the smell of food hard enough it feels as if you are eating it. Honestly! I've had occasion to try it. It makes your mouth water.

---

*The Hollow Man claims to have invented a special language for the Tarabars—to give himself more importance and provide secrecy. Actually, all he does is separate words into syllables and put after each syllable a "k" with its vowel sound. He has trained them to respond to orders *only* when given in this language, but when they sing their theme song, they do this in normal language since that has not been forbidden.

URCHIN (Cont.)

To CLOWN

I saw you swallow that button. . . I don't understand it. How does it get to your ears?

CLOWN

Stop nagging me!

URCHIN

I sneaked into the tailor's house and stole some buttons from him.

CLOWN

Let me have them.

URCHIN

I swallowed them. Imagine, I swallowed six buttons and not one got into my ears! I pushed my finger way deep, but found nothing. . .

CLOWN

Stop doing that or you'll lose your hearing.

URCHIN

I'm not giving up. I'd swallow all the buttons in the world to become a good magician.

CLOWN

I don't think you'll ever become one.

URCHIN

Why not?

CLOWN

To be a wandering clown and magician a person must know how to sing and dance.

URCHIN

I already know how to dance. Not as well as you, but I can learn. But singing—that's a bad business. In one place they even roughed me up when I tried to sing. At first I thought that I sang the wrong song with that chorus, but then I found out that I sang the wrong way. But they shouldn't have roughed me up.

CLOWN

Music takes a lot of practising.

URCHIN

I've got plenty of time.

CLOWN

You also have to be jolly and kind to people. I guess you can do that. But you must get some schooling.

URCHIN

Proudly

I am educated.

CLOWN

How long did you attend school?

URCHIN

Almost a whole year!

CLOWN

Then what happened? Did they throw you out?

URCHIN

Yes.

CLOWN

Why? Were you a hooligan?

URCHIN

No. I didn't have the money for tuition, so they expelled me. But I swear—I know all the letters and can even count to ten. I'm very learned.

The CLOWN smiles, and now he seems to taken an interest in the URCHIN for the first time.

CLOWN

All right. . . If you'll behave yourself. . .

We hear the music of a funeral march, and moving to its rhythm, a stern procession appears, carrying a desert cactus flower on a stretcher. The TARABARS carry the stretcher, the MAYOR heads the procession, and the HOLLOW MAN brings up the rear, singing solemnly and clearly enunciating the words

HOLLOW MAN

Singing

> Death to all the flowers,
> All grasses and cactuses too!
> Death to all the flowers,
> All grasses and cactuses too!

URCHIN

What are they going to do with the poor flower?

CLOWN

Execute it.

URCHIN

What is this, one of their games?

CLOWN

Unfortunately they don't play this game only with cactuses.

URCHIN

With what else?

CLOWN

With people.
The URCHIN's impulse is to rush forward and attack the villains.
The CLOWN restrains him for his own good.

MAYOR

Giving the order
Get rea-dy for the hang-ing!
The TARABARS lower the stretcher, goose-step out and return
with the gallows. They tie the noose around the flower.

HOLLOW MAN

Death! Dea-keath
The TARABARS are about to pull the rope

URCHIN

Stop!
Everyone freezes with surprise, then they all turn toward
the URCHIN.
This is nasty and stupid!

MAYOR

What is nasty and stupid?

URCHIN

What you are doing.

HOLLOW MAN

Bristling
Do you mean to say that you are smarter and nobler than we are?

URCHIN

Yes.

MAYOR

It would be interesting to know what makes you think so.

URCHIN

I attended school for almost a whole year, and I learned that
flowers are. . .are. . .pretty. . .they are nature's jewels!
He is surprised and somewhat embarrassed by his eloquence
And you don't allow grass to grow either. And I learned that
grass is good food for cows and pigs.

MAYOR

We prefer real jewels to pretty flowers. And we feed cows
with their own milk, chickens with their own eggs. . . Therefore
the feeding of our animals costs us nothing. Our city, our
great, inimitable city. . .
The HOLLOW MAN tugs at his sleeve
By the way, how did you get in here?

GUARD

Frightened
The gate was closed.

URCHIN

Right. Gates exist to be locked, walls—to be climbed over.

MAYOR

Do you know what awaits you for your impudence?

URCHIN

What?

MAYOR

The same fate that is about to befall that flower.
He points to the cactus bloom in the noose.

URCHIN

To hang me, you must first catch me! Besides, I don't
like any of you here. You are all mean, and big bores.
A great clown came to your city. He wants to cheer up
everybody. I saw his act in five cities! A person can
just die laughing. And you use him to make money! You
are worse than bandits. You have stolen everybody's fun

URCHIN (Cont.)

from them and left them only hard work. It's like a
school stealing all the kids' fun and leaving them only their
classes. Nuts to you!

He waves his arm in disgust and runs off.

HOLLOW MAN

Catch him!

COMMENTATOR

Did you ever see what happens when several grown-ups try to
catch one real boy? Just look, look!

*The URCHIN slips out of their grasp, kicking and fighting,
and manages to get away. His would-be captors rub their shins
and bruises, looking at each other in consternation.*

MAYOR

I'm afraid that one will escape us.

HOLLOW MAN

He won't get away! I'll see to that.

*But the HOLLOW MAN is in very bad humor because of the
URCHIN's defiance. He snatches the cactus flower from the noose
and tears it to pieces. We hear a plaintive "Oi!" from the torn,
scattering petals.*

MAYOR

At least we've put an end to that flower! Let's go find the boy.

*The MAYOR, the HOLLOW MAN, the GUARD and the
TARABARS leave the stage.*

ANNA

They'll get him!

CLOWN

And you—would you like them to catch him?

ANNA

No, he's fun. Boys like him are very much like swallows.

*She says this so sadly that she is even startled by the
emotion in her voice. The CLOWN takes her hand and
she doesn't draw away. She merely looks at him with questioning
surprise.*

CLOWN

Do you feel sorry that the flower was destroyed?

ANNA

No.

CLOWN

Your hands are cold.

ANNA

They are always cold. . . But yours are so warm. Why?

CLOWN

They are warmed by the heart.

ANNA

How does the heart stay warm?

CLOWN

By feeling kind.

ANNA

It's dangerous to be kind. Very dangerous in our city.

CLOWN

I know it.

ANNA

Do you fear anything?

CLOWN

No, nothing scares me.

ANNA

Not even love?

CLOWN

Why should I fear loving or being loved?

ANNA

Love brings nothing but unhappiness, don't you know that?

CLOWN

I've seen it bring great happiness.

ANNA

How did people act whom it made happy?

CLOWN

They laughed with joy.

ANNA

Making faces like mad dogs.
The CLOWN laughs.
ANNA grimaces a grin—laughter being somewhat contagious
—then, soberly
Sh-h-h. . . If somebody sees us. . .

CLOWN

What will happen?

ANNA

They'll kill you.

CLOWN

And you don't want them to kill me?

ANNA

No. I don't.

CLOWN

Why?

ANNA

I don't know. . . I'm confused. . . Maybe it's because you saved
my swallow.
Suddenly she's gripped by fear. She snatches her cold hand away
from the CLOWN's warm one and jumps away, the way a pedestrian
in the street would jump away from a speeding car.

CLOWN

What's the matter with you?

ANNA

I don't know. . . I'm afraid of you. . .

CLOWN

Take a good look at me. Do I look dangerous?

ANNA

Screaming
Go away! Please go away! Leave our city at once! Save yourself!
She turns from him sharply and runs away
The CLOWN looks after her shaking his head sadly. He looks
warily around, her fear having affected him. The URCHIN
enters

URCHIN

Why did she yell at you?

CLOWN

It's none of your business.

URCHIN

A wonderful answer. The most favorite answer of grown-ups.
But maybe you're right this time. I found out long ago, when
I was still in school that it's better to leave girls alone. Even
when something is the girl's fault, the man (*and he points to
himself*) is blamed.

CLOWN

They didn't catch you after all, did they?

URCHIN

Not a chance!
Now we hear approaching footsteps and the MAYOR's theme song
>   The color of gray! The color of gray!
>   It's the greatest color—Hooray! Hooray!
Pointing to ham
Are you considering donating the ham to a museum?
He holds his stomach to indicate hunger pangs.

CLOWN

Lifting the ham
We'd better eat it away from here. The monsters are coming. . .
*The CLOWN and URCHIN leave, taking the ham with them.
They do so just in time, because the MAYOR and HOLLOW MAN
enter immediately after.*

HOLLOW MAN

Keeping at the MAYOR's heels
Your Immortal Municipalship, I beseech you to set the date for
the wedding right away.

MAYOR

First catch the boy.

HOLLOW MAN

It doesn't pay to get so upset about some urchin. I'll catch him
soon enough.

MAYOR

You catch him first. I feel some danger. . . It will be most unfitting to be ruined by an insolent brat. . .

HOLLOW MAN

You have nothing to fear! Since you are your Immortal Municipalship.

MAYOR

With his usual bombast

Even immortals dislike being ruined. It's good to be immortal while one is alive. Because, what is life. . .it is. . .that which. . . that. . .

The HOLLOW MAN tugs at his sleeve to stop the flow of words.

HOLLOW MAN

Your Immortal Municipalship! If you only knew how I hate your daughter, your Anna. Mine is a passionate hatred! I can't live without it.

MAYOR

Moved by this declaration

Very well. . . I'll order the wedding to take place not later than tomorrow evening.

HOLLOW MAN

I'll be twice as loyal a slave to you!

MAYOR

Tell the dressmaker to make a gray wedding gown for Anna.

He sings

> The color of gray! The color of gray!
> It's the greatest color for a wedding day!
> Hooray! Hooray!

The MAYOR and the HOLLOW MAN exit. Suddenly Lover's Mountain towering over the gray roofs is bathed in light, beautiful as sunrise. We see a profusion of brilliantly colored flowers. We see the CLOWN and we see ANNA on the Mountain. . .

ANNA

As she sees the CLOWN approaching in the distance, with fear in her voice

Who is here?

CLOWN

It's me.

ANNA

Why did you come here?

CLOWN

I got lonesome for the sight of flowers.

ANNA

How did you know that flowers grow here?

CLOWN

On Lover's Mountain there must be flowers—after all, it is this God-forsaken city's only lovers' lane.

ANNA

Yes. . .

CLOWN

And I suppose those who fall in love are drawn here with an irresistible. . .

ANNA

Interrupting him
This isn't true! I came to check whether there was anyone up here. I'm the Mayor's daughter and I have the right to check such things. (*Sadly, almost in tears*) I came only to check. . .

CLOWN

And I came for the same reason. . .to check on someone. . .on you. Down below I thought it only seemed to me that you were falling in love. . .

ANNA

Almost hysterical with panic
Go away! Go away at once! If they see us we are ruined! There is a telescope with a camera that moves constantly over this mountain. It takes pictures all the time and they are checked in the Central Control Room. . .

CLOWN

I'm not afraid to die. But I *am* afraid to live without love.

ANNA

Joining her hands in a pleading gesture
I beg you to leave this place!

*He takes her hands in his and she trembles from the unfamiliar
message of the contact. They are silent for a moment, then speak
to each other in a whisper. Anna is very agitated.*

CLOWN

What's the matter with you? Why are you trembling?

ANNA

I don't know. . .

CLOWN

Are you cold?

ANNA

Let go of my hands. . .

CLOWN

All right. . .

ANNA

No, don't let go of them! Hurry, go away! Leave this city!

CLOWN

I can't leave!

ANNA

Why?

CLOWN

I'm holding your hands. They don't let me go.

ANNA

What are we going to do?

CLOWN

We'll go away together. There are many wonderful cities in the
world, where flowers grow in the park, in flower boxes under
the windows, and right on the streets. In such cities the most
admired people are those who can love. It is the ones who hate
and commit violence that are punished.

ANNA

We are lost!

CLOWN

Let's run!

ANNA

Where?

CLOWN

We'll get away from this dreadful city!

ANNA

They'll lock the gate.

CLOWN

We'll climb over the wall! Let's hurry! I hear footsteps!
*He puts his arm around her and together they run down the
Mountain and disappear from sight.*
The HOLLOW MAN and the MAYOR appear on the Mountain.

MAYOR

Looking around
There's no one here. The telescope must be out of order.

HOLLOW MAN

The photograph clearly shows the shadow of two people.
He inspects the ground
Look, footsteps! A man's and a woman's!

MAYOR

Whose footsteps? Whose?

HOLLOW MAN

Your Municipalship! Give orders to rouse all citizens. Every single
one! Let each person put his stethoscope to his heart. We'll go at
once to the Central Control Room, watch the panel closely, and
without further delay find out who the loving couple is.

MAYOR

Make sure the city gate is closed.

HOLLOW MAN

It's closed.

MAYOR

Then they'll not get away. We'll find them and punish them. We'll
get that business out of the way—then on with your wedding!

HOLLOW MAN

Death to the lovers!

CURTAIN

COMMENTATOR

Here you see it, the Central Control Room, a sinister room in which
the fate of many a citizen of this city has been sealed. And here
the fate of Anna and the Clown is about to be decided. To the eyes
of a modern person there seems to be nothing threatening in this
room. On the contrary, it suggests the excitement of a somewhat
mystifying scientific laboratory in which some wonder of the
Twentieth Century is being created. But you and I also live in
the Twentieth Century, and we know that marvelous discoveries
by the human mind can be used for evil as well as good. . . Here,
in this Central Control Room, evil triumphs. It ominously blinks
its green lights on the electronic panel. And the good?. . . But let
me not be hasty. We'll find out about that a little later.
*We see the HOLLOW MAN and the MAYOR enter the
Central Control Room.*

HOLLOW MAN

Busies himself at the electronic panel
I'm connecting the last square—"Center-Two."

MAYOR

Now they'll be caught. Death awaits them! Death!
*The HOLLOW MAN connects the knife-switch to the panel. There is
only the blinking of green lights. The HOLLOW MAN and the
MAYOR glare at the panel. Both are visibly upset*

HOLLOW MAN

Strange. . .

MAYOR

Again no sign?

HOLLOW MAN

None.

MAYOR

Then the telescope has made a mistake?

HOLLOW MAN

Your Immortal Municipalship, the telescope never makes mistakes.

MAYOR

Threateningly
Then who is responsible for this error? Who set off the alarm? Any
kind of alarm has a bad effect on my liver and could curtail my
life by a day! And life! For me! It is essential! For! Thriving!

MAYOR (Cont.)

The HOLLOW MAN pulls at his sleeve

Tomorrow you'll spend the entire day repairing the telescope
while I busy myself with that Clown and some money matters. . .

HOLLOW MAN

Suddenly on the alert, like a beast of prey on the scent of its victim

Your Municipalship, look!

MAYOR

What is it?

HOLLOW MAN

One of the lights doesn't go on. This means that someone did not
put the stethoscope to his heart!

MAYOR

Maybe that person is simply asleep?

HOLLOW MAN

He is not asleep! The coward is trembling with fear! He knows
he is guilty!

MAYOR

You think so?

HOLLOW MAN

Yes!

MAYOR

Then whose light is it?

HOLLOW MAN

Number M-8.

MAYOR

Who is M-8?

HOLLOW MAN

We'll find out in a moment! (*He grabs a huge, thick volume and
leafs through it*) We'll find out all right!

MAYOR

Pacing the room nervously

Love! How I despise it! There's nothing more repulsive than a
couple in love! I'll punish them personally! All of them! For always!
Everywhere! Up to the last one!

HOLLOW MAN

Frightened by what he has found
Your Immortal Municipalship!. . .

MAYOR

Did you find out?

HOLLOW MAN

Shaken
Yes, I did. . .

MAYOR

Whose light is it?

HOLLOW MAN

Stammering
It—it is. . . It is Anna's light. . .

MAYOR

Impossible!

HOLLOW MAN

Here, see for yourself.

MAYOR

Glancing at the list
No! My daughter couldn't possibly be in love! All her life I have
trained her differently! Every day of her life she has taken hate
pills with her breakfast!

HOLLOW MAN

But it *is* her light. . .

MAYOR

Very likely the child was busy playing and merely forgot to
use the stethoscope.

HOLLOW MAN

She is no longer a child. Tomorrow is our wedding day.

MAYOR

Have her come here and put the stethoscope to her heart, and
you'll see that I'm right.

HOLLOW MAN

Sol-kol-diers-kiers!
Enter the TARABARS

HOLLOW MAN (Cont.)

Bri-king An-ka-na-ka he-kere!
TARABARS run off to carry out the order.

MAYOR

It can't be!

HOLLOW MAN

Your Immortal Municipalship! Remember the curse that hangs over you. . . One couple in love is a sickness, two—an epidemic. If more than three couples in this city should fall in love, they'll arouse the others. Your subjects will rebel. They won't obey you. Then you're ruined! Your rule is finished!

MAYOR

I'm aware of all this—but it can't happen.
The TARABARS lead ANNA in

ANNA

Father, did you want me?

MAYOR

Where have you been?

ANNA

I was taking a walk.

MAYOR

Didn't you hear the siren?

ANNA

I heard it.

MAYOR

Then why didn't your light go on?

ANNA

But *you* never bother to be tested.

MAYOR

I'm the ruler of this city, I'm above suspicion.

ANNA

I'm the daughter of the ruler and I, too, am above suspicion. This machine was invented for us to test others and not so that others may test us.

MAYOR

You're right. I haven't noticed how you've grown up. You've become not only a tough young woman but a clever one as well. How fast children grow up these days!... All right, go back, go on with your walk.

HOLLOW MAN

No, wait! Your Immortal Municipalship, take a good look at her. Don't you see her pallor, and how strangely her eyes shine? These are the symptoms of love. I demand that she be tested!

ANNA

I'm the daughter of the Mayor, and you have no right to demand anything from me.

HOLLOW MAN

I demand that my bride be tested.

MAYOR

Little daughter, do it. What will it cost you? If there's nothing wrong, then there's nothing wrong, and if there's nothing wrong there's nothing to be afraid of.

ANNA

I don't want to carry out orders from him.

MAYOR

All right, I'll permit you not to carry out his orders, but you are obligated to obey my wishes.

ANNA

Suddenly screaming

I hate you all! You are mean, nasty creatures! Yes, you'll die but not from wounds, not from disease, and not from love! You'll die of meanness and dullness! Look! Look at each other—look at how dull your eyes are! (*She grabs the stethoscope and presses it to her chest*) Go ahead, use the knife-switch! It resembles the executioner's axe! In this city everything resembles the axe of the executioner!
The HOLLOW MAN connects the knife-switch and a gleaming red light appears among the weak green ones.

MAYOR

Shouts

Stop it! Remove the switch!
The HOLLOW MAN disconnects the knife-switch and all the panel lights go out.

HOLLOW MAN

Gloating

I was right!

MAYOR

Badly shaken

How can this be? With whom did you fall in love?

ANNA

I won't tell you!

MAYOR

Wait. All is not lost. We must punish the one who aroused her love, but in exceptional cases we can spare the one who responded and sentence her to life imprisonment. (*To ANNA*) Don't despair. I'll build you a darling prison. They'll screen a movie for you three times a day and will grant all your wishes. But him we must put to death. You must tell us who he is.

ANNA

Never! Never in this world!

HOLLOW MAN

Mockingly

That sounds very pretty, and sassy, but you know very well that we have other means of finding out. We'll put them to use, and you'll confess everything.

ANNA

All right, I'll confess right now.

MAYOR

Tell us, tell us quickly who that good-for-nothing is!

ANNA

Points to the HOLLOW MAN

There he is!

HOLLOW MAN

Frightened

It's a lie! It's a lie! You yourself said that you despise me! You declared your hatred of me!

ANNA

From love to have is only a short step. And vice versa.

MAYOR

Soldiers, take him prisoner!
But the TARABARS don't move
Why are you standing there? What is this—a rebellion?

HOLLOW MAN

They don't understand ordinary language.

MAYOR

Then order them to seize you.

HOLLOW MAN

Falling to his knees
Have mercy! She's lying! Have mercy! Spare me!

ANNA

Look, Father, your Hollow Man isn't so tough after all. Listen
to him begging for mercy.

HOLLOW MAN

I never spared the guilty, but I'm innocent! Innocent!

MAYOR

Order the Tarabars to seize you—or I'll do it myself! I'll
personally behead you with your own golden axe!
He tears down the golden axe from the wall

HOLLOW MAN

Crawling on his knees
Wait!. . . Wait!. . . I'll think of something. . .
He suddenly jumps to his feet and utters a cry of triumph
Ah-a-a! Your Immortal Municipalship, there is one other person
who has not been tested.

MAYOR

Who?

HOLLOW MAN

The Clown.

ANNA

He doesn't live in this city and he needn't submit to a test.

HOLLOW MAN

Look how she trembles. I've made a study of trembling—and I know
that this is the way a girl shakes out of fear for the life of her beloved.

ANNA

You have no right to execute him!

HOLLOW MAN

To the TARABARS

Clown-ka *to*-ka *the*-ka *ste*-ka-*the*-ka-o-ka *scope*-ka!

The TARABARS leave, singing their menacing song:

> Love is the cause of all evil—
> It has its price—which must be met
> It is death, death by bayonet!

The fainter the sound becomes, the stronger the fear that grips ANNA. She looks on with terror as the HOLLOW MAN screws a new light bulb into the panel and turns on the power.

Let's watch this light, and we'll soon know everything.

ANNA

In a whisper

If they find him, we are lost!

Suddenly the light begins to blink with a red glow

HOLLOW MAN

All is clear now!

MAYOR

To HOLLOW MAN

Go and get things ready for the execution.

HOLLOW MAN

It's been a long time since I've done it with so much pleasure! (*He leaves*)

We now see again the square in front of the city gate. Here is where the CLOWN will be executed. He has already been tied to a post, and in front of him stands the victorious HOLLOW MAN. Near by is the MAYOR, but he looks thoughtful and even a bit sad.

COMMENTATOR

Strange: a sad fellow-executioner. . . Could it be that he feels pity for his victim?

MAYOR

Calling the HOLLOW MAN to him

Say, couldn't we postpone the execution on some pretext?

HOLLOW MAN

According to law, not for more than two hours.

MAYOR

How about two days? Just two little days?

HOLLOW MAN

No! The law demands that those in love be punished immediately upon discovery of their crime. We destroy love so that it will not destroy us!

MAYOR

It's a pity. A great pity. . . He kept taking lovely gold pieces out of his ears. And I was looking forward so much to benefiting from this economic miracle! (*Turns to CLOWN*) Hey, there, Clown— I had such great hopes about you. I kept seeing the glorious future of this city before my eyes. We would have become so rich that we could have bought up all the neighboring cities. We! Would have become! Rulers! Over squares! Streets! Houses! People! Their hearts! Their souls! Over everything! Their—!
The HOLLOW MAN pulls at his sleeve and the MAYOR speaks in a self-pitying tone
But now none of this will happen. Clown, you have betrayed me! Yes, yes, you are a traitor! For this we shall not merely execute you— we'll do it with a golden axe. That is the symbol of our golden age of cruelty. (*To the HOLLOW MAN*) Bring the golden axe and I'll bring Anna. Now that the magician is to go, let's put an end to him quickly.
He leaves.

HOLLOW MAN

Sol-kol-*diers*-kiers!
The TARABARS enter
Sta-kand *gua*-kuard!
The HOLLOW MAN exits.

THE TARABARS

They bristle their moustaches fiercely and pace back and forth stamping menacingly as they sing:

> The bullet—is dumb! Dumb! Dumb!
> The bayonet's smart—and strikes deep!
> The wolf is always stronger than the sheep.
> Yes, the bullet is flighty, it's dumb!
> Te-ram, te-rum!
> Te-ram, te-rum!

The URCHIN enters the square stealthily. The TARABARS point their bayonets at him.

URCHIN

Low-kow-*er*-ker *a*-ka*rms*!
The TARABARS lower their weapons
A-kat *ea*-kea*se*!
The TARABARS stand at ease
A-ka-*bou*-kout *fa*-kace!
The TARABARS execute an about face. They are now facing the wall

CLOWN

How come you know the language of these hideous soldiers?

URCHIN

That's simple. All school girls nowadays talk in that language
when they tell each other secrets. It is their favorite language.
All they do is put a "k" after every syllable, that's all. For example
if they want to say "Vera loves Misha" they say it this way:
Ve-ka-*ra*-ka *lo*-koves *Mi*-ki-*sha*-ka. Simple.

CLOWN

You're not dumb! In fact, you're a pretty smart sort. Even a splendid
fellow. I think you could become a good clown. But now I won't be
able to teach you my tricks. They're about to execute me.

URCHIN

I know. But you can save yourself.

CLOWN

How?

URCHIN

Start laughing. As loud and as long as you can. Remember how they
were ready to execute a man in that other town? And just then
you came along. You did one of your tricks and broke into laughter.
Then soon everyone began to laugh with you. They laughed and
laughed—and forgave the prisoner. And everything was all right.
You know that happy people can forgive the things for which
angry people or frightened ones will punish. Am I right?

CLOWN

But here they don't know how to forgive and they don't know
how to laugh. That's what makes the Mayor and his Hollow Man
such dangerous scoundrels. (*Sighs*) Well, I'd better tell you the
secret of at least one of my tricks. . .

URCHIN

Later.

CLOWN

Later it will be too late! Hands can only do tricks thought up by the head—and later I will have no head. . .

URCHIN

I'll save you somehow!

CLOWN

But how?

URCHIN

Let me think. . . (*Paces up and down in deep concentration, then stops*) I have an idea! They're not only cruel, they're also greedy. And my history teacher always told us that, through the ages, the largest number of people perished from the plague, and the next largest number from greed. (*Turns and calls out*) Swallow! Dear Queen of the Swallows, I need your help!

SWALLOW comes hopping into the square. URCHIN bends down to her

We must save the life of my friend!

SWALLOW

He's not only *your* friend, he's mine, too! I'll do all I can. But what can possibly be done?

URCHIN

I've heard that once, the Swallows cast a spell over a Crow that stole into their nest—and he could never move again.

SWALLOW

Yes, that's true. And he was as vicious as those two murderers!

URCHIN

Hm-m-m. . . And could you Swallows break the prison wall with your beaks?

SWALLOW

We?—no, we can't. But the Seagulls could do it. They have very strong beaks.

URCHIN

How long would it take you to summon all the Swallows?

SWALLOW

Two hours, maybe less.

URCHIN

Great! And how many Swallows would be needed to lift me up in the air, let me down, and lift me up again?

SWALLOW

On ropes?

URCHIN

It would be better on thin strings, almost invisible ones.

SWALLOW

Oh, about a thousand Swallows I'd say.

URCHIN

Are there that many in this city?

SWALLOW

Yes, there are.

URCHIN

Then gather them quickly, and get some string! As much as possible. (*To the CLOWN*) So long!

CLOWN

Farewell, my young friend.

URCHIN

No, not farewell. We'll see each other soon!
The URCHIN and the SWALLOW run off. A moment later the HOLLOW MAN, the MAYOR, and ANNA enter. The HOLLOW MAN is carrying the golden axe.

MAYOR

To HOLLOW MAN

Why are your soldiers standing with their backs to us? Is this the way they guard our criminal?

HOLLOW MAN

A-ka-bou-kout fa-kace!
The TARABARS turn around.

MAYOR

But, really, those gold coins could come in very handy.

HOLLOW MAN

If this city is stricken with an epidemic of love, gold coins will not save us.

CLOWN

Anna, what are they going to do to you?

ANNA

They'll throw me into prison, for life.

CLOWN

You live in a cruel city, but cruelty will sooner or later destroy those who practice it. Death may bring freedom, but how much better to have our freedom while we're alive. Have faith that you will live to enjoy freedom!

HOLLOW MAN

Cease all conversation!

MAYOR

Ah, those gold pieces! What lovely gold pieces! If we could somehow spare the Clown and kill only his love!

HOLLOW MAN

To kill one's love, one has to betray it.

MAYOR

An excellent idea! I'll try it. . . Listen, Clown, how about selling your love for two gold coins? Just give us a receipt, with the statement that you agree to Anna's marrying the Hollow Man. Write up this document, and you can live.

CLOWN

I prefer death.

MAYOR

Stupid. . . If you die you'll lose her just the same.

CLOWN

If I can save my life only by becoming a scoundrel, then I welcome death!

HOLLOW MAN

Well spoken! Now I'm ready to use the golden axe!

ANNA

Use it on me instead!

HOLLOW MAN

We ought to put an end to both of you, but one at a time. . .

He hefts the axe, getting ready to swing. Suddenly from somewhere above we hear a voice crying: "Stop!" The HOLLOW MAN freezes with the axe in his hands, and the rest look up in surprise. A raggedy old hag, astride a broom, descends to the square. It is the URCHIN disguised as a witch.

"WITCH"

In a lisping hiss

Why are you staring at me as if I were some kind of a puzzle? I'm a witch. A most ordinary witch. I came because I like your nastiness. You're as cruel and pitiless as I am.

HOLLOW MAN

What can we do for you, dear Witch?

"WITCH"

When I need you I'll tell you. . . Oh, how I wish other cities had the same kind of laws as you have here!

MAYOR

We'd like that, too. We had hoped to have a golden windfall to use for this purpose but, unfortunately, the Clown fell in love.

"WITCH"

That's terrible! That's revolting!

MAYOR

He could make such beautiful gold pieces!

"WITCH"

I know.

HOLLOW MAN

How do you know?

"WITCH"

Pointing upward

I can see everything from up there. I can see through walls and from rooftops, so I find out everything about anything, or anyone— even (*glaring at the HOLLOW MAN*) about you!

The "WITCH" shakes her finger at the HOLLOW MAN. He cringes and steps back.

"WITCH"

(*To MAYOR*) I'll help you occupy the neighboring cities. You can let the Clown go free.

MAYOR

Dear Madam Witch, according to our laws. . .

"WITCH"

Yes, yes, I know! Here are two pills. It took me half a lifetime
to prepare each of them. Within two hours they destroy the feeling
of love. In two hours there'll be not a trace of their love left
in them.

MAYOR

Splendid! Then we can postpone the execution for two hours.
For exactly two hours!

CLOWN

I refuse to swallow that pill.

ANNA

And I refuse, too.

"WITCH"

Take them to the prison. There you can force them to take the pills.

HOLLOW MAN

Shouts

No pills!! I'll execute him right now! I refuse to deprive myself
of that pleasure.

MAYOR

You think only of yourself. *I* think of our entire city. Our! Great!
City! Must! Be!
The "WITCH" shuffles over to the MAYOR and pulls his sleeve
Come, let's try the Witch's plan. Maybe it will work.

HOLLOW MAN

Nothing will come of it. It's a useless waste of time.

"WITCH"

Who fashioned that golden axe?

HOLLOW MAN

I did.

"WITCH"

Whispers in the HOLLOW MAN'S ear

Is it made of pure gold, as they say—or did you fake it and put some
of the gold in your own pocket?

HOLLOW MAN

Frightened

Sh-h-h! (*Speaks out loudly*) All right, I agree. But we'll postpone
the execution for only two hours. Not a minute longer!

*The HOLLOW MAN and the MAYOR take ANNA and the CLOWN
off to prison. The "WITCH" casts off her raggedy clothes and
pulls off the gray wig, and the false face, and we recognize the
URCHIN. He calls out*

URCHIN

Swallow! Come, Swallow—I need you.

SWALLOW appears

SWALLOW

You were so restless in the air that the Swallows barely managed
to hold you up. What do you want me to do now? .

URCHIN

Have you summoned all the seagulls? Are they ready to break
through the prison wall with their beaks?

SWALLOW

Yes, there are thousands of them up there in the clouds. They are
awaiting the order to begin. . . But let's think of something that
will get the Mayor and the Hollow Man to the Control Room so we
can cast our spell and wall them in. Can you think of anything?

URCHIN

The Tarabars will help me. I know their language. (*He calls to the
soldiers*) Sol-kol-*diers*-kiers! Ta-ka-*ra*-ka-*ba*-kars!

The TARABARS come goose-stepping in, carrying their rifles

At-kat-*ten*-ken-*tion*-kun! (*They come to attention*) Shoul-kol-der-ker
arms-karms! (*They obey*) Run-kun to-koo the-ke Lov-kov-ers-kers
Moun-koun-*tain*-kain!

*The TARABARS obey the order. They exit, trying to run and
goose-step at the same time*

A few minutes of Stage Time pass. Then we hear the siren

SWALLOW

Horrors! Are there more couples in love?

URCHIN

No, no. Everything is going according to plan. The siren means
that the Tarabars have reached Lovers' Mountain. They have been
seen through the telescope and the alarm has been given. Now the

URCHIN (Cont.)

Hollow man and the Mayor will rush to the Central Control Room.
Have you told your Swallows to cast the same spell on them that
they used on the vicious Crow, so that they'll never again be able
to leave the Control Room?

SWALLOW

Yes, they're only waiting for those two to go inside.

URCHIN

Great! Great! Then you'd better go tell the Seagulls to attack the
prison wall.
She exits and the URCHIN struts off looking very pleased with himself.
Now we hear the noise of swooping wings and the sound of thousands
of beaks striking against the prison wall. Soon comes a thud as
the wall collapses—then the happy crying of thousands of birds.
ANNA and the CLOWN run onto the stage, followed by a gleeful
SWALLOW. The two lovers look happy but bewildered. They don't
yet understand what has happened

CLOWN

Why did the prison wall break open?

SWALLOW

The Seagulls used their beaks to break it, in order to save you.

ANNA

Look, look—the sky is full of birds!

SWALLOW

Those are the Swallows and Seagulls that came to your rescue.

CLOWN

We must escape, quickly—or we'll be caught again.

SWALLOW

Don't worry, there is no one to capture you. The Swallows have
cast a spell on the Mayor and the Hollow Man. They have been walled
up in the Central Control Room, and they can never again leave
that place to do harm in the city.

CLOWN

But what about the Tarabars?

SWALLOW

They are sitting on Lovers' Mountain and crying bitterly with
remorse for their awful deeds.

CLOWN

In that case we'll go the the Control Room and tell the Mayor and the Hollow Man that their rule is at an end.

ANNA

They won't believe it, and they'll find a way to fight us.

CLOWN

They'll believe it all right when they hear the "Song of Friendship and Love!" They'll know then that if they want to save their skins they'd better leave town.

ANNA

But we don't know any such song.

CLOWN

I'll teach it to you. (*He sings*)

> The heart will be warmed, coo like a dove,
> Only through laughter, friendship, and love.
> So come on, come on out,
> Come laugh and shout!
> Bring along brush and paint,
> And without fear or restraint,
> Join the crowd in friendship and mirth!
> Help paint a rainbow over our earth!

Enter the GUARD. He is doubled over with laughter

GUARD

Oh, how funny, how strange. . . For twenty years I didn't laugh, but now. . .I'll never stop! For twenty years I protected the Mayor and the Hollow Man from decent folk, now I'll protect decent folk from them.

He laughs some more, then becomes serious

But, alas! those two won't give in without causing some more grief.

CLOWN

They'll have to give in. We'll make them. Come, let's all go to the Control Room and tell them the news. (*He looks around*) But where is our Urchin? I hope they didn't catch him.

They all exit,

In the Central Control Room the HOLLOW MAN and the MAYOR are pacing frantically back and forth, with lighted candles in their hands. Now they start running about connecting and disconnecting switches, pushing buttons, pulling out and putting in plugs. But the panel lights don't go on, and neither do the room lights

MAYOR

Why don't any of the lights go on? What's the meaning of this?

HOLLOW MAN

There's a power failure.

MAYOR

That hasn't happened in twenty years. Why now—just at the time when
our lives are in danger? Our rule hangs by a hair! I can almost see
this hair—it is thin and gray, very thin. And when one's power
hangs by such a thin hair, it is at the mercy of anyone with a pair of
scissors in his hand!. . . Any scissors!. . . Any hand!. . .
*He extends his arm to have his sleeve pulled, but the HOLLOW MAN
ignores it*

HOLLOW MAN

Calm down, Your Immortal Municipalship. I'll go to the power
station and everything will soon be in order again. We'll execute
the new lovers together with the Clown. We'll not postpone the
execution this time—not by a single minute!

MAYOR

Go! Hurry! We're in mortal danger!
*The HOLLOW MAN tries in vain to open the door. He pushes it with
his shoulder, kicks it with his foot, but the door doesn't yield*

HOLLOW MAN

We've been sealed in, walled in!

MAYOR

Trembling with terror
First the lights go out, then something crashes in the city, and
now the door won't open! Ominous! More than ominous!
Suspicious. . . Open the window, carefully. . .
*The HOLLOW MAN draws the window curtain and we see that it
is dark outside the Control Room although it was just now daytime
in the square at the city gate*

MAYOR

Is it night-time already? Impossible!

HOLLOW MAN

A spell has been cast on us—we're walled in, forever.

MAYOR

Who did it? Let's get him!

HOLLOW MAN

It's the Swallows. I recognize their mischief. They did the same thing to a crow that attacked their nests.

MAYOR

But we are not crows. We are Rulers! No one! No one has! the right. . . Why don't you tug at my sleeve?

Again he extends his arm and walks closer to the HOLLOW MAN for the sleeve to be tugged

HOLLOW MAN

It doesn't matter now.

MAYOR

I'll order the destruction of all Swallows!

HOLLOW MAN

Whom will you order to do it? We can't even call on our loyal Tarabars.

MAYOR

Yes, our soldiers! Our Tarabars! They'll save us! And our loyal Guard of the City Gate!

We hear the song of Laughter, Friendship and Love in the distance and it gains in volume. The HOLLOW MAN and the MAYOR hear it and recognize the voices with alarm

HOLLOW MAN

I hear the Clown's voice.

MAYOR

And Anna's! My Anna's!

HOLLOW MAN

Listen, and the shoemaker's!

MAYOR

And the baker's!

HOLLOW MAN

The tailor's!

MAYOR

The rascal!

HOLLOW MAN

Who?

MAYOR

The tailor! Before he would never sing—about the color
of gray. Said that he didn't have an ear for music. The liar!
I'll order the Guard. . .

HOLLOW MAN

I hear the Guard singing with the others.
Children's voices can now be heard singing

MAYOR

What's that?

HOLLOW MAN

It's the children's chorus from the Gray School.

MAYOR

What an outrage! They are corrupting the young generation! I will
not allow it! I'll order the rebellion to be crushed!

HOLLOW MAN

Too late! A rebellion must be crushed before it gets out
of hand. When it has reached such proportions as this one,
we must run.

MAYOR

I'll drown their damn song with mine!
He sings, his nervous voice quavering
> The color of gray, the color of gray,
> It's the greatest color—Hooray! Hooray!

To HOLLOW MAN
Why don't you sing? Come on, you must sing, too!

HOLLOW MAN

Our song is finished. . .

MAYOR

Finally, limp with hopelessness, piteously
Is it really? What do we do!!

HOLLOW MAN

We escape, if we can.

MAYOR

How? You said we're walled in forever!

HOLLOW MAN

There's a secret passage under the floor. It leads out beyond
the city limits. If the devil is on our side, the Swallows
overlooked the trap door.
He goes to the trap door. He lifts it.
A curse on your head, friend Devil!
*The MAYOR pushes the HOLLOW MAN out of the way
and is the first to jump into the opening.*

MAYOR

Get the secret documents from the safe.

HOLLOW MAN

That won't be necessary. I've hidden them here long ago.
*He points to his chest, and with a slow heavy gaze around
the Control Room, he freezes at the opening to the secret
passage as if unable to tear himself away from this center
of his vicious power.*

MAYOR

Hurry! I hear them coming!

HOLLOW MAN

We'll make it. There are other cities in this world. And
as long as people have heads on their shoulders, there'll be
work for executioners.
*His face takes on a sardonically fierce expression as he lowers
the trap door and disappears below.*

COMMENTATOR

I don't know about other cities, but in this one there
will be no more executions. This I can promise you. The
only good thing about blood-thirsty tyrants is that they
are remembered for a long time. . .

VOICE OF THE CLOWN

From the outside of the Control Room, at the door
Hey there! Mayor! Hollow Man! You're finished. You're no
longer the rulers of this city. Surrender!

VOICE OF ANNA

They've hidden themselves.

VOICE OF SWALLOW

They're speechless with rage.

VOICE OF GUARD

When we can't hear our Mayor's voice, it means he isn't there.

VOICE OF SWALLOW

I'll go down the chimney and find out what goes on in there.
*The SWALLOW comes into the Control Room through
the fireplace. Loudly, to the ones outside, at the door.*
There's no one here! They got away!
*The door is forced from the outside. Enter the CLOWN,
ANNA, and GUARD*

CLOWN

So this is the Control Room. Here is where they set all those
deadly traps for lovers!

GUARD

We must destroy that awful panel.

ANNA

The sooner the better.

CLOWN

No. We'll keep our eye on it and the red lights of those who
know how to love. The one whose light shines the brightest
should be the new Mayor.
He embraces ANNA lovingly
*We are again in the city square at the gate. ANNA, the CLOWN,
the GUARD, the SWALLOW are gathered there.*

ANNA

When will we be married?

CLOWN

Right now.

ANNA

Where?

CLOWN

Here. In this square. Let everyone attend our wedding. These
people need to learn about love all over again.

We hear the URCHIN's voice singing the Laughter, Friendship and Love song as he approaches. He sings at the top of his voice and totally off key. He rushes onto the stage breathlessly. He is carrying two pails of paint and two large paint brushes.

URCHIN

Guess what! In that dried-up field on the other side of these gray buildings a little blade of grass has grown.

He starts to paint the city gate as he speaks, covering it with large strokes of bright yellow and bright pink paint

A little thin blade. And I told the city boys that if they as much as touch it, they'll have to deal with me!

Still holding the brush, he raises his fists and takes the pose of a rough-and-ready prize-fighter. Then he grimaces like a clown and in his euphoria paints pink spots on his cheeks and a yellow one on the tip of his nose.

Everyone laughs. ANNA goes to him, puts her arm around him awkwardly, since she is inexperienced in showing affection, and with her voice breaking with emotion

ANNA

I. . .we. . .are so glad you're safe.

CLOWN

Will you stay and live with us?

URCHIN

Gladly! For a while. . .

CLOWN

And what would you like to do? What would you like to be? I know—a clown.

URCHIN

Teach me to be one! Then I'll work as a clown-school-teacher. That will be very useful. I could teach the kids how to laugh. They never learned how. But first I'll finish painting this gate, then I'll be ready for the first lesson in how to be a terrific clown.

The TARABARS come tripping in—not goose-stepping—holding pails of paint and large brushes attached to their bayonets. One paints the gray walls with orange paint, the other the square pavement with grass-green paint. They work very vigorously as everyone looks on with surprise and approval.

SWALLOW

Exiting
Excuse me.

COMMENTATOR

So you see, everything has ended well. . .
*SWALLOW returns carrying three gray-looking bird-houses,
a small pail of paint, a brush. She demurely starts to paint one
of the bird-houses. The URCHIN and the TARABARS have
been continuing their vigorous painting and the square is
beginning to look colorfully festive, gradually transforming
the gray city.*

And everything will be all right here from now on, for into
this gray and grim city have come Laughter, Friendship, and
Love. . .
*All the players now line up across the proscenium and sing
to the audience which soon joins in*

> The heart can be warmed, can coo like a dove,
> Only through laughter, friendship and love.
>
> So come on, do not doubt,
> Come laugh and shout,
> Bring along brush and paint,
> And without fear or restraint,
> Join the crowd in fellowship and mirth!
> Come paint a rainbow over our earth!

CURTAIN

HEY, THERE—HELLO!

A Play in Two Acts and Eight Scenes
by Gennadi Mamlin

CHARACTERS:

Valerka, a 14-year-old boy

Masha, a 14-year-old girl

Four Mimes

Pronunciation of the names:

    VaLERka — the *a*'s as in *a*rk. Variations: VAlik, VaLERi, VaLERa.

    MAsha — the *a*'s as in *a*rk. Variations: MarIa, MAshka.

    TaIsya, Masha's grandmother — the *a*'s as in *a*rk.

    NikoLAI — the first *i* as in n*i*x, the *a* in LAI as in *a*rk.

Masha in the Moscow TIUZ production.

Hey, There—Hello!   *Scene One*

On the left—extending almost to the proscenium—we see part of a tall board fence. The entire stage from this fence to the right is the backyard of the DOROKHOVS' house. A low wall built of mixed stones separates the yard from the street. In the yard are a table, chairs, a garden swing. These props are adequate for the scene, but the set designer may use his ingenuity in elaborating the decor with objects suggesting a seaside town environment, adding bright touches of southern (Black Sea region) flora.

On the table and chairs are sundry small boxes, rings and swords—a magician's apparatus. In the center of the yard stands a narrow black chest, the height of a man's neck. A tattered picture poster is pasted to it: a magician in a tailcoat, in garish letters his name— Albert Guido.

It is early morning. VALERKA, wearing faded jeans and a blue-and-white striped sailor's jersey, is squatting as he cleans the blade of a sword.

From somewhere in the distance we hear a tune on a trumpet. This melody is the motif for the pantomime scenes. It is therefore important to give it a certain evocative* coloring, to distinguish it from all the other off-stage sounds in the play, such as the ships' whistles, the popular music played on the beach, etc.

VALERKA, dropping the sword, takes a step in the direction from which the trumpet music is heard, but at this instant one of the boards in the fence is moved aside and MASHA sticks her head through the opening.

MASHA

(With the spontaneous friendliness characteristic of simple, good-natured people) Hey, there—hello! My name is Masha.

VALERKA

(Looking at MASHA unenthusiastically) I'll bear that in mind.

MASHA

(Not aware of his irony) I got here Friday. I'm staying with my grandmother.

VALERKA

Taisya?

MASHA

Yes. I lived with her last summer, too, but you weren't here. You were in camp.

VALERKA

It was Mother's idea. . . Why don't you crawl through?

---

*It suggests the emotionality of the flashbacks and VALERKA'S fantasizing in the scenes with the MIMES.

MASHA

(Coming through the opening) I don't have time. I'm doing errands
for our roomers. . . What's that in your hand?

VALERKA

A sword.

MASHA

It is the kind that's swallowed? My grandmother says there's a
sword-swallower living at your place. *(She reads the poster)* "Albert
Guido." Is he a Spaniard?

VALERKA

Ordinarily he's Semyon Semyonovich Leschinsky*, but for the circus
it's better to have a name like "Guido."

MASHA

You know, when he wears a tailcoat he looks like an orchestra
conductor. But in ordinary clothes—he looks like a bookkeeper. I
watched him for an hour. He's old! *(Garrulously)* Yesterday they
showed the circus on television. There were clowns. One was very
short, the other as tall as a telephone pole. The short one was
running away from the tall one, then suddenly he stopped, turned
around, and socked the telephone pole with his fist. The pole fell
down as if he had been hit by a ton of bricks. *(She laughs heartily)*
Wasn't that funny?

VALERKA

How would *I* know? Maybe it was.

MASHA

(With conviction) It was. Grandmother fell out of her chair laughing.
(She walks across the yard) Say, who is that Nikolai who lives with you?

VALERKA

A *homo sapiens.*

MASHA

A who?

VALERKA

A person.

*Pronounced with stresses on capitalized syllables: SeMYON, SeMYONovich LesCHINsky;
the e's are pronounced as the *ye* in yes.

MASHA

He's a strange one. When he fixed our gate Grandma offered him half a ruble. You know, he refused. Then she offered him a whole ruble. Still he refused, saying, "I did it because of your beautiful eyes." What does he do for a living, since he seems to be a millionaire who doesn't need money?

VALERKA

He's a cabinet maker. He happens to be here on vacation, not to earn money.

MASHA

If he's here to rest, then why is he hammering away over there in the shed for the second day now? *(She touches one of the small boxes. The lid pops open and a flower springs up)* Oh! My God!

VALERKA

Get away from there! And, generally, why don't you get lost!

MASHA

I'm sorry! *(She tries to push the flower back down into the box)*

VALERKA

I suppose you came to talk. So, talk. But keep your hands to yourself! There's hardly any space to move around in—Guido's stuff is all over the place. They persuaded him to perform at the Seamen's Club. We're repairing his equipment, Nikolai and me. There's a chest in the shed that's used to separate a person's head from his body. If you poke your head into *that*, it'll be curtains for you!

MASHA

(Peers off-stage at a shed, which is not visable to the audience) Such goings on! Yesterday Vera, one of your boarders, snuck up to the shed and startled Nikolai with a silly riddle. *(Laughs heartily)*

VALERKA

So. . .?

MASHA

It was very funny! There he was hammering away, and she springs this silly riddle on him.

VALERKA

Listen, where are you from?

MASHA

Me? I'm from the Voronezh Region. Why do you ask?

VALERKA

Anyway, you'd better display your Voronezh sense of humor around here in a whisper. People are still sleeping.

MASHA

Yesterday evening Vera wore boots—I notice that boots are very stylish in the city now, even in summer—and she went down the street with Nikolai, arm in arm. And back home she has a husband! The letter carrier says that he sends her a telegram every other day.

VALERKA

What do you do, run a spying service?

MASHA

All evening yesterday I was peeking through a crack in your fence. Our boarders are uninteresting, not like yours. They come back from the beach, eat their dinner, and then take a nap. After that they play cards or some word game. What a mob has poured in from the city this year! It's horrible! Evenings the sidewalk is so full of them, you'd think it was a demonstration! *(She squats down beside VALERKA)* Can I help?

VALERKA

(He hands MASHA another sword, a rag, and a piece of chalk to clean it with) Make sure you don't swallow it!

MASHA

(Laughs. VALERKA looks puzzled. She responds to his look) When I hear something witty I laugh, every time! Sometimes even when it's not funny I laugh, just to be polite. But you—you're such a silent one.

VALERKA

No, not silent—just a man of few words. There's a difference.

MASHA

And me— on the contrary, I love to talk. I open my mouth and the words run on like a piece of driftwood in a strong current.

VALERKA

(Looks at his image reflected in the shining blade of the sword he's been polishing. Suddenly) Mashka! Try to imagine what I'll look like ten years from now.

MASHA

How do I do that?

VALERKA

In your mind's eye, silly! Do you have a mind's eye?

MASHA

Of course I have!

VALERKA

Then go ahead and imagine.

MASHA

(Thinking) Should I close my eyes?

VALERKA

All right, close them.

MASHA

(Closes her eyes and concentrates) I can't. I was looking at the
sun and all I can see is rings swimming before my eyes. Valerka,
where do you eat your dinner?

VALERKA

My mother left money with the cashier at the Oreanda Restaurant.
I go there and eat, and she pays for me.

MASHA

Is it true that your mother's now in Madagascar?

VALERKA

(Nods) She's the navigation officer on a ocean liner.

MASHA

And wny has your father been in the hospital for so long?

VALERKA

That's not exactly your business. Why don't you just go on with your work?

MASHA

Oh! *(Jumps up and listens)* I heard a door bang. Grandmother is
up and I haven't cut the roses yet. I must run. So long!

VALERKA

Gud-bai. *(Evidently VALERKA knows a few English words)*

MASHA

Are you glad that I came to visit you?

VALERKA

Totally!

MASHA

It was yesterday that I pulled the nails out of the fence-board. For a long time now I've been wanting us to become friends.

VALERKA

You're a strange one!

MASHA

What's so strange about me?

VALERKA

I haven't yet given the matter enough thought, but you're strange, for sure!

MASHA

Let's get to be friends first and then you can give me some thought. Those who don't know me might take me for a little fool. To strangers I seem kind of obvious and scatterbrained. Even my own mother criticizes me—says I never keep a single thought to myself. So long!

VALERKA

We've already said gud-bai. Don't let me keep you.

(MASHA dives through the open space in the fence and replaces the board. VALERKA goes up to the poster and stands there, deep in thought. The playing of the trumpet is resumed. Four pantomime figures enter. They wear bright circus costumes. In this scene they are the magician's assistants. They line up behind VALERKA. The FIRST MIME hands him a tailcoat, the SECOND a top-hat; the THIRD pastes a pointed beard on his chin; the FOURTH drapes a silk cloak around his shoulders. There is now the sound of violin music.)

VALERKA

(Addressing the audience) Honorable public, ladies and gentlemen, children, adults, old folks. . .
(The FOUR MIMES noiselessly applaud him)
In the world of illusion it is so simple to make all of you happy. Come here, little girl—no, not you, the other one, with the sad blue eyes. *(He takes a doll that suddenly appears in the hands of one of his assistants and offers it to the imaginary child)* See?—you're happy now. You smiled. . . No, no, I didn't earn your thanks. It is *I* who thank *you* for your lovely smile. . . And you, the worried looking citizen with the brief case, for you I have a little flute—a wonderful little flute. *(He takes the instrument that has suddenly appeared in the hands of the*

VALERKA (Cont.)

SECOND MIME) How you will please your boss with your playing! *(He plays and the FOUR MIMES dance)* You'll see how soon he signs the order for your promotion. . . And what can I do to console *you*, Old Man? It *is* so sad to take leave forever of the sunshine and of your friends. I will give you as a gift that which makes man immortal! *(He takes from the THIRD MIME something invisible and offers it to the imaginary old man)* Take it— please take it! Don't let it bother you that my gift is intangible. I am giving you *talent*. You will write a wonderful fairy tale, and that way you will remain in this world forever. You see how simple it is to make all of you happy, ladies and gentlemen, children, adults, old folks! *(The FOUR MIMES noiselessly applaud)*

MASHA

(Appears at the fence opening. Whispers) Valerka! *(Louder)* Valerka! *The MIMES remove the tailcoat, top-hat, and cloak from VALERKA, pull off the beard, bow to him, and disappear)* Don't you tell my grandmother that I was here! *(VALERKA looks at her without answering. MASHA looks around, climbs through the opening, and carefully replaces the board)* Should I tell you why you interest me?

VALERKA

If you must.

MASHA

Because the old woman doesn't like you. She says, "Those roomers of his—whoever happens to knock on his door is accepted."

VALERKA

You're the ones who have roomers. The people who live *here* are my friends.

MASHA

Friends—what kind of friends are they if you've never set eyes on them before? And is it true that you don't accept any rent from them?

VALERKA

True.

MASHA

You're abnormal! And why no money?

VALERKA

Oh, I don't know. Someone is always living with us. Sometimes relatives, sometimes friends.

MASHA

The letter carrier says that you get whole bundles of letters, like an office.

VALERKA

So?

MASHA

I like that. My grandmother doesn't get *any*. And she says, "There's a mystery for you! They—meaning your family—have friends all over Russia writing to them! And why are they taking all the trouble to write and spend four kopecks on a stamp? What business are they up to? There's something fishy," she says. "The authorities should check on whether he takes money from his tenants or not."

VALERKA

They've already been here to check. The old witch brought a police officer right up to our gate.

MASHA

She certainly doesn't wish you well. "He's not growing up in a normal way," she says. *(VALERKA turns away)* Why did you turn away?

VALERKA

I'm listening to you. Quote on, quote on!

MASHA

"Neither the mother nor the father," she says, "looks after the household. And the tenants spoil him. And that magician—some great artist *he* is! He couldn't even earn enough to have a home of his own. Lives with strangers in his old age!"

VALERKA

(Turns back to her abruptly) Are you through now?

MASHA

(Stopping short) Yes . . .

VALERKA

You worm—that's what you are, a worm! Why did you crawl in here to talk such rot? Slither back into your hole.

MASHA

(Looks back at the fence) Sh-h-h! Valerka, what's gotten into you?
I am interested in you!

VALERKA

Then sit in the crack in your fence and study me!

MASHA

It's not me who's strange. It's you! I've never met anyone
like you.

VALERKA

You hang out in the wrong places.

MASHA

And there's nobody like you in my village, either.

VALERKA

Yes, there *are* people like me—only you wouldn't know them if
you saw them!

MASHA

Valerka, don't mind what I've been saying. . . *(He turns away)*
Don't go away. Come, let's shake hands.

VALERKA

What for?

MASHA

I came over to make friends.

VALERKA

(Faces her again) Let's keep it simple. *(He smiles and shakes her
extended hand)* Are you satisfied now?

MASHA

Yes. After all, I'm lonesome here. I haven't made friends with anyone
yet. And will you promise never to yell at me? I get gooseflesh when
people yell at me. Come, let's go to the beach together.

VALERKA

Can't. I have a rehearsal. I am Guido's "chief assistant."

MASHA

I've only been down to the beach once since I got here. There were
too many things to do for Grandmother. And then she keeps saying . . .

VALERKA

There you go again, quoting her immortal words!

MASHA

This time it's not about you. "And why," she says, "are people so attracted to the South? What's so special about the sea? Seaweed and salt! When I was a kid," she says "we swam in the river and didn't know anything about this nonsense of swimming in the sea!"

VALERKA

She's a hypocrite, that old woman. If you listen to her long enough she'll turn you into a hypocrite as well. If people still preferred rivers, then who would pay her a ruble a day just for sleeping on a cot? So much for your grandmother!

(MASHA looks around anxiously. VALERKA continues, musingly)

And this fence—for her it's an observation-post extending all over town! To get through it to where normal people live, a person has to secretly pry loose a board.

MASHA

Sh-h-h!

(VALERKA waves her off, and turns away)

But she's family! I don't have the right to judge her. . . Valerka, what are these swords for?

VALERKA

(Crossly) To cut the chest in half. A person lies in it and the swords go through him.

MASHA

Sure! Do you expect me to believe that? Ha-ha!

VALERKA

Don't touch that! And don't step on this board or you'll fly off. Living here is like living on a roller-coaster.

(Somewhere near the harbor a clock strikes)

Wow, it's eight o'clock! My people have overslept!

(He goes toward the house)

MASHA

Valerka, I assume we're friends now. Yes?

VALERKA

Go ahead and assume.

MASHA

That means I may come to visit you?

VALERKA

Appear. "Like a transitory vision, like an apparition of sheerest beauty! . . ." *(A line from Pushkin)*

MASHA

(Laughs) You're all such odd-balls—first Vera, then you talk in verse. And old Nikolai sang a song yesterday. "I have just had," sang he, "my seventeenth birthday." He's bald as the palm of your hand, but he sings about being seventeen.

VALERKA

Goodbye, magpie!

(He goes)

(MASHA walks around the yard. Carefully closing her eyes, she steps on the board. Nothing happens. She approaches the tall chest, touches it. Looking around to see whether VALERKA is watching, she opens something like a half-door, peers inside, bends over, and gets into the chest, closing the half-door behind her. Carefully raising her head, she looks around and breaks into song as she dances in place. "I am now seventeen, seventeen, seventeen! I am now seventeen, cha-cha-cha!" She hears approaching footsteps and quickly hides her head. VALERKA enters. He stands erect, lifts the sword and flourishes it as he quotes from a poem by Novella Matveeva: "Oh you Magician, perform a miracle! Make people understand me!" He goes to the chest and, pushing the tip of the sword into a crack, invisible from the distance, he drives it clear through it.)

MASHA

(Screams) A-a-a-a-a! *(She thrusts her head out, looking with terror at the sword hilt, then at the tip of the sword on the other side)*

VALERKA

(At first taken aback, then laughing) You're not a chicken, Mashka, and you're not a worm. You are a sheep! And you'll be turning on a spit while I roast you over the fire! *(He grasps a second sword and drives it through the chest)*

MASHA

(Almost inaudibly) A-a-a-a! *(She rolls out of the chest, touches herself, looking for wounds)* You nut!

VALERKA

(With a third sword in his hand, fencing with an imaginary enemy) And you are a spy—a spy from an enemy courtyard! . . . And for this you'll get, not friendship but death by torture!

(MASHA backs off toward the fence, away from the attacking VALERKA, and slips through the opening. He drives the sword into the fence)

VALERKA

And he nailed her to the pillar of disgrace. Hooray! *(He guffaws)*

MASHA

(Peers momentarily through the opening in the fence) Fool!

"And your eyes are green.
Like our cat's . . ."

The next day.

Even before the curtain rises and before the footlights go up, there is a symbolic sound of the trumpet. We hear its melody.

As the melody ends, the curtain rises. We see a street of the seaside town, running parallel to the shore. There is an iron parapet between the street and the beach. Near the parapet, at one end, stands a large scale for the weight-watching vacationers to check their weight. It is fastened with a big lock. Beside it is a low stool.

VALERKA runs onto the stage, hugging a portfolio to his chest. And, as usual when his imagination soars, the FOUR MIMES appear. At the moment they seem to be running after him, their heads lowered and their knees high, in the manner of sprinters. They are simply imitating VALERKA'S movements. He is evidently imagining himself to be the world's champion sprinter. He is now running with mock speed, going through the motions as stands in one spot. The FIRST and SECOND MIMES outpace him, then stretch an imaginary tape at the finish line. VALERKA tears it with his chest, and now the THIRD and FOURTH MIMES hold the severed tape while the FIRST and SECOND noiselessly applaud VALERKA'S victory. Suddenly the tempo of the music changes. VALERKA picks up the portfolio, which he had dropped. Now he is, first, a noted diplomat, then an astronaut returning from a record-breaking space flight, with the MIMES now acting out a reception by a committee of important officials. Again the tempo of the music changes, followed by a pantomime of a vigorous soccer game, in which VALERKA is a phenomenal goalie.

MASHA enters. She does not see VALERKA. She removes the lock from the scale, takes a white robe out of her shopping bag, and puts it on. It is way too long for her. She sits on the stool and takes a handful of coins from her dress pocket. She counts them.

Up to this moment, VALERKA and MASHA have not yet noticed each other. But soon VALERKA sees MASHA. The music stops. The MIMES leave the stage.

VALERKA

(Sneaks up on MASHA) Your money or your life!

MASHA

(Startled. She quickly hides the money, then looks up!) Damn you!

VALERKA

Business was good today, hey? It's interesting to speculate what your grasping grandmother will do when she has no more cherries to sell. You'd better watch out—she might sell *you*, into slavery!

MASHA

(Continues to count the money) No, she won't. She can't—we
don't live in America.

VALERKA

Really? . . . Oh, Masha, what a wonderful morning! Almost
unbearable! *(Cups his hands and speaks as if into a megaphone)*
O Sea, how noble in strength and beauty!

MASHA

Have you lost your mind?

VALERKA

(In the same tones) O People—how *ig*-noble!

MASHA

(Ignores his rhapsody) No, it just never comes out right. And
the old woman doesn't believe me—she thinks I steal from her
to buy myself ice cream.

VALERKA

Since she's supsicious anyway, you might as well treat yourself.
Gorge yourself on it! By the way, they don't have slaves in America
any more. *(He stands on the scale)* Taisya uses you to sell
everything in sight, and now she also makes you tend the scale. Do
you know that she justifies all this by saying that she works
for the government?

MASHA

She has no time to do things herself. She's too busy with her
summer tenants. She just got a new one.

VALERKA

And where did she put this one?

MASHA

We have a tiny attic.

VALERKA

"A tiny, teenchy attic!" Just wait—before long the State will
build enough boarding houses for vacationers, and then the rubles
will stop accumulating under old Taisya's mattress.

MASHA

They'll never be able to build enough for all of Russia. The
demand will always be greater than the supply.

VALERKA

(After a pause—suddenly) Masha, lend me four rubles until the first of the month.

MASHA

What for?

VALERKA

If you don't, I'll drown myself.

MASHA

Go ahead and drown! . . . Ask my grandmother for the loan.

VALERKA

Fat chance of getting it from her!

MASHA

Then ask your boarders.

VALERKA

What next?—do you have any other brilliant ideas? I don't borrow from friends. *(Sits silently on the parapet for a few moments, then breaks into laughter)* What a sight you were yesterday when you flopped out of that chest! A remarkable acrobatic stunt!

MASHA

Thanks for them kind words! Just the same, any other girl would have shouted, "Help!" Last winter I was skating and fell through the ice. I bet you would have yelled, "I'm drowning!" But not me. I climbed onto an ice floe and lay there without uttering a sound.

VALERKA

Are you lying?—I mean, perchance using poetic license?

MASHA

So help me God! Some boys were playing hockey not far away, and I felt sure that it was impossible for people not to notice when somebody was in danger.

VALERKA

So what happened?

MASHA

They noticed all right. But the next two nights I slept in the school store-room. My mother beats me every time I do anything she disapproves of. She uses our school grading system—from one to five—but in reverse. With her, five is the worst—five blows, that is.

VALERKA

Some teacher! And you—do you follow the custom of the Czarist regime—stretch out on a bench and wait for the lash?

MASHA

Certainly not. I run. But she secretly watches out for me at our cottage door. And no matter what, she catches me in the end, and lets me have it.

VALERKA

From a mother like that, I'd run to the North Pole.

MASHA

I think she's right. When a person is guilty punishment isn't so frightful. So what—so she hits me three times, or four. It hurts—that's all. I think it's much worse to be yelled at. When a person yells, he forgets himself. He looks for the most insulting words, the ones that hurt most. He may even be sorry later for using them. But you remember those words. All your life.

VALERKA

Does your father teach you with blows, too?

MASHA

My father has left us.

VALERKA

Where did he go?

MASHA

Well, he used to go off for a while at a time, to the big city. He liked to play the balalaika. He worked as a mechanic for a living, but he played the balalaika for his soul. Then one day a group of amateur musicians came along. I think they were cooks and waitresses on vacation. One of them sang folk songs. She'd sing and my father would accompany her on his balalaika. She'd sing and smile at him. She fell in love with my father and lured him away from us. He's handsome, it's easy to fall in love with him. . . . My sister and I resemble him—in height and looks.

VALERKA

You'll never perish of modesty!

MASHA

What do you mean? Just see what eyes I have! Believe it or not, I can balance five matches on my eyelashes. Now notice my smile.

(MASHA flashes her best smile. VALERKA refuses to be impressed)

VALERKA

Your nose is shaped like a potato.

MASHA

That's not true! It's pertly turned up. These days, everything Russian is in style—even snub-noses. You wait and take a look at me three years from now! I'll be luscious—you won't be able to tell me from my sister. And she's really something! She sure stands out in a crowd. And what skin she has—peaches and cream! When she walks by, every man in sight turns to look at her!

VALERKA

(Calls out loudly to the crowd on the beach) Hey, people! Listen, everybody! Our town has been honored by a visit from the most celebrated beauty of this century—MASHA . . .
(MASHA drags him away from the parapet)
Tell me, Masha, what is your family name?

MASHA

Do you want to know it for another one of your crazy tricks?

VALERKA

No. I swear! What is it?

MASHA

Balagayeva.*

VALERKA

(Suddenly pushes her away) Now explain something to me, Balagayeva. If you believe that people will not abandon you when you are in trouble—as they didn't when you were clinging to the ice— then why do you tremble over your coins like a miserable miser? Avaricious people don't believe in kindness.

MASHA

I'm not avaricious.

VALERKA

But are you kind?

MASHA

I'm practical. At home, in the village, we're taught to count our money carefully.

*Pronounced with the stress on the capitalized syllable: BalaGAyeva; The a's as in ark.

VALERKA

You have no self-respect.

MASHA

What makes you sat that?

VALERKA

After what happened yesterday, you should've been too proud
to have anything further to do with me.

MASHA

I didn't. It was you who spoke first today.

VALERKA

(Looks at her in surprise) You're right—it *was* me.

MASHA

And, generally, we country folks have more pride than you city
people. That's not surprising. Here you are like ants. You meet
and pass each other, hardly expecting ever to meet again. The way
we live, our conduct is noticed by everyone, and every word is taken
for what it says. So we can't afford to play fast and loose with our
self-respect. . . Now, how about you, Valerka? Why do you need
money—that four rubles?

VALERKA

It's a secret. *(He leaves her abruptly)*

MASHA

(Calls after him) You can just go to hell!

VALERKA

(Turns back) What?

MASHA

Oh, don't bother me! Get away from me!

VALERKA

Ha-ha! Look at her—she's offended! *(He comes closer to
MASHA, stands behind her)* Hey!
(MASHA doesn't answer)
Hey, Sophia Loren! *(Silence)* I'm expecting someone.

MASHA

(Turns around quickly) Who?

VALERKA

The devil knows *who* he is! Some cousin of my mother's. Sent a telegram: "Arriving Simforopol at nine in the morning." It'll take three hours to get him here by bus. I'll meet him at the terminal at about noon.

MASHA

How will you recognize him?

VALERKA

He has the same family name as my mother—Sinko. I'll just run up to every arriving bus and shout: "Comrade Sinko!" Whoever answers will be him.

MASHA

(*Thinking*) Right—but why the money?

VALERKA

We're accustomed to treating arriving friends and relatives to dinner. Well, I looked into our pantry and it's empty— completely empty.

MASHA

Didn't your mother leave you any pocket money at all?

VALERKA

Yes, she did. But I flew up through the chimney and the money got burned.

MASHA

How *did* you spend it?

VALERKA

What difference does it make? I had it, and it's gone.

MASHA

There you go again, being rude.

VALERKA

(*Stands very erect and speaks in the manner of a sergeant reporting to his superior officer*) Sir, I spent it to buy unnecessary trifles to repair the magician's equipment, such as: light bulbs—5, colored paper—5 sheets, black velvet—one yard, to a total sum of 28 rubles, zero kopecks.

MASHA

What were you thinking of! Twenty-eight rubles! Let that
magician pay it out of his own pocket.

VALERKA

Where would he get it? He lives on his small pension. . . Don't you
dare say anything to him about this money. I told him that the
Seamen's Club provided it. . . Don't worry about the four rubles,
Mashka. I looked through all my pockets and scraped together about
a ruble. I'll buy some bread, milk and sausage. We won't die of hunger. . . .
By the way, wouldn't you like to have a magic purse, making money
for you all the time?

MASHA

What for? The old woman would take it away from me anyway.
And how about you—would you like one?

VALERKA

(In a whisper, as if telling her a secret) Me? I—Maria Balagayeva—I
would want one. I'd give all the money to Taisya. Let her use it
to build a granite wall around her, as high as the sky, so that I'd
never again have to hear her voice.
(He grabs his portfolio and starts to leave)

MASHA

Valerka!
(He stops)
I would find a niche even in a granite wall. I'm not curious about
my grandmother, but I'm very curious about you. *(She laughs)* Is
it true that you let a woman and her four children room with you last month?

VALERKA

(Raises two fingers) Yes—I swear it by all the planets
and asteroids!

MASHA

You know, I have a kind of intuition about you. . . . . . You keep on
fooling around, you laugh at everything, play the cynic—but I
suspect that inside there is something sad that eats at you.
*(Somewhere on the beach, in the distance, a loudspeaker plays
jazz. MASHA dances the Twist around the scale)*

VALERKA

So that's what they teach you in your village.

MASHA

The Twist is no longer in style there. The Recreation Center
has gone back to the Shaky. . . And in our school the Komosomol
has issued directives for us not to be seduced by Western influences.
And our phys. ed. teacher has choreographed a different kind of
social dancing. Do you want to see it?

VALERKA

Go ahead, demonstrate.

(MASHA dances a mixture of Twist, Krakoviak, and some
choreographed gymnastic exercises. We hear the trumpet against
the background of the jazz. VALERKA moves away from the
parapet but continues to watch MASHA dance. The sound of the
trumpet is repeated. The FOUR MIMES enter. They wear white
doctor's robes, with sleeves rolled up to the elbows, white caps,
and surgeon's gloves. They stand behind VALERKA. The stage
is darkened as the lights focus on him. MASHA is now invisible,
but the dance music continues to be heard for the entire duration
of the ensuing scene to stress the frivolity of the general seaside
resort atmosphere, MASHA'S being in tune with it—and
VALERKA'S heavy mood)*

VALERKA

(Addressing himself to an imaginary interlocutor)

One day last spring when I came home from school I was surprised
to see my father busy fixing a window frame. Until that day he had
been bedridden since the Fall. I ran toward him and he, too, took
two steps toward me. But he was seized with a coughing spell and,
as always, he stretched out his arm as if to keep me at a safe distance.
He always kept a distance between the two of us—wouldn't let me
touch his things—he was afraid I'd be infected. I don't think that
in all my life he ever touched me. . . . That day some of his friends
came to visit. Mother prepared a nice meal, even serving them early
strawberries, and Father said he was really feeling well for the first
time since he was wounded. Afterward his friends drove us to the
harbor and we all went aboard a battle cruiser. We stood on the
captain's bridge. The Commander was loudly recounting some
incident, trying to make himself heard above the sound of the wind.
Father was so thin and he looked so "civilian" next to the magnificently
uniformed Commander—but I was proud of him just the same. I
knew that once he had stood on just such a bridge as the Commander.
It was during the War. And the present Commander was then one
of his crew.

*An old fashioned ballroom dance originating in Poland, probably in the early 19th
Century, and continuing to be popular in Russia until the Revolution.

VALERKA (Cont.)

(There is movement among the MIMES. A file folder appears in the hands of one of them. It is passed from him to the other MIMES. The one on the extreme left opens it and hands it to VALERKA, who does not look at the papers in the folder)

Yes, Comrade Doctor, I know. You are talking to me as to an adult, and I'm grateful to you for this! But that's only the record of his illness! . . .not the whole story. . .

(The folder disappears. He continues to address the imaginary interlocutor)

I'll tell you why he's now lying in this ward. It happened in the middle of the war. It was winter-time. And he was still, at that time, a very young Commander. His cruiser was convoying a transport ship from burning Sevastopol to Novorosiisk. It was full of women and children and old people, who were being evacuated. And when a German submarine fired a torpedo at the transport, my father steered his ship in the path of the torpedo. Only two men survived— he and the sailor who is now Commander. It was getting dark. The transport picked up the sailor. But they couldn't find my father and thought he had drowned. He was still alive, though, and managed to keep afloat all night in the icy water. The next eight years he spent in hospitals and sanitariums. Each spring they predicted that he would soon die. But one spring he came to this town, almost cured. He met my mother, they married, and settled here for good.

(An X-ray picture appears in the hand of one of the MIMES. It is passed along to the others, and the last one hands it to VALERKA)

Yes, I know, Comrade Doctor. I've seen all your X-rays. But a person can breathe with just one lung. . . Don't you understand?. . . Let him come home, stay with us. . . Even if he has to remain bedridden. But let him be with us—for as long as he lives. . .

(The FOUR MIMES step back toward the backdrop, right)

(Desperately—to the invisible doctor who leaves with the MIMES) Comrade Doctor! . . . Comrade Doctor! . . . There must be something you can do! . . . Something! . . .

(The MIMES disappear backstage. The whole stage is now lit again. MASHA finishes her dance and comments on it)

MASHA

Head up—proudly, with a smile—joyously. And arms this way: as if you were sowing seeds, cutting the grass with a scythe or sickle—sow the seeds—cut the grass. The phys. ed. teacher calls this dance "Virgin Land"! Well, how do you like it?

VALERKA

It's convincing.

MASHA

You think so? We didn't care for it, and the boys even refused to
dance it. But the principal insisted. A "tableau," he would call it, and
say that it "fully expresses the aspirations of wholesome youth
and the ideals of emancipated farm labor!" *(She stops short,
thinks a moment as she dances a few more steps)* Valerka,
what does it convince you of?

VALERKA

Of the fact that we have fools galore! They ought to put your
phys. ed. teacher in a strait-jacket.

MASHA

(Taken aback, then doubling up with laughter) And I thought
that you liked it! You're. . . Oh, Valerka, one of our new boarders
is a telepathist. I swear it! Do you believe in telepathy?

VALERKA

It is considered—mysticism.

MASHA

What difference does it make what it is considered if it actually
exists? *I* believe in it. *(She turns her back to him)* Look at the
back of my neck, concentrate. . . Are you looking?

VALERKA

I'm looking.

MASHA

Now, think and I'll tell you what it is. Concentrate hard. Think of
an object. *(She closes her eyes, gropes the air with her hands)* That's
it. . .that's it. . .yes, it's round—berries—lots of berries. . . Think
harder. A pail. Now the berries are in the pail.

VALERKA

You're off the track.

MASHA

What *were* you thinking of?

VALERKA

Of you. I was wondering whether you are more stupid than
clever, or more clever than stupid.

MASHA

More clever! I'm terribly smart. Only I'm like a dog: I understand everything but I can't express it. . . Now *you* turn around. I'll think of something, and you try to find out what it is. You can make fun of me later. Come on, turn around. *(He does. She looks at the back of his neck with great concentration)* Relax. Close your eyes. Are you thinking of something?

VALERKA

An owl.

MASHA

Why an owl?

VALERKA

I don't know. Just an owl.

MASHA

And I was thinking of a sword.

VALERKA

I think there has to be some contact for this to work.

MASHA

What kind?

VALERKA

Ordinary. Put your palms on my temples.

MASHA

This way?

VALERKA

We'll try it. I'll tell you if it's working. Are you looking at the back of my neck?

MASHA

Yes.

VALERKA

Now telepathize!

MASHA

(Laughs) Oh, Valerka—your ears are burning!

VALERKA

So what?

MASHA

(Not at once, and in a low voice—she is aware of the effect on VALERKA of her touching him) Oh, nothing. *(She removes her hands slowly)*

VALERKA

(Still stands with his eyes closed, then turns around.)
What's the matter?

MASHA

I don't want to do this any more.

VALERKA

Don't you want to hypnotize me?

MASHA

Your eyes are green. Like our cat's. . . It's funny.

VALERKA

Who cares? Come on, let's try it once more. What if it really works?
(He turns his back to MASHA and closes his eyes. But MASHA does not look at him. With a strange abstraction, she stares off at the sea, then lowers her eyes and notices VALERKA'S portfolio. She slowly takes some money from her pocket and puts it into the portfolio. She walks away from VALERKA, and sits down near the scale)

VALERKA

(Continues to guess) Cruiser. . . Wait, wait. . .its outlines are becoming clearer—it's a gunboat!

MASHA

(Absent-mindedly) Yes.

VALERKA

(Laughing) No, it was a cat I saw. So much for your scientific experiment in telepathy! *(He looks at his watch)* I'd better hurry or the store will be closed. *(He takes the coins from his portfolio to put them in his pocket. He feels the five-ruble bill, unfolds it, and whistles)* The materialization of a wish. Masha, look! Five rubles! Ha-ha! And I, in reality a millionaire, lowered myself before you for a miserly loan. Yesterday I ransacked the whole house but I didn't think of looking in the portfolio. Now my guest will have a real party! *(He slaps MASHA heartily on the back and runs off)*
(MASHA remains for a while, deep in thought, then locks the scale and hangs up a sign: "Closed for Lunch")

                                        ". . . tantamount to love."

The following day.

A part of the pier, featuring a plank boardwalk and pile structures. With a fishing-line wound around his finger, VALERKA is fishing for bullheads.

MASHA approaches, carrying a shopping bag.

*It is at once clear that a change has come over her—in the way she walks, the way she speaks, the way she holds up her head, there is a challenging self-awareness about her. Her braids are now wound around her head, giving the impression of a specially chosen hairdo. She wears a pretty light-blue blouse over her jumper (**sarafan**— a sleeveless dress, in this case in the national Russian style). She is wearing high-heeled shoes. She is aware of her femininity.*

(She walks up to VALERKA and watches him fish)

VALERKA

Don't stare, the fish don't like it.

MASHA

What about you—*you're* staring at them.

VALERKA

They're used to me. . . Darn them, they're not hungry. I offer them delicious bait, but they don't bite.

MASHA

(Falls silent, walks away, stares at the sea, and suddenly starts singing the refrain of a corny love song)

                "Oh, what have you done to me,
                What grief have you brought me!
                Oh, why did you, that Monday,
                Give me a white rose?"

VALERKA

(Listens with amazement to MASHA'S vocalizing) What's all this howling about? And why are you all dressed up?
(MASHA dances a bit, clicking her heels)
(Still more amazed) Is this your concert stage?
(MASHA sits down near VALERKA, letting her legs dangle from the pier)
I think I'll use *you* for bait—maybe the fish'll develop an appetite for such a beauty!

MASHA

(Straightens her blouse) Don't I look good in blue?
Grandmother keeps grumbling and scolding, but just the same
she gave me this as a gift yesterday. She bought it at a second-hand
store. It cost seventeen rubles.

VALERKA

She dresses you in diamonds and gold!

MASHA

She's done better than *you* do for others. All you give
people is walking sticks that you whittle from tree-branches.
(She sings again)
   "Oh, what have you done to me. . ."

VALERKA

What a siren!

(He moves away from her and casts his fishing line)

MASHA

Would it interest you to know why I didn't stop by at your
place yesterday?

VALERKA

(Seems to be absorbed entirely in watching the fish) Why
didn't you?

MASHA

Guess! . . . I was testing you, that's why. I even tried
to guess—sort of told my own fortune— will he or
won't he come?

VALERKA

To *Taisya's*?!

MASHA

Why do you put it that way? *She's* not your friend—*I* am. Should
I tell you what fortune I predicted? *(Sings)* "What grief you've
brought me!. . ." I used to sing solo in our Amateur Music Center.
Oh, Valerka, the boys were just wild about me! One of them even
sent me a note. He wrote: "Let's go out on a date after the movies."

VALERKA

Did you go?

MASHA

Yes. He said, "Do you know how to kiss?" I said, "No." He said,
"Then why do you sing love songs—you mislead your listeners. . ."
Should I tell you the rest?

VALERKA

If it's worth hearing—tell on.

MASHA

Then he said, "Let me teach you how to kiss." I said, "Go ahead."

VALERKA

You don't say!

MASHA

(Repeating) He insists: "Come on, I'll teach you." I say: "All
right, go ahead."

VALERKA

Disgusting!

MASHA

He kissed me on the cheek—here. He's peculiar. He writes poetry.
We call him "Yevtushenko." He's shy. He kissed me and ran away!
For a long time after that he'd lower his eyes when he met me.
And then something else happened. A boy in the 11th grade invited
me to a dance. I caught cold, or I would have gone.

VALERKA

You sure are a chatterbox, Mashka! *(There is a pull on the line)*
Oh! Bite, my turtle-dove! Please bite!

MASHA

(Runs over to VALERKA, looks down into the water) How small
he is! Our village fishermen throw back small ones like that.
Our pike are as big as carp—well, at least as big as perch. *(She
yells)* Pull him in, Valerka—pull!

VALERKA

(Pulls up the hook. There's nothing on it) Your voice is enough
to deafen the poor fish! Why do you shout right near my ear?

MASHA

I'm tense, that's why I shout. . . Oh, Valerka, throw your line
in better—look, a whole school of them! Look, look, there's a crab.
You might as well catch him.

VALERKA

Crab are caught by hand.

MASHA

He got away!

VALERKA

And the fish went away, too. They seem to hate food!
(He stands up, stretches, looks at MASHA)
Tell me the truth—how come you got so dressed up so early
in the morning?
(A low steamship's whistle is heard)
It's the "Admiral Nakhimov" taking tourists on a cruise around Europe.
*(The trumpet. The MIMES appear. To the rhythm of a waltz they
carry a Commander's cap, raised high, in the manner of a ceremony.
They halt behind VALERKA and slowly lower the cap)*

VALERKA

(Musingly) The Bosporus. . .the Dardanelles. . .Africa. . .Rome. . .Milan. . .

MASHA

Milan—that's where they have the famous opera. Right?
*(VALERKA assumes an air of importance. The cap has been
lowered almost to his head)*
Valerka! How withdrawn you are! Please don't get lost in
thought when I'm near you.

VALERKA

It's easy to get lost in thought with you around!
*(The waltz music stops abruptly. The FOUR MIMES raise the
cap and tip-toe off into the wings with it)*
What is it *now?*

MASHA

Yesterday the telepathist told me a lot about Italy. An opera
ticket is very expensive—you could buy two pairs of high-heeled
pumps for what it costs. Would you believe it? Two pairs! Only
under capitalism! Generally he evaluates life abroad in terms of
the price of shoes. The price of a movie—a pair of sandals. A
snack in a coffee-shop—the cost of half a shoe. I couldn't resist
asking him, "Why do you always talk about footwear? Are you a
centipede or a man?" He was insulted, and refused to tell me
anything else about Italy.
*(A pause. MASHA gives VALERKA a sidelong glance, paces back
and forth on the boardwalk. She walks like a grown woman,
eager to attract attention, her head tauntingly high)*

VALERKA

You're a one-woman circus! How about coming to work
with our act—as an extra? That way you can show off before
a large public.

MASHA

I don't dare. My grandmother would kill me. She despises all of you
show people. . . . But, here, I brought you something to eat, Valerka.

VALERKA

Me?

MASHA

My father used to like it when I brought him his lunch when
he was fishing. Look—sandwiches and lemonade. Let's sit here.
You eat and I'll look at you.
*(She gets settled near VALERKA. He rubs his hands with
impatience as he watches her spread a napkin and take out the
sandwiches from her shopping bag. Then he falls to, greedily)*
Do they taste good?

VALERKA

Hmm-hmmm! Is today Sunday?

MASHA

Today? No, it's Wednesday.

VALERKA

Then why did you dress up this morning?

MASHA

I didn't dress up. This is an ordinary blouse. And my good
shoes—that's all. Why—do I look that way?

VALERKA

Which way?

MASHA

Festive. "Which way!!"

VALERKA

You look silly. The blouse is too big.

VALERKA

I'll grow into it. In another six months it will fit just right.

VALERKA

Then why don't you wait half a year to wear it? And what a mess your hair is! You look like a scarecrow.

(MASHA snatches the lemonade bottle from his hand and is about to throw it into the sea)

VALERKA

Hey! Hey! Can't you take a joke?

(MASHA lowers her arm)

Actually it's a cute hairdo.

(He takes back his bottle and drinks)

MASHA

(Looks down at her blouse) Maybe it *is* too garish.

VALERKA

(Continues to eat with gusto) It's not important. You should care!

(MASHA takes off her blouse)

That's different. What's important is not to be on display, not to pose as a grande dame, to be your age. You may wear eye makeup that makes you look like an aging woman, but, just the same, you'll be running on the beach like a kid.

MASHA

"Not to be on display," you say. But you yourself wear patches on your pants.

VALERKA

Jeans. They are practical. The "patch" is a trademark. If I had sewn it on myself then you'd have the right to call me a fop. Do you know what I mean?

MASHA

No.

VALERKA

It's the same thing whether you decorate your jeans or let your hair grow down to your knees. It's all the same thing—you're trying to attract attention, to stand out. Do you want some of this? *(Offers her the lemonade bottle)*

MASHA

Okay. *(Takes a couple of swallows from the bottle)* It's interesting—first you drink, now I do. . . Don't you see? The same bottle—the same source. Look: I took a sip, and now *(Offering him the bottle)* you'll drink from the very same bottle!

VALERKA

(Finally getting what she's driving at) You'd better forget
about your idiotic dates. I think they were disgusting. *(He examines
the sandwich)* I've never seen such red bacon.

MASHA

My grandmother hoarded some. And while she was quarreling with
one of her tenants, I sneaked down the cellar and grabbed a piece.

VALERKA

(Gets his back up) I've made it! I've arrived! I'm now
consuming stolen goods!

MASHA

(Insulted) Be careful how you talk. It's one thing to steal—
another to take secretly. Bacon is bacon—isn't it all the
same to you?

VALERKA

(Shouts with exasperation) You're a wooden dummy—with
eyes—that's what you are! Everything is "all the same" to you. But
I'm not used to sneaking things. I don't do it myself and I hate it
when it's done for my sake. It degrades me. Can you understand that?

MASHA

No, I can't. When you anonymously write down a complaint
against a fellow-student in the class book, don't you, in a way,
shout it all over the school?

VALERKA

What a comparison! The class book is about the way people act
toward one another. *(He is about to take another bite of the
sandwich, stops, and then throws it into the sea)*

MASHA

*(Takes the bottle, looks through it in the light, pours out the rest
of the lemonade, and sings in a low voice)*

"Oh, why did you, that Monday,
   Give me a white rose. . ."

VALERKA

All right, don't sulk. . . My uncle—that's my mother's cousin—has
a philosophy of life something like yours. Last night I looked into
his room through the window. He sits there eating candy. He had
kept it under his pillow, and now sat there chewing away. Never
a thought about sharing it. That's why I left the house earlier

VALERKA (Cont.)

this morning. I couldn't stand to look at him. What if he had
noticed that I caught him at his secret feasting?. . . In general
he's a unique type. I moved into the shed and gave him my room.
He had been upset because some of our tenants had rooms facing
the sea and he didn't. "I," he said, "am your mother's cousin. If
you don't have a feeling of kinship for me, I might just as well
live with strangers."

MASHA

And who is he? What does he do?

VALERKA

It's hard to tell. He hints about having an important position.
He is about to retire on a pension. Wants to buy a little house
in our town. That guy won't miss a chance to rake in the rubles.
Ever since I can remember, we never locked our door. But that
one, even when he goes to the store for a bottle of soda, he
latches his window and locks the door to his room.

MASHA

Maybe he brought a lot of cash with him.

VALERKA

Or maybe diamonds! And of course I'd steal them! I, or Guido,
or Nikolai. *(Suddenly he becomes aware that MASHA has put
her head on his shoulder)* So you found yourself a pillow? *(He shakes
her off)* You're weird! We're right here at the beach—it's full of
people who know us. Do you want our names to be written on all
the fences with the immortal words: "Tantamount to love. . .?"

MASHA

Let them!

VALERKA

(Jumps up) Of course you wouldn't care! You're shameless!

MASHA

(Slyly) Valerka, what's that you have in your pocket?

VALERKA

(Preplexed) Nothing.

MASHA

And you claim to be truthful! You have some tickets there. For the movie, "Green Mansions." Slavka*, the postoffice clerk, told me that you bought them for yourself and Vera. That's what you've got there, isn't it?

VALERKA

(Still feigning perplexity) Of course, since you say that I bought them—that's how it must be. *(He takes the tickets from his pocket)*

MASHA

(Snatches the tickets from his hand, stuffs them into her mouth, chews them up, and swallows them) There!

VALERKA

(Extremely surprised) What a maniac! Using woodpulp for food!

MASHA

(Taking some coins from her change purse) Here, you can give Vera her money back.

VALERKA

(Knocks the coins from her hand) Oh!—get lost!. . . Vanish, I tell you! *(She begins to retreat and he calls after her)* Drop dead!
(MASHA stops short)
What's the matter with you? Have you gone and fallen in love with me?

MASHA

(In an awkward pose) That's all I need—to fall in love with an idiot like you!

VALERKA

Just remember—I'm through with all of you women. As for you, don't disappoint me—drop dead!

MASHA

(Now composed) Go ahead, be rude to me. Before, it would have bothered me, but now I couldn't care less. Now I see all your tricks as through a prism—that's how.

**SLAvka — The *a*'s pronounced as in *a*rm.

VALERKA

Through a what?

MASHA

Through a prism. It's like a scientific formula. If you're tired of talking nasty then why don't you pull my braids? This approach is also mentioned. Boys are known to hide their feelings that way. *(She takes a pamphlet from her shopping bag and reads its title)* "The Awkward Age, or Reaching Manhood" by Khmelnitzkii*, who wrote it especially for creatures your age. Read it. It says it right here about hiding feelings. *(Shows him page in book)*

VALERKA

(With curiosity, reading) "At the age of 16, sometimes a little earlier, sometimes later. . ."

MASHA

(Reads on) ". . .you begin to notice girls. You are a bit ashamed as to these stirrings of interest in them, and hide it from your friends. . ." *(Continues reading—louder)* ". . .And when you are attracted to a certain girl, you try to appear cross with her, rude and curt." There— clear enough—black on white. They sell it at the newspaper stand. *(She walks away a safe distance and declaims rhapsocically)* "When a certain girl attracts you. . ."

VALERKA

Just listen to her. You'd think she was memorizing a prayer.

MASHA

(Triumphantly) ". . .you try to be cross, rude, curt. . ."

VALERKA

How disgusting!

MASHA

That's right, go on—spit at me. Reach manhood!

VALERKA

(He jumps at MASHA, grabs the pamphlet, and hurls it into the sea) One more word out of you and you'll be next!

MASHA

(With the unctuousness of a martyr to the truth) You cannot drown the truth.

(VALERKA pushes MASHA into the water. She falls with a big splash)

*KhmelNITZkii — Pronounced with the *e* as in n*e*t, and the *ii* as in m*ee*t.

"Do you know how old Juliet was
when she died? Fourteen years. . ."

Several days have passed. It is late evening.

*A small lean-to, with only two walls. There is a door in one of them
hich is latched on the outside. Inside there is a chest, a small table,
nd a cot. An electric bulb hangs from the ceiling. There is a sign
on one wall: "Don't allow children to play in the street." Next to it
is a lithograph of a schooner at sea.*

*MASHA is in bed, reading a book. She lies facing the wall opposite
the door. We see VALERKA prowling about in the yard. He looks
up at Taisya's house. It is dark. Everyone has retired for the night.
He approaches the lean-to, lifts the latch noiselessly, puts his head
in the door. Seeing MASHA, he knocks on the partly open door and
enters.*

MASHA

(Quickly pulling the blanket up to her shoulders) What are
you doing here?

VALERKA

Who, me?

MASHA

You.

VALERKA

It's a good question. What *am* I doing here? I guess it's just to
satisfy a sporting curiosity. I have a passion for overcoming obstacles.
(However, despite the outward bravado, he is obviously embarassed)
I suppose it was Taisya who nailed down the board in the fence.

MASHA

Yes, she did it.

VALERKA

I tried to loosen it with my shoulder, but it wouldn't give.

MASHA

*(She watches him as he examines her hideaway and, after a
pause)* No, I'm the one who nailed it down.

VALERKA

(Without turning toward her) You certainly did a good job.
(Motions to the sign on the wall) An outstanding piece of art.
Personally, I prefer the exhortation, "Don't hang by your heels."
Especially not before bedtime. . . May I sit down?

MASHA

Go ahead.

VALERKA

(Sits on the floor) It's exotic here. . . Asian countries were the first to have astronomers and philosophers, but they somehow never invented the chair.

MASHA

If you're not comfortable—sit on the chest.

VALERKA

No, I can rough it! The old woman is strict. She's bringing you up like a Spartan. I suppose her chickens live here in the wintertime.

MASHA

It was my idea to stay here. Before I fall asleep, I imagine I'm in a tent, in the woods.

VALERKA

Did Taisya latch the door to protect you from romance?
(MASHA leafs the pages of the book, but does not reply)
And I thought you wouldn't even speak to me any more.

MASHA

(After a brief silence) You opened the door by accident, didn't you?

VALERKA

Did I? *(Looks closely at MASHA)* You're a strange creature. . . .
Tell me, do you, by accident, believe in God?

MASHA

By accident? No.

VALERKA

But you know what the Bible says: "Turn the other cheek."

MASHA

That means that you didn't just happen to open the door—you did it on purpose to get me in trouble.

VALERKA

(After a brief silence) I don't know. . . Maybe I did it without a purpose.

MASHA

Of course. Without a purpose. You're not mean. . .

VALERKA

Actually, I jumped over the fence to come here to ask your pardon.

MASHA

Thank you!

VALERKA

Make believe that I stand before you and bow to the ground
for forgiveness.

MASHA

All right. . . This no longer matters now.

VALERKA

Then what does matter?
(MASHA does not reply)
You said this no longer matters. I am asking you what does?

MASHA

Everything.

VALERKA

(Shouting) Did I come here to take part in a quiz show?

MASHA

Quiet! You'll wake the old woman, and she'll come and lead you
out of here by your ear.

MASHA

(Gets up from the floor, opens the door, and calls out) "The long
white sail in the sea's blue mist!"*

MASHA

(After a pause) Go on—shout some more. You must think it's
heroic to wake up an old woman.

VALERKA

(Threatening) I'm going.
(He gets up and starts toward the door)

MASHA

So go!

---

*The first line of a famous poem by Lermontov, memorized by every school child.

VALERKA

(Hesitates at the door, then returns to his place on the floor) "There is no sadder tale in the world than the tale of Romeo and Juliet."

MASHA

The ballet?

VALERKA

(Smiling) The ballet.

MASHA

Was it you who sent me the book?

VALERKA

(With exaggerated interest) What book?

MASHA

Turgenev's *First Love.* Arlenka, our neighbor, gave it to my grandmother to give to me. I thought it was another bit of your asinine humor.

VALERKA

Personally, I've never met donkeys with a sense of humor. By the way, sometimes people put notes in books.

MASHA

What for?

VALERKA

For many reasons. For example, to declare their love.

MASHA

Not likely. *(However, she shakes the book over the blanket)* Oh, that means that Shurik sent it from Leningrad.

VALERKA

Who?! Who?!

MASHA

Shurik. He arrived here one day with Mother. His family lives in the corner house. Haven't you ever seen him? He's tall and wears a suede jacket.

VALERKA

(Suddenly annoyed) I don't look at people's jackets, I look at their faces.

MASHA

(Calmly) And he has a face that a person would remember. A handsome face. Only he's peeling—got too sunburnt.

VALERKA

(After a silence) With men the most important thing is their character.

MASHA

Of course. . . But their faces, too. He is going to be a physicist. *(Intuitively, she hits a sensitive nerve)* Personally, I consider physicists the most important people on earth. How about you?

VALERKA

That's all nonsense.

MASHA

The Nuclear Age! Whoever has control of nuclear energy has the greatest power.

VALERKA

How narrow-minded you are! Physics, you believe, is civilization. Today we are in the nuclear age, tomorrow we'll be in some other age. Yesterday, we rode in carriages—today, in automobiles—but tomorrow we'll *fly* in private carriages. There's no end to technological inventions, but what's most important is people's happiness. That's it. Whoever does the most to assure humanity's happiness is the most important. But those like your Shurik I don't care for very much. They show off. Even if he calls knowledge a "flow of information," still he's not yet an Einstein.

MASHA

He's not a who?

VALERKA

Not Einstein. Well, I should know better than to start a philosophical discussion with you. Just the same, he's a fool, your Shurik, and that's that.

MASHA

(Looking askance at VALERKA and smiling) He's funny. When he sees me coming, he runs up to the horizontal bar and swings on it to attract attention. My, how dumb you boys can be! When I was in fourth grade, a boy in my class fell in love with me, and to attract my attention he smeared his whole face with ink and walked to the blackboard on all fours.

VALERKA

There you go again about your conquests.

MASHA

Just think of it, in the fourth grade! They suspended him and he hated me for it, thought it was my fault. One day he put a mouse in one of my boots.

VALERKA

What makes you think it was Shurik who sent the book?

MASHA

Who else would it be?. . .

VALERKA

(With a touch of disgust) Maybe he too has fallen in love with you.

MASHA

Who, Shurik? Why should he fall in love with me?

VALERKA

Because you are pretty.

MASHA

Do you think so?!

VALERKA

Who, me? I haven't considered the matter yet. I just remember how you showed off. . . By the way, do you know how old Juliet was when she died?. . . Fourteen.

MASHA

Fantastic! That means she was only in the sixth grade. Nowadays girls don't take poison because of love. To get over an unhappy love affair my sister fell in love with somebody else—that, and to spite her first one. *(Again she looks sidelong at VALERKA and smiles)* Tell me about tonight's show at the Seamen's Club.

VALERKA

(Off-handedly) It was okay. In the first part there were scenes from Schiller's *The Robbers.* Carl Moore was played by the bos'un from the ship "The First of May." *(He envelops himself in an imaginary cape)* "Oh, humanity! False, two-faced, beastly tribe! Your tears are but water! Your hearts—iron!" In the second part we performed in "Forty Minutes in the World of Illusion.". . . Ha! Listen to this— it develops that my uncle's name is Goliaph* Petrovich.

*A very unusual name.

MASHA

Didn't you know that before?

VALERKA

He always refers to himself as "Uncle Goly.". . . In one act we
invited him to come up on the stage. Nikolai asks, "How should I
introduce you to the audience?" He says, "As a representative of
the audience—Goliaph Petrovich Sinko." The audience laughed. Next
to Nikolai he looked like a midget. We have a certain act—we put
someone from the audience, who volunteers, into a chest and we saw
it in half with the person inside. The whole trick is of course in the
saw—but the illusion is complete. The saw buzzes and sawdust
and small splinters blow in all directions. The audience holds its
breath in astonishment and alarm. My uncle was scared
out of his wits. He rolled out of the chest screaming, "Help! Help!"
Ran all over the stage desperately looking for an exit and not finding
it in his panic. Now he has shut himself up in his room and won't
talk to anyone. . . Guido took five curtain calls. Then my friends and
neighbors lined up to shake my hand. "Thank you, Valery
Aleksandrovich," they said to me, "you did the impossible and
unforgettable." As for Guido, it develops that he is not just a Merited
National Artist. He began his career way before the Revolution.
There were stores at that time where magicians could buy their
equipment, but now. . .

MASHA

And now?

VALERKA

Now every magician devises his own. Nowadays you can't fool
the public so easily—you can't get by without electronics.
(And characteristically pretending indifference) Why didn't
you come to the show?

MASHA

(With a slight hesitation) You didn't invite me.

VALERKA

Those who were interested—came.

MASHA

(Again a slight hesitation) I promised someone to go to the
movies with him this evening.

VALERKA

(With sarcasm) Oh, yes?

MASHA

On my word of honor! Shurik invited me, and I went.

VALERKA

(After a pause) All in all, our show was more amateur than professional. Our apparatus is makeshift and the assistants untrained. . . By the way, you needn't have bothered about that "word of honor." I don't care one way or the other about minor matters.

MASHA

Don't you believe me?

VALERKA

What difference does it make? Anyway, once a liar, always a liar. There is a proverb about that. Remember that!

MASHA

I'll remember.

VALERKA

(Sees dishes on the table) Ha! She feeds you from a tin bowl. *(He examines the bowl, sniffs the mug)* Like a jailbird. Gruel, bread, and water. That Taisya—she'll get it from me yet!

MASHA

Sh-h-h!

VALERKA

(Shouting) Don't shush me! You keep silent about her ways and she'll put you on a chain, wait and see! *(He throws open the door and shouts in the direction of Taisya's house)* "Oh, people! Deceitful, two-faced, crocodile race! Their tears are water! Their hearts— iron! A kiss on their lips, a sword in their bosom!" Lions and leopards feed their young. Crows carry food for miles to their nestlings, but she. . .she! *(He flings the bowl into the yard)*

After the bowl bounces noisily in the yard, we hear sounds from the house—a shutter is flung open, a door creaks.

MASHA

That was quite a remarkable bit of acting.

VALERKA

If she comes here—I'll destroy her with the truth—on the spot! Don't listen with such fear for her footsteps! *(Nevertheless he listens for them—and not with indifference)*

MASHA

She's coming!

VALERKA

Let her.

MASHA

Oh, Valerka—hide!

VALERKA

(With less assurance) What next! Let lovers in bedroom farces hide in closets.

MASHA

Valerka, hurry up and hide!
(VALERKA dives under the chest. MASHA pretends to be asleep. A pause. MASHA listens)

MASHA

She went back to the house.

VALERKA

(Crawls out from under the chest) In wartime those who panic are not coddled—they are shot.

MASHA

(With a smile) Valerka, how could your pride let you crawl under the chest?

VALERKA

Your cowardice is contagious.

MASHA

(Leafing her book, then suddenly) There is something underlined here! Oh, Valerka—look! "I am attracted to you." Marked with a red pencil. Other boys push girls into snowdrifts, say vulgar things to them. They'd rather die than admit that they like a girl. But not Shurik. *He* underlined his feelings.
(Overdoing it) In general, Shurik is different from the others. Even in small things. For example, in the movies he changed seats with me so that I could see the screen better.

VALERKA

(Put out) Shurik! Why did you bring *him* up?

MASHA

Because he's the one who sent me this book.

VALERKA

A-a-a. . . *(Stands up)* Goodnight. Pleasant dreams, Maria Balagayeva. Gud-bai! *(He stretches lazily, opens the door)*
(MASHA looks after him silently. With a purely feminine intuition she knows that he'd like to continue their conversation. He pauses, then speaks without turning around)

I'm the one who underlined those words. . .

MASHA

(Pause) I know it. I watched you from the attic and saw you hand the book to Lenka.

VALERKA

(Still not turning around) Is that all you have to say about it?. . .

MASHA

That's all.

VALERKA

Why haven't you been coming to the pier? Why didn't you come yesterday?

MASHA

(With indifference) Yesterday—what was yesterday? It seems like a hundred years ago. I've already forgotten to even think about what happened yesterday. I was just having a little fun with you. What do I need boys for? Half the boys in my village pursue me. I only look at them to show them how disgusted I am. *(After a moment's silence, tersely)* Go away.

VALERKA

Forever?
(MASHA doesn't answer)
Salut!* *(Puts some money on the table)* Here, give it to Taisya.

MASHA

What's that?

VALERKA

Five rubles.

*The equivalent of "Ciao!"

MASHA

What is that for?

VALERKA

Buy your freedom with it. When she yells—the whole town can hear her. Guido told me how she demanded the five rubles from you, how you lied that you lost it, and how she threatened to put you under lock and key until you confessed what you did with the money. Isn't that right?

MASHA

Our relationship is nobody's business. We'll manage. It's all in the family.

VALERKA

(Picks up aluminum mug, waves it in front of MASHA'S face, and flings it to the floor) So, you were at the movies this evening? **Shurik** invited you? She's a monster, your grandmother—not family! *(Pointing to the money)* I hate lying! A dishonest act, even for a noble cause, cannot be justified.

MASHA

Go away!

VALERKA

I'm going!

(MASHA thoughtfully turns the leaves of the book, as the light focuses on VALERKA, who comes forward to the proscenium The FOUR MIMES enter noiselessly. This time they are the robbers from Schiller's play. One of them thrusts a dagger into VALERKA'S belt. The SECOND hands him a plumed hat. The THIRD throws a cloak around his shoulders. The FOURTH gives him a sword)

VALERKA

(In the role of the robber, Moore, bombastically but not without humor) Who lured me here?! Which one of you lured me here—you fiends of hell?! Down with the joys of love! I, who have heard death's summons howl all around me, its poisonous fangs stretching to reach me from a thousand tree trunks, without retreating a single step—am *I* to tremble before a woman? NO! No woman on earth can shake my courage! . . . Blood, blood! I have need to quench my thirst with blood, and then I shall be saved!

(He attacks an imaginary enemy with his sword. The FIRST and SECOND MIMES, standing behind him, clutch their chests and slowly fall to their knees. VALERKA makes his second thrust, and the THIRD and FOURTH MIMES falter, but remain standing, leaning on each other)

(Laughs sardonically) Ha-ha-ha-ha!

(The scene fades into total darkness.)

Hey, There—Hello!   *Scene One*

"... And here are flowers..."

Two days later.

While the stage is still dark, we hear the howl of the wind and the roar of the sea. The lights come up, focusing on the MIMES and VALERKA, who clings to the rail of the Captain's bridge. They all wear Sailor's caps, covered by storm hoods. There is an atmosphere of suspense, danger, tense activity.

VALERKA

(As Commander of the torpedo-boat) Message to Base: "We are half an hour from Novorosiisk. Enemy trying to sink evacuation transport..."
(One of the MIMES begins to operate an imaginary radio-sending key, and we hear the clicking of the Morse Code through the noise of the storm)
"... The enemy destroyer we torpedoed is still afloat—Square 43-B. Are protecting transport with smoke screen."
(A tense silence. We hear the approach of attacking planes)
(Looks up. Addresses crew) Prepare to repel air attack!
(The SECOND and THIRD MIMES aim imaginary anti-aircraft guns)
Fire!
(The guns continue to be fired. The planes sweep back and forth over the torpedo-boat. There is the scream of a falling bomb. Explosion. One of the MIME-gunners drops)
Keep fighting!... Why is one gun silent?
(The THIRD MIME replaces the "fallen" gunner at the silent gun. The sound of firing continues. The roar of the planes subsides)
(Breathing heavily with relief) Message to Base: "Enemy retreating. Submarine to port..." *(To crew)* Prepare for attack! Portside rudder... *(Suddenly)* Too late! Abandon maneuver... Starboard rudder. Full speed ahead! Message to Base: "Torpedo sighted, aimed at transport. Moving to intercept torpedo."
(Clicking of Morse Code Key. Roar of wind)
All hands to port!
(The MIMES do not move)
Life jackets on! At my command, abandon ship!
(The MIMES do not move)
Hard aport! *Harder!* Cut the motors!
(At once there is total silence. VALERKA and the MIMES stand still, eyes fixed on the approaching torpedo. Excruciating last moments.

Then. . .the sound of a record playing a popular song. As always, this happens suddenly, and is very loud.

The MIMES leave the stage. the lights come up slowly, and we now see, not the warship Commander's bridge, but the peaceful deck of an ocean liner, featuring a table and two chairs and part of a spotlessly white bulkhead with a life belt hanging on it bearing the ship's name, "Taras Shevchenko." This is the flagship of the Black Sea Merchant Marine fleet, which, having more than fulfilled its financial quota, is marking the occasion by taking a shipload of vacationers on a 4-hour excursion, affording them the illusion of a luxurious sea voyage. The deck is fitted out as an open-air restaurant. VALERKA, standing near the rail, picks up a pair of binoculars from a table and examines the shoreline. He is wearing dark trousers (not his customary jeans), a white shirt with a bright kerchief tucked into the open collar, like an ascot.

The music from the ship's loudspeaker is muted and we hear the voice of the excursion leader over the public-address system)

VOICE OF EXCURSION GUIDE

If you happen to be looking at the shore, you see before your eyes the famous Livadiisky Palace. Its name, is derived from the Greek word *livadion*, which, translated into our language, means "meadow." In the year 1889 the Livadiisky became the residence of a gang of exploiters and oppressors—more precisely, the Czar and his royal family. In this palace, counting the halls and the servants' quarters, there are 120 magnificently furnished rooms. I should like to call your attention to the splendid location of the palace, constructed by the skilled hands of the common people. Now it is a place of rest and convalescence for 800 workers. . . Please take note that excursionists on this boat are forbidden to use First Class accomodations, they are not to use the music salon, the swimming pool, the bathtubs, or showers. Thank you for your kind attention.

(The loudspeaker is now silent, and the music resumes)

MASHA

(From offstage, right) Flowers! Who will buy these flowers? Gladiolas of all colors. Half a ruble apiece, five for two rubles.

(VALERKA glances quickly to the right, puts on dark glasses, and resumes examining the shore through the binoculars. MASHA enters. She is dressed in the same way as in Act I, Scene 3. She carries a wicker basket and in it, wrapped in a wet cloth, is a bunch of flowers)

MASHA (Cont.)

(She stops behind VALERKA, whom she doesn't recognize and speaks hesitantly) Flowers? Who will buy these flowers? Half a ruble a piece.
(VALERKA, without turning around, places a half-ruble on the table. MASHA takes a flower and offers it to him)

VALERKA

(Removes the glasses) Madam, I beg you not to refuse to accept this beautiful flower as a token of my delight at our unexpected meeting.

MASHA

(Embarrassed, flings the money to the deck) Idiot!
(MASHA starts off)

VALERKA

Hey, Balagayeva, stop! Any minute now they're going to be giving out free and reliable advice here. Don't miss it!

MASHA

(Hesitates, then comes back and sits down) All right, what is it?

VALERKA

Now pay close attention. What is the first commandment for the businessman? *(Triumphantily)* "Money has no smell." *(He picks up and carefully smells the half-ruble)* It doesn't smell like cologne, or like sweat—or like anything else. Do you follow me?

MASHA

(Indifferently) No. *(She has been gazing at the shore through the binoculars, and continues to do so)*

VALERKA

Then I'll explain it all, one step at a time. If you are a private entrepreneur, your business is to trade. But you don't dare offend the customer. You hide your priciples in your pocket. You exchange your goods for the money, which has no odor. If I have money to spend, I'm neither your friend nor your foe—merely a customer. Come, let me have my flower. I'm resigned to sacrificing this wonderful coin for it.

MASHA

If you're resigned, then throw it into the sea.

VALERKA

(Gets ready to do so but changes his mind.) None of your smart tricks! I'd do better to buy ice cream with it. *(He starts off, then stops)* Tell me, how can you make yourself ask fifty kopecks for one flower?

MASHA

Vacationists have lots of money—they'd even pay a ruble and a half.

VALERKA

(With a whistle) Do you mean to say that you are being philanthropic? That you're selling at a loss?
(He starts off)

MASHA

(Laughs suddenly and runs after him. He exits, she remains) And I took him for a foreigner. Thought he was a Frenchman! *(She quickly takes a hand-mirror from her pocket and tidies her hair)*

VOICE OF EXCURSION GUIDE

. . .an enchanting corner of our southern flora. Not without reason did the local people name this beach "Golden." A bit higher you now can see the famous Crimean vineyards which, thanks to the labors of our work-loving, collective farm peasantry, produce the best varieties of grapes. . .such as "Ladies' Fingers," *(Pause)* for example. . .and others. Have a little patience, and soon there will appear before your eyes the "Swallow's Nest". . .
(VALERKA enters with two small bowls of ice cream. He places one of them in front of MASHA and sits down across from her)

VALERKA

Why are you looking at me so closely?

MASHA

We haven't seen each other for a long time. . .

VALERKA

I guess not.

MASHA

Seven days.

VALERKA

As long as that? According to my chronometer, barely two days have passed. It's this strange life you lead—business enterprises, sea voyages, all kinds of boy-friends. *I* condense my time. According to the Einstein theory. You wouldn't understand that. . .

MASHA

(Continues to eat her ice cream, unimpressed by VALERKA'S worldly casualness) Your uncle has gotten into the habit of dropping in on us.

VALERKA

Wonder what he's up to?

MASHA

I didn't expect to find you here. I know you know lots of seamen and can get on any boat. But there was a big demand for tickets on this one—2000 people bought them and 500 more sneaked aboard without.

VALERKA

Well, you see, Balagayeva, I'm democratic. I don't demean myself to ask for special favors from my sea-faring friends. I'm just one of the crowd.

MASHA

Why do you put on an act with me?

VALERKA

I've decided to take up acting. Do you think I'm talented?

MASHA

You're a phoney, that's what you are!

VALERKA

You've noticed that?

MASHA

Like sand in the mouth. . . Are you here alone?

VALERKA

(Off-handedly) There's someone—she follows me around. Begs me to take her to the movies, to the beach. Now it's this excursion. A nuisance. She lives near us.

MASHA

Is it Nina?
(VALERKA shrugs his shoulders in an indeterminate answer)
She's very pretty.

VALERKA

When you take a stroll with her on the boardwalk, it's like being on parade. Everone lines up to admire her.
(MASHA again raises the binoculars to her eyes and inspects the coast.

VOICE OF EXCURSION GUIDE

(The loudspeaker is not functioning properly. The sound comes on like a thunderbolt, then subsides to more normal tones) And now, dear participants in our wonderful excursion, I shall continue to describe the lavish beauty passing past your eyes. . .

(MASHA lowers the binoculars, then puts them to her eyes again, as the description begins)

. . .You have seen many times, on posters and postcards, the scene that is now being displayed before your amazed view—"The Swallow's Nest," built on the promontory, Ai-Todor. . .

(The loudspeaker hoarsely comes to a halt. MASHA and VALERKA look up at it. It remains silent)

VALERKA

(Imitating the lush tones of the Excursion Guide). . . Built on the promontory, Ai-Tudor, in 1912, by the engineer, Sherwood, is this unique and incomparable structure, "The Swallow's Nest." It is the pride of our inimitable, marvellous and amazing region! It suffered in the earthquake of 1927, however. As you can see, part of the cliff was shattered, reducing our pride and joy to a battered condition. . . Thank you for your kind attention. Amen!

MASHA

Some people travel a long way to come here to see this beautiful sight. But it's beneath you, I suppose, to appreciate it.

VALERKA

(Loading the words with oblique meaning) Some people don't value what they have. When they lose it. . .they weep. . .

MASHA

Is that from a poem?

VALERKA

Yes, a poem.

MASHA

(The words have impressed her) I must write that down.

VALERKA

Write this also: "Love me as I love you, then you and I will be inseparable."

MASHA

(Repeating the words to herself) Yes, I'll write it down.

VALERKA

Oh God, why did you—of all girls—redheads, blondes, brunettes, and many other colors. . .? *(Silence)*

MASHA

(Not lowering the binoculars) Go on. . .

VALERKA

(Shrugging his shoulders in puzzlement) I await God's reprieve like a nightingale a summer's eve. . . You dinosaur!

MASHA

(Still with binoculars) My! Valerka, how many rooms do you think there are in this "Swallow's Nest?"

VALERKA

Not enough. You ought to acquire the Livadiisky Palace. Think of what a fortune you could make filling it with summer boarders!

MASHA

An interesting thought.

VALERKA

Listen do you ever let your imagination soar? Let's say, you look at a tree and think, not about how many cubic meters of firewood it would make but, perhaps, that a poet had once gazed at this tree, or that when we are no longer in the world the tree will nightly speak to the stars, its branches stirring. . .

MASHA

Inanimate objects don't talk. What would they talk about?

VALERKA

About eternity, you stupid head!

MASHA

Don't yell, people will hear you! *(Looks around)* Look, Valerka, there's your Nina.

VALERKA

(Annoyed at the interruption of his flight of fancy) The hell with her! Can you imagine what, in the face of eternity, they would say about you?. . .

MASHA

If you are friends, it's nasty of you to send her to hell.

VALERKA

(Exasperated) Whom?

MASHA

Your Nina. She's coming over.

VALERKA

(Quickly bending down low to the deck, turning his head away) I'm sick and tired of her. I don't want her to see me. Let her go by.

MASHA

(Smiling scornfully) Don't panic. She turned in the other direction. So, let's go on—what were you saying about eternity?

VALERKA

Let's change the subject. All this is over your head.

MASHA

How do you know that? Maybe I treasure your every word and store it in a special place in my brain.

VALERKA

When I heard you peddling your wares like a fishwife—do you know how I felt? Ashamed! I felt like running from you.

MASHA

Go on, run. You are a holy-of-holies. . . You were ashamed of me, you say? Didn't you know that I sell at the market-place?

VALERKA

I thought you sold cherries, pickles, or things like that—but not flowers!

MASHA

What's wrong with flowers? They're a respectable product. Better than to sell pickles and soak your hands in pickle brine. And the flower buyer—he is a special kind of customer. He's in a happy mood.

VALERKA

Happy mood! Then why do you overcharge him—because of his happy mood? Asking half a ruble for a single flower! Maybe he earns only three rubles a day!

MASHA

I have other flowers for that kind. They buy violets.

VALERKA

There it is—your barbarian psychology. In the marketplace
there are only two kinds of people for you—if they have money,
they count—if not, forget them!

MASHA

But think how my grandmother breaks her back growing these
flowers. Would you give them away free? Not everyone can fly into
space. Not everyone can be a great scientist. Someone has to
sell flowers. Don't you thinks so?

VALERKA

No. Your grandmother doesn't simply sell flowers—she
gets rich on them. She's greedy! And you, you little fool, are
letting her harness you to a pushcart.

MASHA

There's no law against selling flowers.

VALERKA

Beware, you'll overdo this sort of thing. Instead of friends,
you'll have only customers and boarders, like Taisya.

MASHA

Was it your father who taught you all this?

VALERKA

My father, among others. You're a fool—it's no use talking to you!

MASHA

Talk to me anyhow.

VALERKA

Why are you looking away?

MASHA

(*Pushes her flower basket under the table with her foot*) Do you
see that seaman with a band on his sleeve? He's got his eye
on me. He's been following me.

VALERKA

What for?

MASHA

He wanted to take the flowers away.

VALERKA

You said the law was on your side.

MASHA

In the market—but not on board ship.

VALERKA

Don't hide your face! It makes you look like a sneak! Does it pay to lose your self-respect for the sake of an extra ten rubles? You disgust me, Masha! You disgust me—do you hear?

MASHA

I hear, I hear. Don't yell.

VALERKA

He's gone. Went down the ladder. You win. Go on and do business "Only half a ruble apiece. Five for two."

MASHA

(Lifts the basket, starts to walk away, then stops) And I hoped that you and I would become friends.

VALERKA

So you hoped. . . Wait—how many do you have left? Are they all gladiolas?

MASHA

About twenty. What is it to you?

VALERKA

(He takes money out of his pocket) Here. It happens to be just the right amount. Ten rubles. My uncle has become generous. Here, I'm buying them all.

MASHA

Don't act the big capitalist.

VALERKA

(Grabs the basket from MASHA, pushes the money into her hand) Money for your merchandise.

MASHA

(After a pause) Show-off!
(VALERKA doesn't answer. He turns around and walks away. toward backdrop. He stops, turns, and flings the basket at MASHA. It rolls to her feet)

VOICE OF EXCURSION GUIDE

Splendid and matchless is Nature in our marvellous region. Just
as the Armenians are proud of their Mt. Ararat, we take pride in
our Mt. Ai-Petri, which you have the opportunity to admire at this
very moment in our captivating sea excursion. Notice how proud
and unreachable is that granite wall, almost covered with our
matchless flora! Many are those who scale the summit of Ai-Petri
to enjoy the rising of our Crimean sun and our inimitable
sea panorama—

*(The Loudspeaker hisses, attempts two or three times to emit
the rhapsodic speech of the Excursion Guide, but utters only
fragments of his words)*

. . .the. . .elaborated poet, Al. . .ushkin said. . .bewitch me. . .
oh. . .utiful elements!. . .

*(Silence. Then to lessen the embarrassment caused by the
malfunctioning Loudspeaker, a phonograph begins playing a
silly popular song: "In our backyard." MASHA picks up the basket
and spreads the flowers on the table. She examines each one to
see if they have been damaged. Then she stands there, lost in
unhappy thought, and, looking out to the sea, she throws the
flowers into the water, one at a time.
The deck of the excursion ship is darkened as the lights go down)*

". . .And I almost believed in your selflessness. . ."

The following day.

The DOROKHOV'S yard. In the foreground, an easel and a stool, with a box of paints and a brush. It is a hot day. We see VALERKA peering through a crack in the fence. Soon MASHA'S head appears above the fence. He does not see her. She looks at him for a while without smiling, then throws a cypress cone at him and disappears. VALERKA is startled. He looks around and, seeing no one, resumes looking through the crack into Taisya's yard.

MASHA

(Crawls through the fence, studies what is painted on the canvas—not looking at VALERKA) Hello!

VALERKA

(Abruptly stops looking through the crack, straightens up, then, without turning, draws a line across the fence, steps away from it. After a moment of thought, he draws another line, perpendicular to the first one, admires his handiwork, and slowly turns his head toward MASHA) Did you rise from the bowels of the earth?

MASHA

Yes. Do you paint?

VALERKA

I create! I'm painting an abstract study of what goes on on the seamy side of this fence.

MASHA

(Nodding toward the easel) Did you paint this, too?

VALERKA

Oh, that? It's a mere jest of genius, a sketch. *(He goes over to the easel)* War in the Crimea—everything is up in smoke.

MASHA

(Pointing) And what is this?—here?

VALERKA

Not "what" but "who." A boy. In contemporary art what is most important—is to avoid photographic likeness.

MASHA

Do you think you're talented?

VALERKA

Who knows? A fool was once asked: Can you play the violin?
He answered: I don't know, I never tried. It's the same with me.

MASHA

(Continuing to examine the "painting") And who is this—the
boy's grandfather?

VALERKA

What makes you think it's an old man?

MASHA

He's got a beard.

VALERKA

(Thoughtfully) Have it your way—only it happens to be a tree,
and not anybody's grandfather. You're looking at an autumn landscape.

MASHA

(After a pause) Go on with your creating. I didn't come to see
you anyway. I came to see Nikolai. Your uncle sent me to tell him
to come and help carry some fruit to the post office—he's shipping
it home. *(She looks penetratingly at VALERKA, seems to be
about to say something, but controls herself)* Is Nikolai home?

VALERKA

Take a look. Lately they've all been disappearing first thing in
the morning. I wake up—there's no one around. I'm abandoned.
They return after dark and fall into bed. If it weren't against
the law, they'd probably just live on the beach.

MASHA

What is there for them to do here? Sit around and chew the
rag with your uncle?

VALERKA

I suppose it's better to get sunstroke. Or to drown.

MASHA

Where did you get the paints?

VALERKA

Vera gave me her easel and paints and these canvases. She left
suddenly, an hour ago, and said I should keep her things so I
wouldn't forget her.

MASHA

(As if stating a simple fact) You know, you really are a rat!
I mean, a real rat!

VALERKA

What's the matter, Balagayeva? What's eating you?

MASHA

I swore I wouldn't get mixed up in this! That I'd pretend I didn't
know anything about it, that it's none of my business. But since
hypocrisy has become your second nature. . .I almost believed in
your selflessness. Because a person would like to believe that
he's surrounded by real people, not crummy ones. You keep carrying
on about my grandmother. Her pension is only 60 rubles a month.
She doesn't pretend to be a holy-of-holies. You're right, she
has nothing but money on her mind. But tell me, how much
does your mother earn?

VALERKA

(Not understanding what she's driving at) I don't get it.
What *is* eating you?

MASHA

Don't try to evade my question. A navigator on an ocean liner
must bring home plenty of pay. And your father's war pension
is a lot bigger than what my grandmother gets.

VALERKA

I wouldn't know. We don't talk about money in my family.

MASHA

Why talk about it when you have it? *(Mimicking him)*
"Vera left suddenly." At least if you showed some
shame when you lie. But no—you have developed your
hypocrisy to a fine art. You lie without blinking an eye.
You pretend not to know why Vera packed in such a great
hurry, and took off in five minutes flat.

VALERKA

What crazy nonsense you're talking, Masha. What's come
over you, anyway?!

MASHA

Go on pretending, acting simple-minded. Your uncle at least
lacks your pretenses. Yesterday evening he blurted it all out.
He even boasted about it to my grandmother. He says his
cousin ought to be grateful to him, that a man is in charge now
who's put some sense into her son's head—yours!. . . No, my
grandmother doesn't have enough imagination to charge ten kopecks
for a free local call made on her telephone. But you planned
a dirty scheme like that with your uncle.

VALERKA

What ten kopecks?! What are you raving about?!

MASHA

Are you trying to tell me you weren't the one who nailed a box beside the telephone for the purpose?

VALERKA

(With growing bewilderment) My father nailed it there—for bills, receipts, papers.

MASHA

It *was* for papers. But now—if your "friends" use the phone they have to put in a coin. "We don't intend to pay for your conversations," your uncle tells them, "and if you've unburdened your heart, talked a long time—put in two coins."

VALERKA

(Beside himself, roars) WHOSE HEART?! WHOSE COINS?!

MASHA

Guido's. Vera's. Anyway, you know better than I do *whose!* It wasn't for *me* that your uncle deposited ten rubles in the savings bank!

VALERKA

(Now with sad suspicion) You say that Vera packed and left— for *what* reason?

MASHA

What an actor you are! *(Mimicking him)* "It's friends, not boarders, who live in my house!". . . You know as well as I do that she left because you and your uncle raised the rent for her room—to three rubles a day. He said there was space in that room for *three* cots. But where was she, a student, to get that kind of money?

VALERKA

(Holding his head) Masha! Stop! *(After a pause)* Do you mean that my uncle has been collecting rent money from Guido, from Nikolai, from Vera?

MASHA

(Now she is bewildered) For a whole week now. A ruble a day. And he's also insisting that they pay up for the past use of the rooms.

VALERKA

What a lowdown rat! The damned extortionist! The Kulak!

MASHA

Did you really not know about all this?

VALERKA

What do you take me for, you bird-brain! *(Paces widly up and down in a state of outrage)* That's all we need! How low can we sink?! And I kept beating my brains out thinking, why have they been avoiding me—giving me the cold shoulder?. . . He's a rotten swindler!

MASHA

He says he doesn't keep the money for himself, that he deposits it in the bank, in your name.

VALERKA

That doesn't exactly make me feel any better. *(Shouts)* Just think! Guido barely manages on his pension, but won't charge for his performance!. . . Enough of this!

MASHA

(Upset) Oh, Valerka! I'm not even glad that I told you all this.

VALERKA

Would you be glad if I belonged to the same gang as you and your Taisya? If I did, I'd pray for a storm, throw myself into the sea, and swim till a wave knocked me against a rocky cliff. *(He runs into the house and comes back almost at once with a large suitcase. He throws it onto the table and runs back into the house)*

MASHA

What are you up to now?

VALERKA

(Comes out carrying an armful of his uncle's underwear and bedding) Put all that into the suitcase.

MASHA

Are you out of your mind? Chasing your own uncle out of the house! A relative!

VALERKA

(He is now back with a second batch of things) Relative? What makes him a relative? "Relative" means being close—in thought, in behavior. Right?

MASHA

But he's your mother's cousin.

VALERKA

So what?! Am I accountable because his cousin gave birth to me? If he claims to be my kin let him first behave so that I won't be ashamed of being related to him! Guido is my kin! Nikolai! Copernicus, who was burned at the stake—*he* is my kin! But that one is no relative of mine! He's a thief!

(VALERKA runs back into the house. MASHA, dumbfounded, clasps her hands in amazement, then starts to pack the suitcase. VALERKA brings out more of his uncle's things)

Hurry up! Why are you standing there? Get on with the packing!

(He sits at the table, takes a pencil and paper from his pocket, and starts writing a note. MASHA hesitates, then resumes packing. VALERKA continues to write)

He's shrewd. He knows Mother is on a voyage and Father is lying sick in the hospital. Neither one of them would have allowed him even to step into our house. They despise money-grubbers like him!

(The telephone rings in the house)

MASHA

The telephone.

VALERKA

Answer it.

MASHA

(Goes, then calls from offstage) It's the hospital. For you.

VALERKA

(Continuing to write) It's on a long cord—bring it out here. *(Pause. Then, realizing what MASHA has said, he is frightened)* The *hospital?!* (MASHA brings out the phone and hands it to him) Yes?. . . Yes, Doctor, it's me. *(Dazed)* When?. . . In a car? What car? *(He drops the receiver, and after a brief pause turns to MASHA)* I must hurry! *(Dashes off)*

".. . Oh, stars! Listen to me, stars!. . ."

A dead-end street overlooking the sea. It ends in a steep curved incline, covered with gravel. There is a boulder at the top right forming a kind of bench. Near it, covered with dust, stands a dwarf cypress. The incline ends abruptly, on the left side, facing the sea, and the ground falls away sharply. Though the vacationists never come here, a railing fences off the steep declivity.

It is six o'clock in the evening.

VALERKA stands with his back to the audience, elbows resting on the railing. In this scene, the actor who plays VALERKA must test the nuances of his speech and gestures with a fine tuning fork, so that even his kidding evokes a feeling of sadness in the audience, but never any laughter)

MASHA

(Offstage) Valerka!. . .

(VALERKA does not move or respond)

Valerka!. . .

(MASHA appears from left, breathing hard from the climb. She sits on the rock and looks around)

What a hill!. . . Lenka told me that you went this way, or I would never have found you. . . How strangely the world is shaped: Where I live, there's not even the lowest hillock—and here, there's a hill on top of a hill. If I were God, I'd allot a mountain for every plain. That would be only fair, and there would be something to rest your eyes on. *(Pause)* What got into you? No one had left the table yet, but you jumped up and ran off. Where I come from it is considered almost a sin to leave the table before the guests.

(VALERKA doesn't turn around. He mumbles something)

Oh, Valerka, I, too, have my troubles. Nothing compared to yours of course. It's really more a disappointment than trouble. It happened two days ago, but I wasn't going to even mention it to you then. My telepathist, it turns out, is a robber. When you threw your uncle out, he moved in with us. You know that small bag he always kept with him—well, he locked it up in the closet of his room, and put the key under his pillow. When he woke up in the morning the bag was gone, and so was the telepathist. Your uncle said he had two thousand rubles in it. . . That's probably a lie—how would he come by two thousand rubles? And my grandmother. . . Well, I'll tell you, I've come to a decision. . . Why don't you listen when I talk to you?

(VALERKA continues to mumble)

All right, have it your way. I'll tell you the rest another time.

MASHA (Cont.)

(Pause) Our house looks so tiny from here!. . . And the cemetery. . .
(With careful detail) It's a fine cemetery. Serene. And it is so well
tended. Just the way it should be, really. . . Oh, Valerka, I never
before saw such a beautiful funeral as Gagarin's in Moscow. I saw it
on television. With flowers! So many people! and when the sailors
fired their salute over his grave, everything inside me trembled with
grief—and exaltation. . . And the funeral repast was fine, too. He
had well-to-do friends, but they didn't act greedy at the tables. He had
as many friends as your father. . . *(She is silent for a moment, glances
at VALERKA)* You just stand there. Don't pay attention to a word
I'm saying. I'm just talking to make a noise, you know. *(She sighs)*
Ah! The sea! What an element of nature! You look at the sea and
feel as though there is nothing else in the world. . .

VALERKA

(Without turning around, suddenly) He streaked into the firmament
and gleamed like a silver ribbon in the sun. *(He stands erect, waivers,
and quickly grabs the railing)*

MASHA

Do you feel sick?

VALERKA

"He didn't die, he broke into a laugh!". . . "Strange birds!. . ."
*(VALERKA raises an arm to gesture, wavers again, and almost
falls. MASHA goes over to him and holds him steady)*

MASHA

Valerka, are you drunk?

VALERKA

(Proudly) It's alcoholics who get drunk. I am a teenager, hardly
more than a boy. Health authorities forbid me to get drunk. . .
Hello, Masha!

MASHA

We've already met today.

VALERKA

I greet you in Eternity. Like the Stars, like the Moon! Don't
hold me up. A sense of self-worth obliges a man to stand on his
own two feet, not to crawl on all fours.

MASHA

My God! What's wrong with you?

VALERKA

Three cheers for our glorious naval power! Hurrah!

MASHA

But you only drank tiny glasses of wine.

VALERKA

So you were watching me! I refuse to shake hands with spies and informers! Don't hold me up!

MASHA

The last resort—drowning your troubles in wine!

VALERKA

You're a real philosophizer. You're loaded with copybook truths. . . I'll explain: After the funeral, when they raised their glasses to drink to our naval might, I picked up a tumblerful by mistake. Then they stood up and said, "Bottoms up!" So I drank up—emptied the tumbler.

MASHA

So you drank too much. They why do you hang around in this condition? Better go to your little shed and sleep it off.

VALERKA

A certain writer said: "We live among people—we die alone." Unlike you, Masha, I'm a well-read person. . . As soon as I saw that the others were going to go on with the drinking, I made myself scarce. *(Shaking his head)* Disgusting! Drunks—those big heroes! I couldn't take it.

MASHA

(Leads him to the rock seat) Sit here awhile, Valerka. Sit quietly and it will pass.

VALERKA

It will *not* pass! I've been standing here for twenty long minutes. What's so dreadful is that I can't lose consciousness. It urges me to use my will power and conquer the dizziness. But the will is powerless. The human will can't win over a glass of liquid! Masha, I'm going to jump off this cliff! *(He tries to stand up)*

MASHA

(Holding him down) Sit still. Let me rub your temples. *(Rubs his temples)* It'll make you feel better.

VALERKA

Masha, ask me the question.

MASHA

Which one?

VALERKA

This one: Why do good people die while swine like my uncle live
on? And why doesn't anyone have the imagination to answer
this question except with corny platitudes?

MASHA

(After a pause) Valerka, don't mind me—go ahead and have a good cry.

VALERKA

(Shouts) "Strange birds. . ." What do they understand?. . . *(In a normal
voice)* What rot were you talking before? "People! Flowers! Rich
friends, lavish funeral repast. . ." *(After a silence, he continues)*
One day last spring I came home from school and saw him
repairing a window frame. Until then he had not been out of his
sickbed since autumn. . . *(He wants to go on, but can't. Tears
choke him. He waves it off and is silent)*

MASHA

Go on, talk about it, Valerka—talk!

VALERKA

(Regains control) A week ago I said to him, at the hospital, "Dad—"
He likes it when I call him Dad. "Let me stay here with you. We'll
ask them to put up a cot for me on the balcony—that way it will
be more cheerful for both of us." And he smiles and says: "So you're
afraid I'll sneak off and die when you're not around. Don't worry.
Until I see your mother, I'll hang on for dear life. I'll mount an all out
defense and will not surrender. I'll hold out till the last bullet. . .
(Bitterly) And you! . . .you carry on like that old woman did at
his funeral. She kept counting the wreaths, counting the little
pillows on which his war medals were carried in the procession.
She kept cackling, "This town has never before seen such a funeral!"
She was bursting with pride, as though they were honoring *her*
as she was about to be buried. . . Death—it is an abyss, leading
nowhere! But all our foolish vainglory feeds even on it.

MASHA

Goliaph Petrovich—your uncle—said that they shouldn't have
hurried with the funeral—they should have waited until your
mother got back.

VALERKA

(*Rages*) Don't you dare mention that filthy name in my presence!
(*In a normal voice*) She's on the Atlantic. Two thousand miles from
land. . . I noticed on some people's faces in the cemetery that they
were thinking nasty thoughts. They looked relieved, saying to themselves:
"How lucky that it isn't me. . ." And I, Masha, I swear I'd die for
any of them if it would bring them immortality! Without fear!
Do you understand what I'm trying to say? I'd die for them—that's all.

MASHA

You're saying that out of conceit. You think you're stronger
than anyone else—that others don't have the strength, but you
can take on anything.

VALERKA

Again you're talking nonsense.

MASHA

All right, maybe not out of conceit. Maybe out of sympathy—kindness.

VALERKA

(*Rising*) I'm not kind, Balagayeva. Would you like to know
what I am? An egotist!

MASHA

Sit down, sit down! What kind of an egotist are you when
your house is full of people living in it free of charge?

VALERKA

So what? What *is* an egotist? What makes a person one?—
tell me! It's that he does not neglect his own satisfaction.
Some people experience the greatest satisfaction from
getting the biggest piece of the pie, others from putting a
fence around their place so that no one can set foot on their
ground. For me it is seeing the people around me feeling good.
But I'm not against this kind of selfish motive. Do you
understand me?

MASHA

No.

VALERKA

How could you? My father had a favorite saying: "Enough is
enough.". . . I don't think I'm dizzy any more.

MASHA

Good! Then let's go home.

VALERKA

(Stands up, but feels dizzy and sits down again at once) I think
I'll sit a while longer.

MASHA

Yes, rest. You're tired from all the talking. Keep still. Open
your eyes wider. Look harder.

VALERKA

At what?

MASHA

Oh, at whatever will please you.
*(Pause. There is the sound of the trumpet. The FOUR MIMES appear.
They wear astrologer's headwear, and huge glasses with cardboard
frames. VALERKA gets up. The four link hands and with serious faces,
with frozen smiles, move in a circle around him. Soft music—
strings and flute)*

VALERKA

(He's completely sober, and addresses the heavens) Listen to me,
Stars! There are myriads of you—more of you than there are atoms
on all of our earth. And you, Milky Way! You are like a motionless
cloud. But *I* know—you are like the sand in an hourglass. You
pour from one end of the universe to the other. And every grain
of your sand is immortal compared to me, because it is a star. I am
only a man. . . Come nearer! Nearer! I want to reach you. . .
Thank you, Stars! *(He takes an imaginary star from the sky and
puts in his pocket.)* I thank you! I know that a single star brings
life to only one person. *(Hides another star in his pocket—and
another—and another.)* Thank you! Thank you! So many people
on my earth will be happy because of your priceless gift! They
will forever marvel at your kindness as a gift to man. . . Oh, you
countless, blindingly beautiful, magnificent Stars! *(He shakes an
imaginary tree)* Oh, how many billions of stars have covered
the earth! With magic radiance you have filled this world!
*(He covers his face with his hands. The music stops.
The MIMES leave.)*

MASHA

(To VALERKA, who is again sitting near her) Valerka, what are
you looking at? At the cloud? That one?

VALERKA

(Not at once) Your eyes. They *are* beautiful. However,
Mashka, I may be lying. . .

MASHA

Not you, Valerka. I've never met a more honest person.

VALERKA

I lie. Remember what I said about Nina, on board that ship?

MASHA

I know.

VALERKA

What do you know—bird-brain?

MASHA

That you were kidding. I know it because my window faces hers. I knew that the two of you weren't even acquainted. She has real boyfriends—college students.

VALERKA

Exactly. Only I wasn't kidding—I was lying. I played up to my false pride—it betrayed me. And I lied another time. When my father's friends toasted our Navy, I did drink with the others from a small wine glass. But the rest I guzzled down later—I went to the kitchen and gulped down a whole tumblerful. Just for spite! I thought to myself, to hell with it. If I'm going to the dogs, I might as well go all the way.

MASHA

(After a silence, and without raising her head) You are shameless and a big fraud.

VALERKA

Watch out—you are kicking a man when he's down.

MASHA

(Rises with difficulty, stunned with disappointment) My God, what a terrible creature you are! You didn't even respect the memory of your dead father. On such a day!. . .to get stinking drunk! And here I was, soothing you in your grief, coddling you like a nurse—talking to you like a stricken child. Life gave you its first blow—testing whether you'd stand up to it, on your feet. And you—you crumbled! You fell flat on your face." "You're kicking a man when he's down. . ." Ha! You can stumble home by yourself. *(She starts to go)*

VALERKA

(Calling after her) Mash-ka!

MASHA

(Stops) What?

VALERKA

I can't. I can't make it down that hill and across the intersection.
I need help!

MASHA

(Mockingly) In your own home town! "These paths I could follow
blindfolded. I'll jump from cliff to cliff like a mountain goat!"
—those were your own words, you soused mountain goat. . .

VALERKA

Now you are showing your true feelings. Never mind your pretenses.
You bother about me only because of my father's death. About *me*—you
couldn't care less. So, Balagayeva, what makes you so different
from the rest of the skunks on this earth?

MASHA

(She comes close to him) Valerka! Some people become weaklings
from grief. Others become evil. Watch out—let meanness get hold of you,
and it's like diving into a deep well. It's not easy to get back up.

VALERKA

(Rises with difficulty) And who are you to preach to me?

MASHA

A human being.

VALERKA

And what's so human about you? Your legs? Your eyes? Monkeys
have those, too—my Consoler! Oh, get lost, why don't you?

MASHA

(Trying to control herself) Valerka—don't! It's your worst
self, your lowest self, that speaks that way. Even in grief, a
man mustn't lose his dignity.

VALERKA

There you go again with your lectures. How would you like a fast
roll down this hill? *(He raises his fist threateningly)* I'll
give you a good start with this!

MASHA

I must warn you that I forget myself when someone shakes his fist at me.

VALERKA

(Ignoring her threat) I spit on your feelings! Why do you hang
on to me? Pest! I keep running from you—an ass would get the

VALERKA (Cont.)

message—but you hang on, as if on a leash, following me all
over and braying elementary truths.
(MASHA slaps him. He feels his cheek, amazed)
Just look at her—slapping away just like in the movies.
(He looks for a more insulting word) You—tramp! That's
what you are!
(MASHA slaps him again, first on one side of the face, then the other)

MASHA

There's more where that came from—you'd better say your prayers!
*(MASHA gives him a sharp kick, and bears down on him with fists
flying. VALERKA falls beneath her blows. She stands over him
for a while, then sits down on the rock and, covering her face, weeps)*

VALERKA

*(Gets to his feet slowly, feels his cheek-bone, then sits down beside
MASHA)* Something nasty gets hold of me. . . Forgive me!
(MASHA nods silently) You're right—it lowers me—way down to
the ground. I play the superman. . .I feel rocky, not from the
liquor but because of my misfortune. . . My legs don't feel like my own.

MASHA

(Wiping her eyes) It'll pass, Valerka. Not all at once, but it
will. Time will heal the hurt.

VALERKA

There you go again with your maxims. *(Almost tenderly)* My
little fool.

MASHA

Let's go, Valerka. Hold on to my shoulder. It's steep.

VALERKA

I can make it—without any help.

MASHA

Of course you can. But it would help *me*—calm me down.
(She places his hand on her shoulder, leads him down)

VALERKA

(Sadly) "Strange birds. . ." *(Stops)* His forehead was as cold as ice.
Strange! A heat-wave outside, and he—a piece of ice.

(They exit)

". . .Hey, there—hello!"

The time is early morning, a few days later.

We see the DOROKHOVS' yard from a different angle than in ACT 1, Scene One. The fence is featured.

When the curtain rises, the lights are focuseed on the fence and the area immediately around it, but the rest of the stage remains dark.

We hear MASHA'S voice, and other noises, coming from Taisya's yard, on the other side of the fence.

MASHA

(Offstage) At the Dorokhovs' they could leave gold around on the table and no one would take it. But you—you surround yourself with tall fences, put locks on everything in sight—yet thieves come running!
(She jumps through the opening in the fence, and shouts back, from this side)

It's too bad they didn't steal you, as well as the pigs!
(Some time passes, while the noise subsides, then she sits down. There is the sound of music. MASHA gets up, goes to the fence, and drags a suitcase through the opening. She carries it toward the house, and calls up into the wings: "Valerka! Valerka!" No answer. She waits, then calls again, louder: "VA-LER-KA!" Still no answer. She opens the suitcase, takes out a kerchief, spreads it out and is about to lie down and sleep when she notices a note on the table. She picks it up and reads. The music stops)

"Semyon Semyonovich *(Guido)*: The "Kerch" is in port. They are waiting for me. The Captain said he would cast off at 6 a.m. If Masha asks, tell her I'll be back on Saturday. The buttermilk is in the cellar. See you soon. Valerka."

(MASHA jumps up, runs to one side of the stage, and calls again down to the pier: "VALERKA! VALERKA!" Then she runs to the other side and calls again. She gets no answer. She picks up the suitcase and begins to put the kerchief back—then drops it and runs off. Music accompanies her movements)

(The lights now come up on the right side of the stage, and we see the pier jutting out at a distance from the yard. MASHA runs onto the pier)

Valerka!

(We now see VALERKA at the end of the pier. They approach each other at a run)

VALERKA

Entrez! What got you up with the roosters?

MASHA

I looked in your litle barn—and you were gone. In the
shed—gone. Your cot on the balcony was still made up.
I found your note.

VALERKA

I wish you lots of business, Maria Balagayeva. May you have little
spoilage! Three cheers for gladiolas at a half-ruble apiece,
five for two. I'll be back on Saturday.

MASHA

Great! But I won't be here Saturday.

VALERKA

Okay, then come on Sunday.

MASHA

I won't be here Sunday, either.

VALERKA

Where *will* you be—are you flying off to Mars?

MASHA

No. I'm hurrying to catch a bus. It's leaving in three hours.

VALERKA

How come? You said you'd be staying the whole summer.

MASHA

I told you—you weren't listening. I had a fight with my grandmother.

VALERKA

So?

MASHA

The telepathist turned out to be a thief—remember? He
stole your uncle's money. The old woman started to scream
at me, saying I was the one who brought him into her house.
So I had it out with her.

(*A ship's whistle. VALERKA is about to run off, but he stops*)

VALERKA

Masha, stay here and live on our balcony. Tell Nikolai to take
you to the restaurant for your meals.

MASHA

No. I'll leave. I've already bought my ticket.

VALERKA

Does that mean you'll never come again?

MASHA

I'll come.

VALERKA

She won't forgive you.

MASHA

If she doesn't, then maybe I'll come and live at your place.

VALERKA

Masha, leave me your address.

MASHA

I left it—it's on your cot.

VALERKA

Masha, remember?—you said a person might take you for a little fool, I mean—I did take you for one then. But later I thought about it more carefully, and I began to see what you're all about. Do you get me?

MASHA

Yes, I do.

VALERKA

But—how do you feel about me?

MASHA

About you? This way: my first thought when I wake up in the morning is about you. When I give change to my customers, or do household chores, it's the same thing—either I remember something you've said, or what I've said to you.

VALERKA

Hey, there—hello!

MASHA

Hey, there—hello!

VALERKA

And may the sun rise each morning. . .

MASHA

And may we always be honest with ourselves, and everyone else. . .

VALERKA

And may I be like my father—have faith like him, hate evil like him.

MASHA

And, most important, don't bow your head.

VALERKA

Right! Small people, like my uncle, walk around with their heads down. The sun melts the snow—and they grumble: "Mud." What's important is that it means spring is near. . .

MASHA

Yes. May everyone know happiness. . .

VALERKA

Whoever makes people happy is important.

MASHA

(To VALERKA)
Hey, there—hello!

VALERKA

(To MASHA)
Hey, there—hello!

(Music. VALERKA and MASHA, holding hands, bow to the audience.)

THE YOUNG GRADUATES

A Play in Three Acts and Five Scenes
by Victor Rozov

CHARACTERS:

Pyotr Ivanovich Averin, Doctor of Biological Sciences, 50 years old

Anastasia Efremovna, his wife, 48

Arkady, their son, an actor, 28

Masha, Arkady's girl friend, 24

Andrei, their son, 17

Aleksei, a cousin of Andrei and Arkady, 18

Galya Davidova ⎫ Andrei's classmates who just graduated from a
Vadim Rozvalov ⎭ Moscow 10-year school.

Katya Sorokina ⎫ Aleksei's friends who just graduated from a
Afanasy Kabanov ⎭ provincial 10-year school.

Pronunication of names:

PYOtr IVAnovich

AnasTAsia EfREmovna

ArKAdy

MAsha

AndREI

AlekSEI

GALya

VaDIM

KATya

AfaNAsy

The *a* as in M*a*m*a*; the *e* as in p*e*t the *ei* as in r*ay*; the *i* as in b*ea*m; the *ya* as in *ya*cht; the *y* as in b*ea*m.

Originally produced at the Central Children's Theatre in Moscow, under the title, V dobryi chas (Good Luck!).

Aleksei, Andrei and Galya in the Moscow Central Children's Theatre production.

The living-dining room in the home of the AVERINS. It is an apartment in a new high-rise building in Moscow. The furniture is of good quality, expensive and mostly new, but there are also an antique or two, for instance a tall grandfather clock, in a corner to the left. To the right, a grand piano. The apartment is new-looking and spacious. It has a balcony. There are doors leading to the other rooms. The outside entrance is at the end of a narrow hall leading from the living-dining room.

It is mid-summer, the time when college-entrance examinations are given.

ANDREI darts in from an adjoining room—the room he shares with his older brother ARKADY. He is pursued by ARKADY, shoeless and in his undershirt, carrying an open book. ANDREI is holding a necktie in his hand.

ARKADY

Put it back, do you hear?!

ANDREI

Don't shout. Father is working. Sh-h-h!

ARKADY

I said—put it back!

ANDREI

Do you think I'll eat it up, or what?

ARKADY

Give it to me!

ANDREI

It's a gift from Masha, isn't it?

ARKADY

None of your business.

ANDREI

It *is* from Masha, that's why it's so precious. Here, take it!
He tosses ARKADY'S tie up to the chandelier, where it remains hanging.

ARKADY

Reaching for the tie.
That's all you can think of—dressing up and running off to parties. Wait and see, you'll flunk your exams and come to a dead end—with no future.

ANDREI

And I suppose *you* have a future. . . You call yourself an actor!
You only appear in crowd scenes. It's embarrassing to see you
on the stage!

ARKADY goes back to their room. ANDREI shouts after him.

It's a disgrace—you're a disgrace to the family!

*He paces the room, goes to the piano and standing, plays Chopsticks
with one finger. He stops abruptly, closes the piano-lid. He
resumes his restless pacing. The doorbell rings. He runs to
answer it. He returns to the room with MASHA.*

MASHA

(Referring to ARKADY) Is he busy?

ANDREI

(Scathingly) Doing what?! He's sprawled on his bed reading the
biography of some theatrical celebrity.

He starts toward their room.

MASHA

Don't tell him it's me.

ANDREI

(Shouting) Hey, Actor! You have a visitor.

ARKADY

(From offstage) Who is it?

ANDREI

Come and see. *(To MASHA)* He'll be a while getting ready to
make his entrance. He lies around in his undershirt all the time.

MASHA

Why do you needle him?

ANDREI

He asks for it. It's not in my nature to put up with failures.
They're always bellyaching, as if the world is against them.

MASHA

Are you disappointed in him?

ANDREI

After all, he's my brother. . . I care. . . How can anyone have so
little self-respect? He sticks with that theatre. . . And. . .where
will it get him?

MASHA

And you?—how are you spending your time?

ANDREI

As usual—being bored. Have you noticed, Masha, how deadly it is around here?

MASHA

No, I hadn't noticed.

ANDREI

Of course the place is clean, neat and comfortable. . . Mother keeps trying. *(He goes to the table and picks up a large ugly sea-shell ash tray and turns it disparagingly in his hand)* Look what a monstrosity she's bought! Who needs it? No one smokes in this family. She says—it's for guests. And look at that antique clock! It's too bad you didn't come a few minutes earlier—you would have heard it bang out eight o'clock. It makes me jump at night every time it strikes. When I was a child we stayed with relatives in Siberia. I remember nothing so well as the log walls and the ordinary clock with its soft ticking. Somehow it was comforting to listen to that tick. . . And here?. . . *(He waves his hand in disgust)* There are times when I feel like going from room to room and planting a little dust in every corner and hanging a few spiderwebs. . . I can't stand this place. . . In school at least there is always something going on. I wish the kids would show up. They're late. . .

MASHA

What college did you decide on?

ANDREI

Mother is making me apply to the Bauman Technological Institute. Says it is "respectable." And what makes her think they'd accept me? So—I'll blow it. Guess they'll let me in at some other college.

MASHA

But what school do you prefer?

ANDREI

None.

MASHA

None? Don't you have any ambition—any favorite profession?

ANDREI

I'll tell you, Masha—last year they asked the Junior Class to
state what they wanted to be. Well, they all answered—
but many of them lied. Fed'ka Kuskov, for example, said he
wanted to be a pilot. And why did he say that? Just to show
off. Now, after goofing off in the senior year, he'd be glad
to attend any school that would take him. Volod'ka Tsepochkin
answered even more hypocritically: "I want to become a person
who could help his country." And he is a first-class jerk—
nothing but a sponger and a parasite! I answered honestly—
I said I didn't know what I wanted to be. Some fuss they raised!
"A komsomolets* in the ninth grade, and still doesn't know!"
Practically the whole school was indignant about it! That sort
of thing can make a person disgusted for the rest of his life
with any calling! *(He notices that MASHA is glancing
toward the door, anxious for ARKADY to come into the room)*
Am I boring you?

MASHA

Don't be silly.

ANDREI

Tell me, Masha, but for Pete's sake be honest about it —
you are a photographer. It's not exactly the most brilliant
profession. Well, is being a photographer the height of
your ambition?

MASHA

(Laughs) Of course not. . . It was my fate to become one. But I
like it now—believe me, I even like it a lot!

ANDREI

No, Masha, I don't believe you.

MASHA

I know—at the age of seventeen you all insist on becoming
someone great. But what if by chance you should remain just
an ordinary mortal—a bookkeeper, a pharmacist. . . or a
photographer?

ANDREI

Categorically

Not a chance! *(Somewhat more calmly)* What hopes did you
have? What did you want to be?

*A member of the Young Communist League, a national organization for 15 to 28
year-old Soviet youth.

MASHA

A concert pianist, and—a famous one, nothing less would do!

ANDREI

Are you kidding?

MASHA

Not at all.

ANDREI

Play something.

MASHA

I haven't touched a piano in two years.

ANDREI

Why?

ARKADY

(Enters) Oh, it's you?

MASHA

No more, and no less.

ARKADY

(To ANDREI) Go and clean up your desk—it looks like a pigsty.

ANDREI

My desk is my business, and if you want me to leave, I can go without a phony excuse. *(To MASHA)* It was good to talk with you. You're not stupid. . .
He exits.

MASHA

(Laughing) Andriusha takes himself very seriously these days.

ARKADY

It's not funny. . . He's growing up to be a fool, and his head is full of mush.
A pause.

MASHA

I have discovered that there is no malice in me—I went over in my mind all your arguments but I still don't understand why we shouldn't see each other any more.

ARKADY

I've made up my mind.

MASHA

Firmly?

ARKADY

Yes.

MASHA

Forever?

ARKADY

Yes.

MASHA

Why?

ARKADY

It is difficult for me to tell you why, but if you want the whole truth. . .

MASHA

(With sarcasm) I virtually hunger for it!

ARKADY

I don't love you.

MASHA

That's not true!

ARKADY

(Laughs) . . .Well, right now there's no room in my life for love. Can you understand that?

MASHA

Not without an effort. You say Andriushka's brain is filled with mush. At his age it's to be expected, but at yours? Do you have any idea what has been happening to you? Here, I've brought fascinating evidence of it. . . *(She unwraps the package she is carrying. It contains two large photographs. Shows them to ARKADY)* Actor Averin fours years ago—a jolly young fellow. . . And now—a middle-aged grump. . . I worked half the night over these. . .

ARKADY

(Looking at the photos) Yesterday they assigned the parts of a new play. For me—again nothing. But Vasya Mishkin got the lead role again. He never showed much talent at the drama school. . .

MASHA

Evidently he has grown.

ARKADY

And what about me?—have I shrunk?

MASHA

Some people move ahead easily, Arkasha, others with difficulty, more slowly.

ARKADY

Why don't you simply say that you, too, consider me untalented, why pretend?

MASHA

(Sadly) Dear Arkasha, don't be angry! It's so hard on me to see you this way. . . Before, you'd talk to me about your theatre as a bright, beautiful, light-hearted world. . .

ARKADY

Light-hearted! That proves how stupid I was! How naive!— it's the most gloomy. . .

MASHA

Do you yourself believe in your abilities?

ARKADY

(Stubbornly) I do.

MASHA

That's what counts! Arkasha, an author I've been reading expressed a wise thought. He wrote: "Talent is never wasted."

ARKADY

So, what about yours?
MASHA does not answer.
It's an empty phrase. At our theatre. . .

MASHA

Let's not talk about that, Arkasha.

ARKADY

Yes, yes. . . *(He paces the room. A pause)*
This morning I woke up at five, the room was full of sunshine. . .
I lay there feeling good. Then the same thought, the same worry

ARKADY (Cont.)

begain to haunt me, and I remembered everything. . . I wanted
to fall asleep again but couldn't, kept tossing about till nine.
(Goes over to MASHA) Oh, don't mind me. . . Of course I have
changed. A lot?

*MASHA is silent. ARKADY again picks up the photographs,
looks at them, puts them aside.*

A lot! And I'm being objective. . . I'm leaving the theatre!

MASHA

Why?

ARKADY

Yes, I'm quitting. And soon. I'll make one more effort and
then I'll be through.

MASHA

What kind of effort?

ARKADY

I'm studying a part—a big one. They gave me permission. I'll
read for it and then if I don't succeed, I'll leave—you'll see!

MASHA

When is the reading?

ARKADY

I won't tell you. The audition will be during the day. Outsiders
will not be allowed.

MASHA

Maybe you shouldn't do it, Arkasha? You play small roles.
You play them well. You've even been mentioned in the papers
several times.

ARKADY

Is that why I went to drama school, is that why I was born into
this world? Please don't persist. It's easy for you to talk. You've
managed to resign yourself. . .

MASHA

Resign myself?!

ARKADY

Well, you've managed to accept your loss. . .

MASHA

Accept! When that miserable accident happened, you came to me, you kissed my broken fingers and talked, and talked. For days! Do you think I even heard what you were saying to me? I wanted to die then and there. But I never permitted myself to insult you. *(She starts to leave)*

ARKADY

Masha!

MASHA

That's enough!. . . You've lost your taste for life. You're beginning to love yourself, not your art—and its taking its revenge on you! I am *not* resigned, I love. . . And I'm much happier than you! *She exits.*

ARKADY

Paces from one end of the room to the other.
What's the difference! What difference does it make!
PYOTR IVANOVICH enters. ARKADY goes to his room, opens the window, stretches, and breathes in deeply. ANASTASIA EFREMOVNA enters, and flops into a chair in a state of exhaustion.

ANASTASIA EFREMOVNA

I've been running around trying to find things out for Andriusha. He hasn't bestirred himself much. It's very difficult to get into the good colleges. There's a flood of applications. I even went to the Sazonovs—wanted to discuss it all with Vasilii Ivanovich. But it develops he no longer teaches at the Bauman. *(To her husband)* Petrusha, are you looking for something in here?

PYOTR IVANOVICH

No, I've been sitting down too long. I'm stretching my bones a bit. *ARKADY enters, carrying his actor's bag.*

ARKADY

I'm walking to the theatre. Want to get some air.

PYOTR IVANOVICH

Wait a few minutes. Let's have a brief family council. *(He takes a letter from his pocket)* From our Siberian relatives. *(Reads)* "Dear Petrusha, Anastasia Efremovna, and Boys: I have a favor to ask you, a big favor. Especially you, Anastasia Efremovna. And this is what it's all about. My Aleksei has finished high

PYOTR IVANOVICH (Cont.)

school and hopes to enter a school in Moscow. Could you let him live with you while he pursues his studies, that is, if he passes the entrance examinations, for which I don't have much hope. I am asking a great deal, I know, and I even hesitated to write you, but Aleksei kept after me, and I gave in—he's a stubborn one! But don't hesitate to refuse, and let us know right away if it is impossible. I won't hold it against you. I'll write you another time about our life out here. The children and I embrace you. Your Olya." There. . . *(He looks at his wife and son)* So, do we welcome our guest?

ANASTASIA EFREMOVNA

As you wish, Petya. Olya is—*your* sister.

PYOTR IVANOVICH

No, Nasten'ka, the letter is addressed mainly to you, and you'll be bearing all the responsibilities—so yours is the deciding voice.

ANASTASIA EFREMOVNA

I can't understand how people can be so inconsiderate, so shameless! Everybody flocks to Moscow, as if the city is made of rubber—can be stretched and stretched. As it is we suffocate from the crowds. But no, they keep coming and coming!

PYOTR IVANOVICH

I see what you're driving at. . .

ANASTASIA EFREMOVNA

And where would we put him?

PYOTR IVANOVICH

That's no problem. He can share the room with Arkady and Andriusha.

ARKADY

No, thank you. Andrei is all I can handle. *(To his father)* You have a couch in your study.

PYOTR IVANOVICH

All right. Let him stay there.

ANASTASIA EFREMOVNA

(TO ARKADY) Don't even suggest it. Your father works till late at night. People often come to call on him. And there he will be, the young scholar, snoring away. No. How can people be so inconsiderate! . . .

PYOTR IVANOVICH

But during the war you and the children lived in their small home for two years!

ANASTASIA EFREMOVNA

(With sarcasm) All right, then. Let's put up a cot right here in the middle of this room, why don't we!. . .

ARKADY

Mother, calm down!

ANASTASIA EFREMOVNA

How can I be calm? Who is this Aleksei? What is he like? Andrushka is so impressionable, so unstable. . . Most of all I'm afraid that he'll be a bad influence on him. And then, there will be constant traffic here—of school friends, some kind of girls. . .

PYOTR IVANOVICH

Don't exaggerate!

ANASTASIA EFREMOVNA

That's unavoidable, Petya, and even natural. Furthermore, why should I have to make breakfasts, dinners, and suppers for someone else?—worry about him, look after him. After all, I'll be fully responsible. That same Olya will later expect me to answer for him. And we don't know how he will behave.

PYOTR IVANOVICH

You are really over-anxious about it all.

ANASTASIA EFREMOVNA

Yes, Petya, I am anxious. We've got problems of our own. We must get Andrei into a good school. But how? I've been wracking my brains. . . *(To ARKADY)* And I'm heartsick about you. Do you think I don't notice how you suffer? I'm exhausted with worry. After all, I'm not twenty. . .

ARKADY

Oh, decide for yourselves. My opinion is that the kid should come. *(He starts to go, then stops)* You may set him up in my room. I don't object.
He exits.

ANASTASIA EFREMOVNA

I understand, Petya, it's not easy to refuse, it's embarrassing. But think, we can get into worse trouble. You have an enormous

ANASTASIA EFREMOVNA (Cont.)

amount of work; what if I overlook something you need, neglect things. . . No, I'll write to Olya quite frankly, she won't be offended. The boy can find a school out there, in the provinces. There are many colleges everywhere, now. . . I'll write her this very day. . . I'll even send her a telegram. Yes, yes, it has to be a telegram, or Aleksei might to too late in applying elsewhere.

PYOTR IVANOVICH

When we lived in one room, Nastya, you were somehow more generous, kinder.

ANASTASIA EFREMOVNA

I simply had more energy then. Don't think all this is pleasant for me. But I assure you it's better to act at once—at once, and without beating around the bush.

PYOTR IVANOVICH

Well, I suppose Aleksei will not perish. . . *(He starts to go back to his study)*

ANASTASIA EFREMOVNA

Petya, do you know anyone at the Bauman Institute?

PYOTR IVANOVICH

No, I once met Korobov at Nikolai Afanasievich's, but just that once. We have only a nodding acquaintance.

ANASTASIA EFREMOVNA

Korobov?! The Dean?!

PYOTR IVANOVICH

Yes.

ANASTASIA EFREMOVNA

Is Nikolai Afanasievich a close friend of his?

PYOTR IVANOVICH

I think so. Why?. . .

ANASTASIA EFREMOVNA

We must somehow use influence to get Andrusha into the Bauman.

PYOTR IVANOVICH

Let the boy study harder—that'll do it for him.

ANASTASIA EFREMOVNA

He studies—but the competition is fierce. . .

PYOTR IVANOVICH

I don't like this business of "using influence". . .

ANASTASIA EFREMOVNA

It's nothing unusual, Petya. We are not the only ones to do it. . .
Will Nikolai Afanasievich be back in Moscow soon?

PYOTR IVANOVICH

In a few days. *(The doorbell rings)* If it's someone for me, tell
them I'm not at home.

*He exits, rather in disgust. ANASTASIA EFREMOVNA goes to
the door. She returns to the room with GALYA and VADIM.*

ANASTASIA EFREMOVNA

Come in, come in, future college students. How's everything?

VADIM

Our nerves are stretched to the breaking point, Anastasia
Efremovna. We are making our career choices, you know. At a
time like this it's dangerous to take a false step.
ANDREI enters.

ANDREI

Oh, it's you—at last! You promised to come at seven, and it's
almost nine. And here I was, dying of boredom. . . And you
call yourselves friends! *(To GALYA in a whisper)* Why didn't
you come yesterday?

GALYA

I wasn't feeling well.

ANDREI

(Suspiciously) Are you sure?

GALYA

All right then—I didn't feel like it.

ANDREI

Don't mind my asking, Galka—it's only that I waited and waited
for you. . . Let's go, Comrades.

VADIM

(To ANDREI) Here are the physics and chemistry abstracts.

ANDREI

Don't you need them?

VADIM

I've browsed through them. The exact sciences are not exactly my vocation.

ANASTASIA EFREMOVNA

You're the lucky one, Vadya! You'll be going to the Institute for Foreign Trade. . . How nice it sounds!

ANDREI

Mama, don't worry! The Bauman—is not inglorious either.

ANASTASIA EFREMOVNA

If only they would accept you! *(To GALYA)* What a pretty blouse!

GALYA

(Animatedly) Do you like it?

ANASTASIA EFREMOVNA

Yes, it's very smart.

GALYA

The tucking gives it a lightness, and the color of the buttons adds a lot to its chicness.

VADIM

Galya, don't get started on your favorite obsession, we must hurry.

ANASTASIA EFREMOVNA

Don't let him tease you, Galya.

GALYA

Oh, they don't count.
GALYA, ANDREI, VADIM start toward ANDREI and ARKADY'S room.

ANASTASIA EFREMOVNA

Vadya!
VADIM remains, the others exit. He is very polite and enjoys being a "model young man."
When is Nikolai Afanasievich expected back?

VADIM

I don't know. Father always leaves and returns without notice.

ANASTASIA EFREMOVNA

Do you think he'll be back by the first?

VADIM

Very likely. I'm waiting for him impatiently, myself.

ANASTASIA EFREMOVNA

How well you always carry yourself, Vadya! Always neat and courteous. Smart, too.

VADIM

(*Very pleased*) You embarrass me, Anastasia Efremovna.

ANASTASIA EFREMOVNA

How do you manage it all?!

VADIM

"The wish is father to the deed," some wise man said before I did—and I live accordingly.

ANASTASIA EFREMOVNA

If only your nice ways would rub off on Andriusha!

VADIM

Anastasia Efremovna, don't you worry about him—he's really not that bad, I assure you.

ANASTASIA EFREMOVNA

Never mind defending him, Vadya, don't excuse him. . . Where are you all off to?

VADIM

To Gorky Street, to the "Ice Cream" cafe.

ANASTASIA EFREMOVNA

It's always safe to let him go with you.

VADIM

I hope so.

ANASTASIA EFREMOVNA

All right, go along. Have a good time.
VADIM exits, to join the others in ANDREI'S room.
Andriusha!

ANDREI

(*Entering and speaking gruffly*) What do you want?

ANASTASIA EFREMOVNA

(To herself) What a difference! *(To ANDREI)* You are all going out soon—send off a telegram for me, would you?

ANDREI

O.K., let's have it.

ANASTASIA EFREMOVNA

Do you have a piece of paper?
ANDREI empties his pockets of their assorted junk, finds a piece of crumpled paper and gives it to his mother together with his fountain pen.

ANDREI

There! *(As ANASTASIA EFREMOVNA writes)* I'll send the telegram, and you give me twenty rubles.

ANASTASIA EFREMOVNA

Ten will do.

ANDREI

I sure can't wait to earn my own money! I'm so sick of begging!

ANASTASIA EFREMOVNA

(Handing the message to ANDREI) Don't forget to send it. . .
Come, have some tea and eat a meat cake. I'll warm it for you.

ANDREI

Let's have it, quick.
She starts toward the kitchen.
Mom!

ANASTASIA EFREMOVNA

What?

ANDREI

How about the money?

ANASTASIA EFREMOVNA

Oh, I forgot!. . .

ANDREI

What a memory!

ANASTASIA EFREMOVNA

(Giving him some money) You're pretty rude, Andriusha! You might learn a few things from Vadim.

ANASTASIA EFREMOVNA (Cont.)

She exits. ANDREI exits to his room. Enter, timidly, ALEKSEI, KATYA, and AFANASY. They are carrying their baggage in improvised suitcases (boxes). They look around the room uneasily. Their appearance, clothes, and manner mark them as youngsters from the provinces. They've just arrived in Moscow from Irkutsk.

ALEKSEI

No one. . .?

KATYA

The door wasn't locked—that means someone's home. . .

AFANASY

Combs his hair, but a stubborn cowlick stands erect. To KATYA
Is it down?

KATYA

No, it's still up.

AFANASY

Damn it! *(Looks around)* What a place! What a break for you, Aleksei, to live in such a mansion!. . . And such quiet. . . You can study till the roosters crow!

ALEKSEI

Are we in the right place?

KATYA

I saw the card on the door: "Doctor of Biological Sciences, AVERIN, Pyotr Ivanovich."

ANASTASIA EFREMOVNA

(Enters and stops short) Who let you in?

AFANASY

The door wasn't locked. . .

ANASTASIA EFREMOVNA

Whom do you want?

ALEKSEI

(With a smile) Aunt Nastya. . . *(Goes to her)* I am Aleksei!
(Laughs with pleasure at surprising her)

ANASTASIA EFREMOVNA

You've arrived. . .already. . .

ALEKSEI

Yes.

KATYA

Aleksei kept worrying about whether you would be in Moscow, at home.

ALEKSEI

Mother said—don't go before we hear from them, but I thought: why wait, might as well go. *(Pointing to AFANASY and KATYA)* They left, and I with them. Decided to chance it *(To KATYA and AFANASY)* Put your things down.

AFANASY

(Pulling the knapsack from his back) My, what a city, this Moscow—enormous! We almost missed it!

KATYA

(Putting down her "suitcase") I made a mistake—we got off three stops too soon. We had to walk and walk. . .

ANASTASIA EFREMOVNA

(Pointing to AFANASY and KATYA) And. . .they are with you, too?

ALEKSEI

Yes, we were in the same class. *(Introducing them)* Afanasy Kabanov and Katya Sorokina. You remember her—she lives right near us. *(To AFANASY and KATYA)* This is Anastasia Efremovna, my aunt. *(KATYA and AFANASY shake hands with ANASTASIA EFREMOVNA)* Isn't Uncle Petya home?

ANASTASIA EFREMOVNA

No. . . I mean, he's home, in his study, working. Don't make so much noise, children.

ALEKSEI

(Softly) Ah. . .

AFANASY

We understand.

ALEKSEI

(Laughing uneasily) You didn't recognize me?

ANASTASIA EFREMOVNA

You've grown up. You're tall. . . So you've all come to study?

AFANASY

As my Pop said when he saw me off: Now you're off on life's journey. Give it a try, Son—see how it tastes, how it feels to the touch. . . So. . .we went.

ANASTASIA EFREMOVNA

(To KATYA) Are you also going to stay with us?

KATYA

Of course not! I have a sister in Moscow, I only came along to help them find their way. This is their first trip to Moscow, they could easily get lost.

ANASTASIA EFREMOVNA

(To AFANASY) And you?

AFANASY

Me? I also have relatives here. A whole bunch! On Tverskoy Boulevard, 42—Apartment 2. No. . .thank you for offering your hospitality, but I have a place to stay. . .

ANASTASIA EFREMOVNA

(To her nephew) You know, Alyosha, I must be frank with you, speak to you like a close relative: I don't think you'll be comfortable with us. . . .

ALEKSEI

Don't worry, Aunt Nastya, I don't need much. All I need is a place to sleep.

ANASTASIA EFREMOVNA

(To ALEKSEI) I understand—a place to sleep. . . No I couldn't very well put you up here. This is the living room, and in your Uncle's study—well, you can see how inconvenient that would be for him. We seem to have lots of space. . .but. . .

ALEKSEI

Are you saying that I can't. . .

ANASTASIA EFREMOVNA

I haven't said that. . . Uncle and I simply decided that we'd put you up. . .

ALEKSEI

Aunt Nastya—tell it to me straight. . . Mother made me promise that I wouldn't take things for granted. . .

ANASTASIA EFREMOVNA

Of course you did come sooner than we thought. We got your mother's letter only today. . . Everything happened so unexpectedly. . .

ALEKSEI

I get it. . . *(He picks up his knapsack and his "suitcase" and gets ready to leave)* Forgive me. . .

ANASTASIA EFREMOVNA

Wait. . . Olya was right—she wrote that you were strongheaded.

ALEKSEI

No, I'm not.

ANASTASIA EFREMOVNA

I'm telling you to wait. *(ALEKSEI stops his preparations for leaving)* Just a minute— I think the meat cakes are burning. I'll be right back. *(Exits)*

ALEKSEI

Oh, I wish the ground would swallow me!

AFANASY

If the truth be told—all this means that you shake hands and say good-bye.

ALEKSEI

Let's go!

KATYA

Don't do that—wait. . .

ALEKSEI

Wait for what? I rushed here. . .wanted to give them a big surprise! It's embarrassing as hell! Hurry up, Afansay.

AFANASY

(Fussing with his knapsack) The strap broke.

KATYA

Where will you stay, Alyosha?

ALEKSEI

Somewhere.

KATYA

I'd take you to my sister's but it would be kind of awkward to stay in the same room with the two of us girls.

ALEKSEI

What an idea!

AFANASY

No space, huh! You could put twenty cots in this room.

ALEKSEI

That's none of your business. Come on, move—you can fix it on the street.

AFANASY

Relax! Every obstacle serves as a challenge—lifts the spirit—my Pop says so.

ALEKSEI

Hurry up!

ALEKSEI, AFANASY, KATYA put the knapsacks on their backs, pick up their "suitcases" and aim for the door.

ANDREI

(Entering, stops short with surprise) Whom did you want?
The young visitors stop.

ALEKSEI

No one.

ANDREI

Then *what* did you want?

ALEKSEI

Nothing.

ANDREI

You sure are vague.

KATYA

(To ALEKSEI) Is he your brother?*

ALEKSEI

Probably.

ANDREI

Whose brother?

KATYA

(To ANDREI) He's your cousin from Irkutsk—Aleksei. *(To ALEKSEI)* Say hello—you can't go without saying hello!

*Traditionally Russians refer to cousins as "brothers."

ALEKSEI

(Going over to ANDREI, shakes hands) Hi. You are Andrei?

ANDREI

I am Andrei. . . Wait a minute. . . I do have some relatives somewhere. I was thinking about it the other day. So that's you?

ALEKSEI

That's me.

ANDREI

Well, what do you know!. . . Amusing.

AFANASY

A touching reunion!

KATYA

Alyosha came to Moscow to enroll in a college.

ANDREI

Oh, yes, I'm busy with that dismal business, too.

KATYA

He hoped to stay with you people, but it seems that's impossible.

ANDREI

Why?

AFANASY

Why don't you ask your mother?

KATYA

We've just been talking with Anastasia Efremovna—she said that you were too crowded.

ANDREI

We—crowded?! You must be mistaken. Look at this big room.

KATYA

What difference does it make—she said. . .

ANDREI

You must have misunderstood something. Take off you knapsacks!

AFANASY

We already took them off once.

ALEKSEI

Hold everything. . . I'm not staying.

ANDREI

What in the world did she say to you? First of all, pay no attention to her. Secondly, Arkady and I have our own room and we can do what we want there. You are staying with us, and that's final.

KATYA

He's right, Aloysha. Stay for a while, then we'll see. You can't sleep in the street.

AFANASY

After all, you didn't come this far for trivial reasons—you'll have to sit on your pride for a while.

ANDREI

What's the problem?—I don't understand.

KATYA

(To ALEKSEI) It's getting dark. A person has to have a roof over his head. Stay at least till tomorrow, then we'll see. *(Softly)* Please, Alyosha.

ALEKSEI

It's embarrassing, but, all right, I'll stay for the time being.

AFANASY

Right—not all people are alike—you have to know how to get along.

KATYA

Carefully taking a folded shirt from her "suitcase".
I almost forgot—it's your good shirt. *(To ANDREI)* His suitcase is small and crowded and the shirt would have got ruined. And it's his best one. *(She gives it to ALEKSEI)* Here! And your physics notebook. *(To ANDREI)* We crammed all the time on the train, terribly hard. . . *(Softly to ALEKSEI)* Smile, Alyosha. *(Loudly to AFANASY, nearly in tears)* Let's go. I'll help you find Tverskoy Boulevard.

AFANASY

Never mind! I won't get lost. I have the exact address: Tverskoy Boulevard, 42. . .

KATYA

(To ALEKSEI) I'll drop by tomorrow.

AFANASY

(*To ALEKSEI*) Take it easy now—mind your own business around here. Maintain total neutrality. This is only the beginning, just a petty annoyance. What's ahead will be far worse—the exams! See you.

KATYA, AFANASY say good-bye and exit.

ANDREI

Do you have some place where you could've spent the night?

ALEKSEI

No.

ANDREI

Then you planned to sleep on the streets?

ALEKSEI

Why not?

ANDREI

(*Scrutinizing ALEKSEI*) Interesting. . .

ALEKSEI

Why are you staring at me?

ANDREI

You're a giant!

ALEKSEI

Yes, I grew pretty tall.

ANDREI

(*Animated*) That was a great idea, to come here—in this place there isn't a single live soul. What boredom!

ALEKSEI

Why, has Arkady already moved out?

ANDREI

No, he's still here, but he's mad. Obsessed. Yes, he's looney about his theatre. You can't talk to him about anything else. Imagine—he thinks it's the only thing worth living for in this world. In my opinion the theatre— is just an entertainment medium that's all. What do you think?

ALEKSEI

I have no opinion. I haven't given it enough thought.

ANDREI

What is there to think about? If the play is funny you go, if it's a bore you stay home.

ALEKSEI

Aunt Nastya is cooking meat cakes for us. . .

ANDREI

O.K., we'll check it out, there's time. Come to my room.

VADIM

(Entering) Andrei, you said you'd bring an ash tray.

ANDREI

There it is—on the table, get it for yourself—the sea shell. My brother has just arrived.

VADIM

Do you have another brother? You never told me.

ANDREI

I forgot about it. A first cousin—a Siberian. Get acquainted— Aleskei.

VADIM

(Shaking hands with ALEKSEI) Rozvalov.

ANDREI

(To ALEKSEI) Have you heard about the Academician Rozvalov?

ALEKSEI

A geologist.

ANDREI

(Pointing to VADIM) His son.

VADIM

Andrei, how many times have I said to you—skip the advertisement. What significance does it have—son of an Academician? My father is a celebrity. I don't represent anything.

ANDREI

You'll be a celebrity, too, don't worry.

VADIM

(To ALEKSEI) It's very difficult to have a famous father!

ALEKSEI

Probably. . . It's a responsibility.

VADIM

Yes, you're absolutely right.

GALYA

(Entering) Where did you all disappear to, one by one?

ANDREI

An extraordinary event! My cousin has just arrived. Let me present you. . .

GALYA

(Going over to ALEKSEI) Galya. I've seen you somewhere.

ALEKSEI

Hardly.

ANDREI

Maybe in your dreams. . .

GALYA

Maybe. . .

ANDREI

(Quoting a line of poetry) "You were an apparition in her dreams. . ."

ALEKSEI

(As he shakes hands with GALYA) Aleksei.

ANDREI

Her mother sings at the Bol'shoi Theatre. She's a People's Artist.

GALYA

Stop it, Andrei.

ANDREI

Galochka, you never objected before.

ALEKSEI

Did you say it's dull here?

GALYA

(To ANDREI) Hey, you—host! Your cousin is probably tired from the trip, would like to wash up. . .

ANDREI

Yes, yes. . . In a minute.

VADIM

(Picking up ALEKSEI'S "suitcase") Are the rest of your things in the entry?

ALEKSEI

That is all I have.

VADIM

(Shaking the "suitcase") Not much here!
They all exit to ANDREI and ARKADY'S room.

ANASTASIA EFREMOVNA

Enters, stops short, realizing there's no one in the room. She hurries to the window, looks down to the street.

He left!. . . What was so terrible about what I said to him? How badly it all turned out! *(Calls)* Petya!. . .

(Voice of PYOTR IVANOVICH offstage) "What?"

Are you alone?

(Voice of PYOTR IVANOVICH offstage) "Alone."

This is terrible! My-my-my! Andrusha!. . .

(Voice of ANDREI offstage) "What?"

You haven't left yet?

(Voice of ANDREI offstage) "We're just leaving."

How proud that Aleksei is! What a mess! What now? *(Calls)* Andrusha!

ANDREI

(Running in) What is it?

ANASTASIA EFREMOVNA

What did you do with the ash tray?

ANDREI

Vadim is using it.

ANASTASIA EFREMOVNA

Didn't I ask you not to touch it? It's hard to clean the cigarette butts out of it.

ANDREI

You said yourself that it was for guests! Oh, you're impossible!
He exits.

ANASTASIA EFREMOVNA

(Shouting after him) Don't forget to eat! My-my-my!
She exits to the kitchen.
All the young people now enter, ready to leave for the cafe.

ANDREI

(To ALEKSEI) Now, don't you get stuck here.

ALEKSEI

(Softly, to ANDREI) You ought to tell your mother I'm still here.

ANDREI

Right! *(Softly, to GALYA)* Do you mind if I don't go along?
You understand—my cousin has just arrived. I've got to get
him settled. O.K.?

GALYA

Of course I don't mind.

ANDREI

(Relieved) Honestly?

GALYA

Cross my heart.

ANDREI

You're a real human being—I think. . . Go ahead with Vadim.

GALYA

He bores me. He's forever mouthing words of wisdom.

ANDREI

Come around tomorrow.

GALYA

I'll come.

ANDREI

You're not going to stand me up again?

GALYA

No, I promise. *(Aloud)* Vadim, I'm not going.

VADIM

(To ANDREI) Too bad you broke up the party. But I suppose
you must stay—duty dictates.

ANDREI

Yes. . . Look, my mother asked me to send off this telegram. Could you take care of it for me? *(Searches his pockets, finds the right piece of paper)* Here it is. *(Reads)* "Irkutsk Region. . ." *(Reads the rest to himself)* No, that's not the right one. *(Tears it up)* I must've lost it. Never mind, I'll send it tomorrow myself. Adieu!

VADIM

You're always into some mischief.

GALYA

Good-bye.

GALYA and VADIM exit.

ALEKSEI

I spoiled your plans, didn't I?

ANDREI

I'll survive. Do you like Galya?

ALEKSEI

She's pretty.

ANDREI

She's mine.

ALEKSEI

What do you mean—yours?

ANDREI

Don't you know?—are you still a little boy, or what? And the one who came with you, she's not so bad either—your Katya. . . Right?

ANASTASIA EFREMOVNA enters, carrying the meat cakes and a tea kettle. She see ALEKSEI.

There they are—the meat cakes! You're probably ready to wolf down a plateful after such a long trip. Do you realize, Mom, that Aleksei was about to leave?—you hurt his feelings.

ANASTASIA EFREMOVNA

I did nothing of the kind! Can't an aunt speak openly?. . .

ANDREI

(To ALEKSEI) You want to wash up, don't you? *(Points)* Over there, down the hall, to the left, the second door—the bathroom. Use my towel, with the light blue stripe, the shaggy one.

ALEKSEI exits. ANDREI turns on his mother.

What were you thinking of?!

ANASTASIA EFREMOVNA

What do you mean?

ANDREI

I read your telegram. . . You ought to be ashamed!

ANASTASIA EFREMOVNA

A lot you understand.

ANDREI

There's nothing to understand. Go bring the folding cot to my room.

ANASTASIA EFREMOVNA

You are the hospitable host, but it's Mother who has to "give," "carry," "clean up". . .

ANDREI

All right, we'll get along without your help. Let's have a blanket and a pillow.

ANASTASIA EFREMOVNA

Where will I get a pillow?

ANDREI

There are only three of them piled on your bed!

ANASTASIA EFREMOVNA

And what right has anyone to sleep on my pillows?. . .

ANDREI

(Exasperated) Stop carrying on this way! If you don't give me some bedding for him, I'll sleep on the bare floor, without a blanket or sheet, on the bare boards—I warn you!

ANASTASIA EFREMOVNA

You'll flunk your exams—don't you forget that! You shouldn't get involved in anyone else's business. You must study, worry about your future. Don't think it's that easy to get in, these days. If you don't watch out, you'll be a nobody, you'll find yourself working in a factory.

ANDREI

O.K., don't try to scare me!

ANASTASIA EFREMOVNA

This year there's a larger flood of applicants than last year. Nine for each place—I made it my business to check on this. Now only the very best will be accepted. The rest—after finishing high school will go straight to work. And don't you forget it!

ANDREI

Oh, give up! What a wet blanket you are! Must you ruin a guy's mood all the time? I just managed to cheer up, and then you. . .

ANASTASIA EFREMOVNA

And you'd better watch out—find out what sort of person Aleksei is. You saw the kind of company he keeps. . .

ANDREI

What about them?

ANASTASIA EFREMOVNA

That red-headed one, with the mop of uncombed hair and the strange face. . . And already they bring a woman along with them! They'll be hanging around here. . .

ANDREI

So what? They won't eat me up!

ANASTASIA EFREMOVNA

The worst elements are attracted to you. Where did you hear those coarse words: "gobble up," "O.K.," "let's have it". . .

ANDREI

You know, if I were to list your faults—you'd be surprised. . .like your mad attachments to objects—that ash tray, for instance.

ANASTASIA EFREMOVNA

Oh, talking to you is a waste of time. You'd better feed him. What's one meat cake for the likes of him?—just a mouthful! *She exits. ALEKSEI enters.*

ANDREI

My mohter has a headache. I'll serve you your supper. Generally, don't pay attention to her—she has bizarre ideas. Sometimes she says such things. . .

ANDREI

Stop that!

ANDREI

What?

ALEKSEI

You shouldn't talk about your mother that way.

ANDREI

I'm not exaggerating.

ALEKSEI

It's not right, anyway.

ANDREI

Oho!. . .*(Exiting to the kitchen)* Aha!. . .
*ALEKSEI goes to the window, sees the evening lights illuminating
Moscow. ANDREI enters, carrying a small saucepan, a plate with
pieces of pie, and a spoon.*

ALEKSEI

(Looking out the window) Beautiful!. . .

ANDREI

Me, I'm tired of it. I wish I could go away—some place at the
other end of the world!

ALEKSEI

When you're through with college—then you can go.

ANDREI

No, I'll have to stick around here.

ALEKSEI

Maybe they'll send you.

ANDREI

That's all I'd need! No, I'll somehow beat the system—make sure
I'm not sent anywhere. *(Tastes the food in the saucepan)* Tasty!
I'll have this soup, and you eat the pie. Sit down.
*He makes himself comfortable and continues to relish the "soup."
ALEKSEI continues to stand at the window.*
Where do you want to study?

ALEKSEI

At the agronomy institute—the Timiriazevsky.

ANDREI

Did you graduate with honors?

ALEKSEI

No.

ANDREI

Do you have many B's?

ALEKSEI

I even have a C.

ANDREI

Too bad!. . . They won't take you. You know how tough it is these days. Of course I didn't finish with honors either, but C's?—not a single one! Just the same, I think I'll flunk the entrance. Why are you going in for agronomy?

ALEKSEI

It interests me.

ANDREI

Your chosen profession?

ALEKSEI

I don't know. . . But I'm interested.

ANDREI

You won't make it.

ANASTASIA EFREMOVNA

(Entering) Andrei, what are you doing?!
She rushes to her son and snatches the saucepan from him.

ANDREI

What's gotten into you? Give it back!

ANASTASIA EFREMOVNA

I cooked this for the cat!
She exits to the kitchen, carrying away the "soup".

ANDREI

(Laughing hard) Not bad! Our cat lives pretty well!. . . In that case, let's share the meat cakes fraternally. You don't object?
He divides them into equal portions.

ANASTASIA EFREMOVNA

Enters with a plateful of meat and places it on the table.
Here, have some cold veal. *(She exits)*

ANDREI

Look at this! We're lucky. . . *(Cutting the meat)* Do you have trouble with your studies?

ALEKSEI

No.

ANDREI

Were you often sick?

ALEKSEI

No.

ANDREI

I get it. . . I just skimmed the surface, myself. I could have done better, but had no urge to do it, was bored with it—you understand.

ALEKSEI

We are a large family, and there's no father—you know how that is!

ANDREI

And where's your father?

ALEKSEI

How come you don't know?

ANDREI

How would I know?

ALEKSEI

Mother writes your family regularly.

ANDREI

I never read any of her letters. I agree that was nasty of me. Go on. . .

ALEKSEI

Do you remember, when all of you stayed with us?—they drafted Father into the army.

ANDREI

Yes, I seem to recall something vaguely. . .but nothing specific.

ALEKSEI

Well, he never came back. Was killed at the front. And at home, not counting Mother, there were four of us. Well, why are you staring like that? Money—there was none to spare. So I decided to help out—do odd jobs after school. I swept sidewalks, chopped wood. In the summer I hauled logs out of the river—there's a saw-mill nearby. The last two summers I worked in a shop. So there just wasn't enough time for homework.

ANDREI

Aha. . . I see. . . Come on, sit down and eat.

ALEKSEI

But I'll make it yet. I'll work like a dog, and I'll pass!

ANDREI

Yes, maybe you will. . . Eat, eat. . .

ALEKSEI

No, thanks. Let's have an understanding, right from the start.
I won't eat in your home.

ANDREI

What?!

ALEKSEI

Don't be offended. I have money, I planned everything carefully.
I'll have enough.

ANDREI

Of all the looney. . . You've thought of everything! *(Laughing suddenly)* My mother will have a fit!

ALEKSEI

Why?

ANDREI

You'll see. . . So you plan to go to sleep on an empty stomach?

ALEKSEI

I brought along something to eat—my Mother baked it.
He exits to ANDREI'S room.

PYOTR IVANOVICH

(Entering, calls) Nasten'ka!

ALEKSEI

(Returning with a package in his hand) Hello, Uncle Petya!

ANASTASIA EFREMOVNA

(Entering) What is it, Petrusha?. . . This is Alyosha. Imagine—he's here already. Says he wants to look around.

PYOTR IVANOVICH

Smart boy. Welcome! *(He kisses his nephew)*

ANASTASIA EFREMOVNA

I'm having him stay in the boys' room.

PYOTR IVANOVICH

Smart girl. *(Kisses his wife)* You see how simple it all is! *(To ALEKSEI)* How is the rest of our family—out there?

ALEKSEI

Thanks, they're fine.

PYOTR IVANOVICH

Have some supper. Then come to my study—we'll have a good talk. *(To his wife)* Nasten'ka, let me have some coffee.

ANASTASIA EFREMOVNA

Right away. *(She exits)*

PYOTR IVANOVICH

(To ANDREI) And you—go back to your studies! You must work harder. What else do you think will see you through? I'm ashamed for you!

ANDREI

I try, Papa.

PYOTR IVANOVICH

You don't exactly kill yourself at it!
He exits.

ANDREI

You see how they keep badgering me? I'll get out of their clutches somehow! *(Pours the tea)* Won't you at least have some tea? Basically—it's just water. . .

ANDREI

Go ahead and pour.

ANDREI

(Eating the pie) Will you have some?
ALEKSEI shakes his head, refusing.
Tasty! Have some? *(Goes on eating)* By the way, you could eat the meat without compunction—it's for me.

ALEKSEI

It's not yours. . .

ANDREI

Aha! You mean I didn't earn it. . . Stop kidding! I tell you, stop that comedy or I'll tell Mother, this very minute. Don't be so pious! Eat—or else! *(Calls)* Mom!

ALEKSEI

Cut it out!

ANASTASIA EFREMOVNA

(Enters, carrying bedding) What?

ANDREI

Aleksei doesn't like cold veal.

ANASTASIA EFREMOVNA

If you like, I can warm it, or make you an omelette.

ALEKSEI

No, thank you, Aunt Nastya. I like it very much. He's just kidding. *(Begins to eat)*

ANASTASIA EFREMOVNA

Here, take these, Aloysha. If you like to sleep high, I can bring another pillow.

ALEKSEI

No, one will do. Thank you.
ANASTASIA EFREMOVNA exits.

ANDREI

In the Middle Ages, when you were asked how much a guest should eat, the answer was: When visiting you should eat a lot. If you were in the home of a friend—it would give him pleasure. If in the home of an enemy—it would annoy him. Clever—huh? So, relax and eat up.
They both eat.
Are you tired—want to go to bed?

ALEKSEI

It's early. I'll write Mother a card. I promised to send one right away.

ANDREI

You write while I make up your bed.
He exits, carrying bedding.

ALEKSEI

(Writing) "Dear Mother, I got here without any trouble. I am with our relatives. They received me well. . ."
He stops writing, is lost in thought.

ANDREI

(Enters) You must have a low opinion of me—I suppose you think I'm a carefree fool? I'm not—this is the way I see it all: it's a colossal bore! How many of us, all over the Soviet Union, at this time, are saying good-bye to our schools, to old friends?—Thousands! We're all deciding on our future. . . Worry, argue, cram, run here and there for information about colleges. Everyone wants to succeed at something. But me—somehow everything got screwed up inside of me. Damn it!. . .
Overcome, he coveres his face with his hands.

ALEKSEI

What's the matter?

ANDREI

Don't mind me. Nothing's the matter!. . .
He exits quickly to the hall and comes back at once with a folding cot. Pretending to be cheerful, he hums a lively tune to which he does a few dance steps, as he exits to his room, carrying the cot.
ALEKSEI continues to write his postcard.

Curtain

The Young Graduates   *Scene One*

> Two weeks later. ANDREI and ARKADY'S room. Afternoon.
> *ANDREI and ALEKSEI are studying for the entrance exams.*

ANDREI

Don't you feel as though your brains are being twisted?

ALEKSEI

Yes, I do.

ANDREI

(Slamming his book shut) A break—till evening?

ALEKSEI

A break—till evening!

ANDREI

(Spits on his books) You're wasting your time trying to get into
that agronomy institute. It only sounds interesting—because they
call it an "academy," I suppose. When you are through there they'll
put you on a leash and send you to some Godforsaken collective
farm. That will bring you mighty little satisfaction.

ALEKSEI

I'm not a beast, to be led off on a leash.

ANDREI

All right, all right, then they'll send you on a train.

ALEKSEI

Then, I'll go.

ANDREI

To improve farm production, I suppose? It's boring as hell out there.

ALEKSEI

Have you ever been in the countryside?

ANDREI

I've heard about it.

ALEKSEI

Moscow is beautiful, but the woods and fields, especially where
there's a wide river. . . Did you ever catch fish with a net?

ANDREI

No.

ALEKSEI

Did you ever go spear-fishing at night?

ANDREI

Where do you expect me to have gone spear-fishing? In the
Park of Culture and Rest?

ALEKSEI

And did you ever hunt bobcats?

ANDREI

Hunt what?

ALEKSEI

Catch bobcats—alive?

ANDREI

How about you?

ALEKSEI

But you do like ice cream and cake—the easy life?

ANDREI

(*Laughing*) You're a comedian! Listen, what if I, too, were to apply
at your agronomy institute? We'll study together and both of us
will pass. You know, it's all the same to me where I go. . .

ALEKSEI

You sure can gab! I've been observing you these two weeks—and
I haven't yet decided—whether you're still just a young punk, or
already a full-fledged phony.

ANDREI

I can't tell, myself. Probably a mixture of both. . . I'm probably so
shallow because everything has been handed to me on a silver platter—
the family is well-off. . .they feed and clothe me. . .

ALEKSEI

Is that so? You've found a great excuse for yourself! Afanasy's
old man is the captain of a barge fleet on the Enisei River. They
also live pretty well—but Afanasy doesn't make excuses for
himself the way you do. Katya's dad is a prize-winning author
with a good income. . . Listen, brother, don't blame others for
your hang-ups. Instead, take a good look at yourself. . . Come, let's
go out for some air. . .

ANDREI

Let's wait a while. Galya is coming over soon. We'll all go some place.

ALEKSEI

Why does she hang around you so much?

ANDREI

That should be obvious to you. . .

ALEKSEI

You ought to discourage her.

ANDREI

Why?

ALEKSEI

Because I intend to take her over.

ANDREI

You're damn sure of yourself. . .

ALEKSEI

It's only fair to warn you. . .

ANDREI

Then I'll also warn Galya.

ALEKSEI

Oh no, you don't! Anyway, what are you—a man or a mouse? *(A pause, then ANDREI changes the subject)*

ANDREI

Listen, Alyosha, what will you say if I do pass my exams after all? Won't you be surprised!

ALEKSEI

Not really. You grasp things quickly. I don't.

ANDREI

Quickly? Not quite—I only master the surface. You get into your studies more deeply. For you it's vital. . .

ALEKSEI

Right now I wish I could do it your way. I'm damn tired!

ANDREI

That's not within one's control. It depends on how a person's brain works.

ALEKSEI

Maybe. I should probably have listened to my mother—and not tried. From a distance everything seemed a lot simpler. Here, when I see how many have come from all over the country for the exams—I often stop and ask myself what chance do I have.

ANDREI

You know, Alyosha, you don't write well. You make lots of mistakes.

ALEKSEI

When I write fast, without thinking, I make fewer mistakes. But when I stop to consider grammatical rules—I'm sure to botch it up.

GALYA

(Entering) Hi, boys. How are things?

ANDREI

We are making heroic efforts. *(Looking her over)* You are very chic today—all decked out!

GALYA

I was just in the subway. Some bespectacled youth, pale and wan, carrying a load of notebooks and texts, is sitting across from me—he keeps gaping at me, can't take his eyes off. I can't resist, I go over to him and ask: "Are you getting ready for the exams?" He opens his mouth with surprise, can't breathe in or out. . . Luckily for him the train pulls into the Hunter's Ground Station— and he dashes out.

ANDREI

Many boys gape at you.

GALYA

Yes, it's amazing. . .

ANDREI

Do you enjoy it?

GALYA

Of course. But don't let that worry you, Andriusha—you know that I have strong fists as well as pretty curls.

ANDREI

Aleksei trips up on grammar.

GALYA

Really! I thought he knew everything there was to know.

ANDREI

Kidding aside—you ought to help him.

GALYA

Gladly.

ANDREI

(To ALEKSEI) She could. They didn't give her a silver medal because of her pretty eyes.

GALYA

(To ALEKSEI) Do you trip with both feet or just one?

ALEKSEI

You won a medal?

GALYA

Why?. . . Do I look like a moron? Do you need help with morphology or syntax?

ALEKSEI

I'll manage by myself, don't trouble. . .

ANDREI

Alyoshka, you shouldn't throw away an opportunity. . .

ALEKSEI

I said—I'll manage.

ANASTASIA EFREMOVNA

(Entering) Are you finished studying, boys?

ANDREI

Unfortunately, not forever. Mama, I want to enroll at the agronomy institute.

ANASTASIA EFREMOVNA

Where?

ANDREI

The Timiriazevsky. Do you think it's not too late to drop off the application forms?

ANASTASIA EFREMOVNA

Are you out of your mind?

ANDREI

Aleksei is urging me—says we'll hunt bobcats. . .

ANASTASIA EFREMOVNA

What bobcats? *(To ALEKSEI)* Alyosha, why do you try to confuse
Andrei? Leave him alone.

ANDREI

(Embracing his mother) I'm only teasing. For your sake, Mom,
I'm ready to become whatever you wish, even a circus clown.

GALYA

That's exactly what you're best suited for.

ANDREI

Why not? *(In a high-pitched voice, imitating a clown)* Good evening,
friends! I've just come on foot from the North Pole. . . Br-r-r-r!

ANASTASIA EFREMOVNA

Oh, stop it! *(To ANDREI and ALEKSEI)* Boys, come and eat,
I've prepared some food for you.

ALEKSEI

But Aunt Nastya, we ate only a couple of hours ago. I'm not hungry.

ANDREI

I am. No matter how aggravating life is, I never lose my appetite.
Galya, come keep me company—I'm sure there's something tasty. . .

GALYA

No, thanks. I ate just before coming.
ANASTASIA EFREMOVNA and ANDREI exit. A pause.

GALYA

Come, amuse me.

ALEKSEI

Will a dance solo do?

GALYA

How did you get that scar on your cheek?

ALEKSEI

A cat scratched me.

GALYA

Poor you! I hear you plan to become an·agronomist?

ALEKSEI

Maybe.

GALYA

A famous one—someone like Timiriazev?

ALEKSEI

An ordinary one—not "like" anybody.

GALYA

Do you like Andrei?

GALYA

Yes.

GALYA

And Vadim?

ALEKSEI

He's smart.

GALYA

And me?

ALEKSEI

Why do you put on airs all the time—call attention to yourself?
Where I come from someone like you would be called before
a Committee.

GALYA

And they'd re-educate me, I suppose.

ALEKSEI

They don't bother *that* much about your type.

GALYA

You're right. Not about my type. . .

ALEKSEI

And what's so special about you?

GALYA

First of all, I'm cute. . .

ALEKSEI

(Exploding) Really? Some idiot in the subway gives you the eye—and that makes you happy, you start imagining. . .

GALYA

(Casually) Get me my purse—from the table.

ALEKSEI

Get up and get it yourself.

GALYA

(Reaching for her purse) By the way, when I dropped my kerchief the other day, when we were walking on Red Square, you bent down and picked it up before Andrei had a chance to.

ALEKSEI

Did it mechanically.

GALYA

Innate courtesy—I see. *(Looking at herself in a pocket mirror)* I'm not bad. . . Do you like my dress?

ALEKSEI

Tell me, why do you want to enroll at a Teacher's Institute? Here in Moscow, I hear, they need live models—you ought to apply.

GALYA

A splendid idea! I'll think about it. I understand the pay isn't bad.

ALEKSEI

How did you manage to get a silver medal?

GALYA

Through pull. Why are you so mad?

ALEKSEI

You exasperate me.

GALYA

Who, me? How?

ALEKSEI

You are common through and through!

GALYA

Incredible! Through and through. . .how quickly you took that X-ray of me. I also have a detailed photographic impression of you!

ALEKSEI

Don't bother to tell me about it. I'm not interested.

GALYA

A perfectly stalwart oak!

ALEKSEI

And where did you see a picture of perfectly stalwart oak trees?

GALYA

All right, a pinewood mast.

ALEKSEI

That's in the feminine gender.

GALYA

You *do* remember *some* grammar! All right, you're as stiff as a lamp-post—will you settle for that?

ANASTASIA EFREMOVNA

(Enters) Alyosha, would you please take out the garbage?

ALEKSEI

With pleasure.
He exits.

ANASTASIA EFREMOVNA

What's eating him?

GALYA

He flared up—insisted that since I got a medal I shouldn't apply to a Teacher's Institute but to a university.

ANASTASIA EFREMOVNA

Galya, I would like you to keep an eye on Andrei. I'm afraid Aleksei might be a bad influence. Did you hear that nonsense about the agronomy school? Andrei might. . .he's so unstable. . . You must tell Vadim about it. . .

ANDREI

(Entering, saying to his mother) What was the idea?

ANASTASIA EFREMOVNA

What?

ANDREI

Why did you make Aleksei take the garbage out?

ANASTASIA EFREMOVNA

What's so terrible about that?

ANDREI

I could have done it.

ANASTASIA EFREMOVNA

I can never get you to do it. Next time, just pick it up and take it out.

ANDREI

Oh, nuts! *(Exasperated with her)* What else do you have for me to eat?—I suppose some wholesome cooked fruit?

ANASTASIA EFREMOVNA

Jello.

ANDREI

O.K., let's have some.
ANASTASIA EFREMOVNA exits. ANDREI, to GALYA.
It's really hot in here. You're so flushed.

GALYA

It's stifling outside, too.

ANDREI

What have you two been doing here?. . .

GALYA

I've been listening to the preaching of the stuffed shirt! Your cousin. He's full of criticism. . . According to him, I ought to wear a skirt down to my ankles and display it all over Moscow.

ANDREI

Well, he has his own standards. . . Of course, he's behind the times, but generally, he's an all right guy!

GALYA

Really?. . . He can't stand me—acts as if I were some kind of viper.

ANDREI

(Eagerly) You mean it?

GALYA

You ought to have heard him. . .

ANDREI

Galka, you must be wrong! I swear it! Just before you came he even said. . . No, I mustn't tell you!

GALYA

Did he say something—about me?

ANDREI

Yes.

GALYA

What?

ANDREI

I can't tell you.

GALYA

Are you hiding something from me?

ANDREI

Galka, don't make it hard. I'd like to tell you. . . You'd scream. . . But. . .I can't.

GALYA

All right, then don't. . .

ANDREI

Don't be offended. It's a matter of male honor. . .
ALEKSEI enters.
I'll be quick—I'll just gulp down some jello.
He exits. GALYA and ALEKSEI sit in silence. KATYA enters

GALYA

Katya, come to the rescue of your fellow-townsman.

KATYA

What's wrong?

GALYA

He's been overworking.

KATYA

What kind of work?

GALYA

Amusing me.

KATYA

(*Laughing*) Oh, and I thought. . . (*To ALEKSEI*) It's not easy
to fool her. (*To GALYA*) Has he told you how he hunted bobcats
with my Dad—in the taiga? That's how he got his scar. . . They
caught one alive.

GALYA

He's told Andrei, but he's only promised to tell me.

KATYA

It was interesting, you know—when they set out. . .

ALEKSEI

(*To KATYA*) Never mind that! Did you happen to run into Afanasy?

KATYA

No. Has anything happened to him?

ALEKSEI

I took a trolley-bus to Tverskoy Boulevard, number 42—there
is no such house!

KATYA

(*Worried*) Where can he be?

AFANASY

(*Entering*) Right here, alive and kicking! (*Waves hello to
ALEKSEI and KATYA, introduces himself to GALYA*)
Afanasy.

ALEKSEI

Where have you been staying?

AFANASY

With relatives on Tverskoy.

ALEKSEI

Number 42, apartment 2?

AFANASY

Yes.

ALEKSEI

What do you mean? There is no such address. The street ends
with No. 28.

AFANASY

You got it wrong. It's not 42, apartment 2—it's house number 2, apartment 42. I stayed there only three days. When they found out I was in Moscow—there was a big family reunion. Everyone wanted me! Aunt Vera said, "Move into my place." Uncle Kalya, "No—to mine!" Aunt Sasha drags me off to her digs. *(Points to his baggage, which he has been carrying around with him)* Now I'm moving in with Aunt Vera, on the Mozhaisk Road. I stopped off here on my way. How are things?

KATYA

We're all scared.

AFANASY

(To ALEKSEI) And how's everything here?

ALEKSEI

Bearable.

AFANASY

Sitting down on one of the couches (which converts to a bed).
A roof over your head, brother, is a great thing. Don't forget that. . . There's a huge mob wanting to get into the Aviation Institute—unbelievable!

ALEKSEI

At my Academy, too.

KATYA

I'm sure I'll flunk. I went inside that school, to look around. It's an enormous building, everything so hushed. . . Some kind of dignified people walking about gravely. . . It's scary!

AFANASY

You little coward! But you're an omniscient little coward—you know everything. *(Sprawling luxuriously on the couch)* Bliss!

KATYA

(Handing ALEKSEI a small notebook) Here, I copied rules and sample sentences from the grammar textbook. What gives you the most trouble?

GALYA

I offered to help him—but he proudly declined.

KATYA

(To ALEKSEI) Why? You must make use of every opportunity!

GALYA

(TO ALEKSEI) You see?!

ALEKSEI

Stop showing off! Oh, look—Afanya is asleep. His old weakness. . .

KATYA

(To GALYA) We used to pour cold water over him to wake him up in the classroom.

ALEKSEI

(Shaking AFANASY) Hey, citizen, wake up! Hey, citizen!!

AFANASY

(Jumps, grabs his knapsack) I'm looking for my train coach. . .No. 39. . .50. *They all laugh. He looks around in bewilderment.*

Damn it, what the devil! I was dreaming about some railroad station.* Well, I'm off. . . *(Gets up)* Studied all last night. . . That couch—it's a corrupting influence. . . *(Sits upright on a chair in an effort to keep awake)*

ANDREI runs in, slams the door shut after him, and holds the door handle so as not to let anyone in. He shouts to the people on the other side.

ALEKSEI

I'm sick and tired of all of you! *(To ALEKSEI and AFANASY)* Save me, you guys, they're working me over!. . . *(He lets go of the door handle. ANASTASIA EFREMOVNA and VADIM enter)* Let's get out of here! Let's go swimming.

VADIM

(To ANDREI) Why do you argue? Anastasia Efremovna is absolutely right—you jump like a flea from one plan to another. You must stop and do some thinking.

ANDREI

(Upset, almost distraught) To the swimming pool, my friends— what do you say?

ANASTASIA EFREMOVNA

Vadya, is your father back?

---

*Evidently the homeless Afanasy has been spending the nights illegally at Moscow railroad stations, posing as a traveller waiting for his train. He's only bluffing about many relatives.

VADIM

They tell me he is.

ANASTASIA EFREMOVNA

What do you mean—"They tell you?"...

VADIM

Father arrived at eight this morning and left for work at ten—
I was still asleep.

ANASTASIA EFREMOVNA

That means he's not at home?

VADIM

Not yet.

ANDREI

(Feeling trapped) Come on—how about that swim?

VADIM

You'll have a chance to even drown—at the exams. . . Aleksei,
Anastasia Efremovna says you have influence over Andrei. Won't
you try to pound it into his head that nowadays to study just
hit-or-miss is stupid.

AFANASY

(Softly, to ALEKSEI) Don't get involved.

ALEKSEI

He knows that himself.

ANDREI

Pious words!—I know everything myself. . . What do you all want
from me anyway? I am going on with my studies. I'll finish
college, I'll go to work—be of some use. Does that suit you all?

VADIM

(To ANDREI) Now you think you are someone special. But just
wait till all you become is a nonentity—an average little engineer—
then you'll have the rest of your life to wail about it.

ALEKSEI

There's nothing disgraceful about being an engineer.

VADIM

Just an average one?—what's so enticing about that?

ANDREI

(To VADIM) And you—are you planning to become a special specialist?!

VADIM

Frankly, yes. The soldier who doesn't dream of becoming a
general isn't much of a soldier. You owe it to yourself to aim
high and to reach that goal.

ANASTASIA EFREMOVNA

Take Arkady as an example!

ANDREI

I don't intend to become an actor.

VADIM

In any profession you can vegetate, or you can become somebody.

GALYA

That's absolutely so!

ALEKSEI

Does that mean that I must despise ordinary mortals?

VADIM

I know as well as you how we must treat simple people. But there
is work and work, and I certainly feel more respect for Professor
Averin, Pyotr Ivanovich than for our janitress, Klava, although
I treat her correctly.

ANASTASIA EFREMOVNA

Vadya is absolutely right: you must all think both about your
doctorate, and your professions as professors.

VADIM

It's not so much a matter of our ultimate professions, Anastasia
Efremovna. But if we don't aim high now, reach out for something
big—we'll remain nobodies.

KATYA

What about those who have less ability?

VADIM

In addition to ability there are such things as will-power,
determination to reach one's goal. It seems to me that's what
we've been taught at school and in the Komsomol organization.

AFANASY

That's true.

VADIM

Only with some, it all went in one ear and out the other. I remembered—
and I've chosen a high goal. I'm enrolling at the Institute of
Foreign Trade, and what's more, I don't intend to get buried
later in some minor job at the Ministry.

ANDREI

Yes, you will be the ultimate and most authoritative representative
of the etcetera, etcetera. . . Right?

VADIM

Why not? In any case, I'd like to visit France, Italy, England,
even America. . .*

ANDREI

Tell me, Valya—and will you also spy for some foreign power?

VADIM

Fool!

ANASTASIA EFREMOVNA

Everything is a joke to you, but just wait: Vadya will get a major
position—he'll have an apartment, a high salary. . .

VADIM

(Unctiously) The material rewards don't interest me,
Anastasia Efremovna.

ANASTASIA EFREMOVNA

You're still a youngster, Vadya, but sooner or later you'll all have
to think about apartments, about money, and a family. . .

VADIM

(To ANDREI) You are just lazy. Take me—I'm slaving away at Italian,
French—English, I already know well. All this isn't easy, you know.

ANDREI

Well, you are a genuine genius. You even have already adopted
a diplomat's mannerisms for yourself.

VADIM

Pointing to ANDREI.

More of his mordant irony! I suppose he is referring to my sitting
up straight in a chair instead of sprawling like a frog, *(the sleepy*

---

*As in the case of Vadim, it is the secret hope of many young Soviet careerists to
choose a calling that offers opportunities for travel abroad. They are generally
criticised, even despised by socially dedicated people.

VADIM (Cont.)

AFANASY sits up even straighter) to my greeting people courteously to my refusing to rush about school corridors as if my tail was on fire. . . I chew instead of chomp, I keep my hair combed. . . *(AFANASY tries to smooth his cowlick)* all this evokes flashes of humor in our Andrei. *(To ANDREI)* And what generates this subtle humor? —an urge to justify your own slouchy ways and indifference to everything. Yes, Yes! To learn to sit at the dinner table properly, to offer one's seat to a woman, to help her—all this one must learn, and to learn—means to make an effort!

ANDREI

He has memorized the book *Good Poise*—and lent it to me to read. It hasn't helped.

VADIM

It's an awful book—it's dated. But it would do no harm to bring it up-to-date. There are many who could benefit. . .

ANASTASIA EFREMOVNA

You're smart, Vadim—smart! *(To ANDREI)* Listen to him!

AFANASY

Your ideas are good, there's no denying it. But what am I to do with my hair? It sticks up naturally. Do I have to shave it off?

VADIM

I wasn't speaking about you.

AFANASY

Why not? There was a great deal that applies to me.

GALYA

You are right, Vadim. To be just some kind of agronomist is the life goal of a limited person.

ALEKSEI

I'd consider him a fool who, as a beginning writer, went around saying, "I'll be another Lev Tolstoy!"

VADIM

But he can hope for this—he can and he must!

ALEKSEI

Maybe—secretly.

AFANASY

(Sensing trouble, to ALEKSEI) Be careful. . .

KATYA

Aleksei is right. I think there are certain feelings, high aspirations, which must be guarded in secret. You dream, you hope, quietly. . . then you sort of forget about it! You hope for such a dream to come true as you would for some great happiness which, maybe, you'll never experience. . . But if a soldier appeared before his platoon and suddenly proclaimed out loud: "I want to become a general!. . ." It would be ridiculous. . .wouldn't it?

ALEKSEI

Yes, they'd consider him abnormal, give him a psychiatric examination, and an honorable discharge.

ANDREI

Vadya, look out—I think they've got you cornered.

VADIM

It's amazing what devices people use to avoid the truth! I see, fine intentions must be held in deep secrecy. . .so deep that they're sometimes unnoticeable. A particularly provincial theory. . .

ALEKSEI

There is also the kind of device—very fashionable—to build high fences with high-falutin words, but what is behind those fences?— who knows? Probably not much.

VADIM

So, get up on your toes and take a good look if you are curious.

GALYA

Alyosha, do take a look. But be careful, he'll club you over the head with some heavy quotations!

ALEKSEI

And when a person boasts about himself—I do this, I do that— that's also suspicious. . .

VADIM

(To ALEKSEI) Yours are dangerous ideas. . .

AFANASY

Watch out for that accusation!

VADIM

Dangerous! As it is Andrei is badly confused about the most elementary things in life. I started this discussion for his benefit. He can lose his way without your help, what he needs is clarification.

ANDREI

Vadya, you are my only beacon light! Shine on!

ANASTASIA EFREMOVNA

Really, Alyosha, you might keep your thoughts to yourself.

ALEKSEI

Aunt Nastya, I'm not defending Andrei—he does have some sawdust in his head, but. . .

ANASTASIA EFREMOVNA

What do you mean, sawdust? It's not your business to find fault with him! I don't see anything so bad about him. First of all, Andriushka has good potential—he must strive exactly the way Vadim says.

PYOTR IVANOVICH

(Entering) Nasten'ka, give Nikolai Afanasievich and me a bite to eat. *He exits.*

ANASTASIA EFREMOVNA

(Eagerly) Is Nikolai Afanasievich here? At last! *She exits.*

VADIM

Oh, all right—let's go swimming. *(To ANDREI)* It's useless to argue with you. Damn it, we get excited, quarrel—and why? These are wild days—we think that we are deciding our futures. But why bother? All doors are open to us—every institute—all we need to do is enter.

AFANASY

There's a popular saying, you know: "first pass the entrance exam."

VADIM

That can't be helped. It's a lottery one has to play. *(To ALEKSEI)* I understand school was tough for you, and for very honorable reasons—Andrei has told me about it. But one can't outline one's life history to the Admissions Committee—so naturally you are nervous, on edge. . .

GALYA

Vadim, you're not telling it like it is. You do well in your study of foreign languages, you enjoy it, but in other subjects. . .

VADIM

Look, I have outgrown my childhood, and if I am convinced that in
my chosen profession I'll have no use for certain school subjects,
I have the right to be less serious about them.

GALYA

No, you're lying to us—and to yourself. If you had to compete
like the rest of us, you wouldn't feel so smug. You know very
well that your father will probably make a phone call, and for
you a special little door will open.

KATYA

(Astonished) And they will admit him?!

ANDREI

You sure are naive!. . .

GALYA

They'll hardly refuse Academician Rosvalov. As an exception. . .
they'll somehow manage. . .

AFANASY

Hey!. . . You mean he'll be accepted without taking the entrance?!

GALYA

Yes—in a sort of round about way. By diplomatic dispensation. . .

ALEKSEI

This means that some of those who do take the competitive exams
will be doing it in vain—one place will already be taken. Maybe
ten people are now working their heads off for that place!

VADIM

Don't worry, you and I are interested in different schools. You
are not competing with me.

ANDREI

Galka, Alyosha—you're wrong about this! To have a loophole is a
a great thing! Ha! If only someone would put in a good word for me!
I'd go down on my knees, prostrate myself before him! I'd barter
my honor and conscience!. . . Ah-h-h. . . Enough! Let's go.

VADIM

(To ALEKSEI in a conciliatory tone) Of course there is an element
of deception in all this, but which of you would swear that he'd refuse a
similar opportunity? Only say it simply, without high-flown words.

KATYA

It's a rotten business. . .but tempting. . .

AFANASY

(To KATYA) Then what are you waiting for? Your father is famous—ask him to write you a little letter to the right person.

VADIM

Let's go, friends.

ANDREI

Come on. *(To ALEKSEI)* Why do you look so sad?

ALEKSEI

(Suddenly shouts furiously at VADIM) "Will power!" "Determination!" "The Komsomol has taught us!" Why do you besmirch such good words?

VADIM

Have you gone mad, or what?

ALEKSEI

(In the same vein) "All doors are open!" "We are entering upon life!" Then why creep into it through the back door?

VADIM

What do you mean, "back door"?

ALEKSEI

(Still furious) You don't un-der-stand? When it suits you, you are shrewd—when not, you are as innocent as a saint. . .

VADIM

Do you know what is really behind your nasty words?

ALEKSEI

What?

VADIM

The meanest little. . .

ALEKSEI

Go on—say it!

VADIM

What for? You know, yourself. . .

ALEKSEI

Are you afraid to say it?

VADIM

I have no desire to insult you. . .

ALEKSEI

You were going to say, "The meanest little emotion". . . You mean envy?

ANDREI

Alyoshka, Alyoshka, don't turn him into a cause—a social evil. He's an exceptional case.

ALEKSEI

(To VADIM, still in the same vein) You have no decency, no honor. You're a cheat!

VADIM

(Almost speechless) I. . .me. . .I am. . . *(Is about to strike him)*

ALEKSEI

Go ahead, hit me! Go on! You swine!

KATYA

Aleksei, stop it!—that's not the way.

AFANASY

In a case like this, it is. The same rules must apply to everyone. If there is a competition, it should apply to all—if there's a line, no one must push his way ahead out of turn.

ALEKSEI

(To VADIM) Swine! Cheat!

VADIM

You are all hypocrites! I am sure—if you had the possibility, you would, as Andriusha said, prostrate yourselves! You think you wouldn't? *No one answers him. He exits.*

GALYA

(To ALEKSEI) You ought to thank *me*. . .

ALEKSEI

For what?

GALYA

Helped you climb up on that fence, to take a good look. Didn't I? *She exits.*

AFANASY

(Wearily pulling himself up) Come, Katya, let's go. *(Picks up his baggage)* Off to Mozhaisk, to Aunt Liuba.

KATYA

But you said—Aunt Vera!

AFANASY

I'm getting all the relatives mixed up.

KATYA and AFANASY wave good-bye and exit.

ANDREI and ALEKSEI exit. ARKADY enters, throws himself on his couch. He looks despondent.

ANASTASIA EFREMOVNA

What's the matter? What are you doing here at this time of day? Why aren't you at the theatre?

ARKADY

I quit. I gave in my resignation.

ANASTASIA EFREMOVNA

Quit? Why did you do a thing like that? Why? How could you? What will you do with yourself? After all you're no longer seventeen. . . Oh, Arkasha! *(ARKADY is silent)* But don't look so lost. . .

MASHA

(Entering) Hello, Anastasia Efremovna.

ANASTASIA EFREMOVNA

(Coldly) Hello.

MASHA

I'll only be a minute.

ANASTASIA EFREMOVNA

Suit yourself. . .

She exits.

MASHA

Hello, Arkady. *(ARKADY is silent)* At least you are consistent. Not a word from you—before or now.

ARKADY

(Casually) Hi.

MASHA

Thank you! For two weeks now I kept hoping that you would come, apologize. . . I even looked for excuses for you—he's busy at the theatre, maybe he got sick. . . Unfortunately, you are well. . . I brought these. . . Maybe you'll soon meet another girl and you would not want me to keep this "evidence." *(She unwraps a package, from which she takes a packet of letters and hands them to ARKADY. In a business-like tone)* This—the first year, when you were in Kiev and Poltava, touring. This—when I was South, on vacation. These—from Vladivostok, Khabarovsk. . . Messages for me when I was in the hospital. . . These are tapes, negatives which I developed, and photographs. And all kinds of little mementos—for New Year's, birthdays, Woman's Day *(She nervously drops several of the gifts and small knick-knacks)* Oh, they've scattered!. . . *(Bends down and takes too long to gather the things, trying to get her emotions under control. She finally stands up, puts the things on the table)* That's all. *(She is about to leave, smiles wryly)* No, don't bother to see me to the door.
ANDREI and ALEKSEI enter.

ANDREI

Hello, Masha. I want you to meet our guest.

MASHA

Hello.

ANDREI

This is our cousin, Aleksei.

MASHA

(Shaking hands with ALEKSEI, routinely) Have you been here long? Where are you from?

ALEKSEI

From near Irkutsk.

ANDREI

He arrived the day you were here last.

MASHA

(Withdrawn) Ah!. . . *(She is about to leave)*

ANDREI

Are you upset?

MASHA

Why?

ANDREI

What do you mean—why? Don't you care?

MASHA

About what?

ANDREI

(Pointing to ARKADY) That he left the theatre!

MASHA

Left?

ANDREI

Didn't he tell you?

MASHA

Arkasha, wasn't it today that you did the reading?

ARKADY

Yes.

MASHA goes to ARKADY. The entire ensuing scene is observed by ANDREI and ALEKSEI in stunned silence—they glance at each other at times, afraid to breathe.

MASHA

(With great tenderness and compassion) I've just been in Sokol'niki Park. . .walking around. . .to familiar spots. . .that bench is broken, only the frame is left. . . Oh! It's so lovely there. . .so quiet. The same fat woman has the ice cream stand. Only, the pavilion is now painted blue. Let's go there this evening, have supper at the restaurant. . .I have some money—saved it up for a dress. Let's blow it! What do you say? We've been planning to go out on the town for a long time. Or let's just walk around the streets. You know, we must walk and walk. . .where there are lots of people. . . yes, people. . . It makes you feel less anxious—there are all kinds of reassuring noises around you. . . I love you very much. . .very! No, don't say anything. We'll go out and I'll do the talking—I'll tell you lots of things about myself that you don't know. . . You needn't say anything—you needn't bother to explain anything. . . For the past four years I've hardly told you anything, but I have so much. . .so much!. . . Come, get up! *(She raises ARKADY)* Don't bother about a tie—you'll feel freer without one. . . There, let's walk to Sokol'niki along Gorky Street, then Kirovskaya, past the railroad stations. . .

MASHA, her arm around ARKADY, leads him out of the room. ANDREI and ALEKSEI stand riveted.

ANDREI

They teach us a lot in school, and everything is more or less clear.
Then you stumble on a real life situation—and you understand
absolutely zero.

ALEKSEI

I agree.

ANDREI

At least that's one good mark to my credit.
ANASTASIA EFREMOVNA enters and hands ANDREI a note.

ANDREI

Who's this from?

ANASTASIA EFREMOVNA

It's for the Dean. Go and thank Nikolai Afanasievich. Now, thank
God, I don't need to worry about *you* any more! But where is Arkady?

ANDREI

He left with Masha.

ANASTASIA EFREMOVNA

What a weakling! Now go and thank Nikolai Afanasievich.
She exits. ANDREI reads the note.

ANDREI

You may count me in—at the Bauman Institute. *(ALEKSEI says
nothing)* Do you think it's okay for people like Vadim but not
for the likes of us?. . . All right! *(He puts the note in his pocket)*
Phew! My heart is going pitter-patter. . . *(Looks at ALEKSEI for
his reaction)* All right, I'll think it over. . . *(ALEKSEI turns away
from him, goes to the door)* Where are you off to?

ALEKSEI

To take a walk.

ANDREI

I'm coming with you. You understand. . .

ALEKSEI

Why do you hang on? We're not Siamese twins, you and I.
Leave me alone.

ANDREI

Now you are furious.

ALEKSEI

Suddenly turns on ANDREI, grabs at the Komsomol pin on ANDREI'S shirt.
Take that off! What do you need it for?

ANDREI

(Pushing ALEKSEI away) Take it easy—I'm not Vadim!

ANASTASIA EFREMOVNA

(Entering) Andriusha, Nikolai Afanasievich is leaving—hurry!

ANDREI

I'm going to take this note to the newspaper.

ANASTASIA EFREMOVNA

Stop talking nonsense!

ANDREI

I'm really going to do it.

ANASTASIA EFREMOVNA

Don't you dare make a joke of it, do you hear!

ANDREI

I'm not joking.

ANASTASIA EFREMOVNA

There's nothing funny about it. Give me back the note.

ANDREI

No.

ANASTASIA EFREMOVNA

I'll call your father.

ANDREI

Go ahead and call him.

ANASTASIA EFREMOVNA

Do you realize what you are doing! *(To ALEKSEI)* He learned this from you. You have taught him. . .

ANDREI

No one "taught" me.

ANASTASIA EFREMOVNA

I don't believe it—you wouldn't have enough sense. . . *(To ALEKSEI)*
You came here to stay with us—so, please, respect our way of
doing things. We sheltered you. . .

ANDREI

What are you saying? There you go! You dredged up some
damned word—"sheltered!" No one has "sheltered" him. He
came—and that's all!

ALEKSEI

Aunt Nastya, I didn't say anything to him—about the note. . .

ANASTASIA EFREMOVNA

You are a bad influence—bad! Don't forget that to confuse a
creature like him—is doing him no favor. *(Calls)* Petya!. . .
She exits.

ANDREI

So, did I make the right decision? Yes? *(ALEKSEI says nothing)*
Let the Vadim's play that game. . .

ALEKSEI

Give back the note.

ANDREI

What?

ALEKSEI

I say, give it back.

ANDREI

I won't!

ALEKSEI

Do you hear me?!

ANDREI

The hell with you!

ALEKSEI

(Moving toward ANDREI manacingly) I say, give it back!!

ANDREI

What's with you? I said—I won't!

ANDREI (Cont.)

ALEKSEI grabs ANDREI and they struggle. ALEKSEI takes the note by force, twisting ANDREI'S arm. ANDREI cries out.
Mama!

ANASTASIA EFREMOVNA

(Comes running in) Stop that at once! Aleksei, let go of him! I must ask you to leave. Go away—wherever you wish—but get out of here!!

PYTOR IVANOVICH

(Entering, to his wife) Why did you do it? So, while I was looking in the closet for a manuscript you made Nikolai Afanasievich. . .

ANDREI

Made him!

PYTOR IVANOVICH

Don't you dare say anything against him! Will any of you become such a scholar? Hardly!

ANASTASIA EFREMOVNA

Petya, I. . .

PYTOR IVANOVICH

Did you cry in front of him? You did—didn't you? *(ANASTASIA EFREMOVNA is silent)* Go at once and apologize. Do you hear?
ANASTASIA EFREMOVNA and PYTOR IVANOVICH start to exit.

ANDREI

(To his parents) Here, take your note.

PYTOR IVANOVICH

(Turning back, speaks from doorway) You may keep it as a souvenir. . . "I'll take it to the newspaper"! You trash! If you studied properly your mother would not go out of her mind worrying about your future. You brought her to it. You're to blame!
He exits, followed by ANASTASIA EFREMOVNA.

ANDREI

You see—they bungled it, now they are all down on me. *(He tears up the note)*

ALEKSEI

I'm leaving this place, tomorrow.

ANDREI

Oh, yes? And leave me here for them to plague me to death?
You're a fine one!

ALEKSEI

What do I have to do with it?

ANDREI

Listen to him—the soul of innocence! If not for you, I would
probably have taken the note, and everything would have been
finished and done with. Now. . . Oh, hell!—three more days before
exams—and now no crutch to lean on. . . Well, I'm not about to
shed any tears.

Curtain

The Young Graduates   *Scene Two*

> *The same as Act I—the living-dining room. No one is in the room.*

ANASTASIA EFREMOVNA

(Enters, calling) Arkady!. . .Arkasha!. . .

PYTOR IVANOVICH

(Coming in from his study) There's no one else home.

ANASTASIA EFREMOVNA

Arkady hasn't been back?

PYTOR IVANOVICH

No, where did he go?

ANASTASIA EFREMOVNA

On some excursion boat—along the canal—with Masha, of course.
He's surprisingly casual about his situation! Oh, I'm so tired.
(She sits down) Have been running around to all the schools.
Andrei will probably be able to enroll at the Fishing Institute.

PYTOR IVANOVICH

But he's taking his examination today. He just left.

ANASTASIA EFREMOVNA

He'll never make it at the Bauman—he has one B and will probably
end up with another. And they will not accept anyone with two
B's. . . I found that out today. It's appalling—the rules they
make these days.

PYTOR IVANOVICH

But why the Fishing?. . .

ANASTASIA EFREMOVNA

Where else?

PYTOR IVANOVICH

What if he objects?

ANASTASIA EFREMOVNA

When he flunks, he'll have to settle for what he can get. He
must continue his education, mustn't he? Of course, the business
with the note was very embarrassing, but if. . .

PYTOR IVANOVICH

Forget it, Nastya.

ANASTASIA EFREMOVNA

Is Nikolai Afanasievich in better health now?

PYTOR IVANOVICH

Somewhat. But he had a quarrel with his son—Vadim asked him to phone the Institute of Foreign Trade in his behalf—Nikolai Afanasievich almost hit him.

ANASTASIA EFREMOVNA

How awful!

PYTOR IVANOVICH

It certainly is—when your son grows up to be a scoundrel. . .

ANASTASIA EFREMOVNA

I suppose Alyosha will be living in student housing—in the outskirts.

PYTOR IVANOVICH

Aleksei will stay right here. He's a quiet fellow, steady, and Andrei can only benefit from his living with us.

ANASTASIA EFREMOVNA

(*Smiling sarcastically*) Of course. . .

PYTOR IVANOVICH

Why do you smile that way?

ANASTASIA EFREMOVNA

He's a quiet one, you say? The quiet Alyosha is already after girls—Galina, for example.

PYTOR IVANOVICH

Which Galina?

ANASTASIA EFREMOVNA

Davidova, the daughter of the National Artist—the soprano at the Bol'shoi Opera.

PYTOR IVANOVICH

So what?

ANASTASIA EFREMOVNA

Andriusha fancies her, she's an interesting girl. . . But our Andriusha just winces and says nothing. . .not an ounce of pride in that boy.

Enter KATYA and AFANASY. He still has his baggage. They greet the AVERINS.

KATYA

Alyosha isn't back yet?

ANASTASIA EFREMOVNA

No.

KATYA

And Andriusha?

ANASTASIA EFREMOVNA

He's not back either.

AFANASY

Then excuse us.
KATYA and AFANASY turn to leave.

PYTOR IVANOVICH

Why don't you wait for them? They'll probably appear soon.

ANASTASIA EFREMOVNA

Have a seat.
KATYA and AFANASY sit down.

PYTOR IVANOVICH

Have you been taking the examinations?

AFANASY

We are.

PYTOR IVANOVICH

Are you doing well? How is it going?

KATYA

Well enough.

PYTOR IVANOVICH

You expect to get in?

AFANASY

It looks like it.

PYTOR IVANOVICH

That's the way. *(To his wife)* You see, some make it.

ANASTASIA EFREMOVNA

Petya, you seem to be blaming me?. . .

PYTOR IVANOVICH does not answer. Goes off to his study,
ANASTASIA EFREMOVNA following him.

Don't worry. If worse comes to worst he can enter the Fishing Institute.
She exits.

AFANASY

Aleksei shouldn't have stayed here.

KATYA

Where else? You are lucky—a relative on every street.

AFANASY

Not quite. . .

KATYA

You ought to fix him up with one of them.

AFANASY

Impossible. Besides, he has one B and will likely get another.
That means good-bye to the Agronomy Academy and "Hello,
Mama, I'm back."

KATYA

Oh, dry up! What a thing to say!

AFANASY

I wouldn't mind drying up if it helped him any. He's had enough
trouble—and now Galina's on the make for him.

KATYA

You mean it?!

AFANASY

I saw how she looked at him when he was having it out with Vadim.

KATYA

How did she look at him? How?

AFANASY

The same looks you give him—only. . .more dynamic.

KATYA

I dropped by here yesterday, they told me he had gone with her
to the Museum of History.

AFANASY

Yes—"history". . . They're writing their own. . .

KATYA

I don't believe it! Andrei is his cousin, and he knows that Andrei and Galya. . .

AFANASY

In such matters the status of a relative loses its traditional importance. You've read enough novels to know that.

KATYA

And what about me? Alyosha knows that I. . .

AFANASY

Did you tell him?

KATYA

How can you even ask such a question? I'd rather die! But he's not blind—he can see.
ALEKSEI and GALYA arrive. ANASTASIA EFREMOVNA enters from another room, at the sound of the door.

ANASTASIA EFREMOVNA

Is that Andriusha?. . . Oh, it's you, Alyosha—how did it go?

ALEKSEI

All is well, Aunt Nastya.

ANASTASIA EFREMOVNA

Did you get an A?

ALEKSEI

An A.

ANASTASIA EFREMOVNA

Congratulations. We should wire Olya—tell her the good news. . . Call me when Andriusha comes, will you?
She exits.

GALYA

(To ALEKSEI) You're doing brilliantly.

KATYA

Not so brilliantly—he got a B in his written.

GALYA

How awful! So smart and then—ay, ay, ay!

ALEKSEI

She'd love it if I failed.

GALYA

Yes, very much. It would be fascinating to see you come down
a peg or two.

ALEKSEI

Is that why you came to the Academy?

KATYA

(To GALYA) Did you go to meet him there?

GALYA

It's Alyosha's overworked imagination that made him think so.
I passed the place on my way home—I live nearby. *(Admiring
herself in the mirror, to KATYA)* Do you like this style?

ALEKSEI

Listen, Galya—couldn't you choose a more fascinating topic?

GALYA

Maybe I could. *(To AFANASY)* Afanasy, if I don't scare you, come
along with me. I'd like to ask you two or three questions.

AFANASY

Why should I be scared—you are not a shark and I am not a fish.
AFANASY and GALYA go off to ANDREI'S room.

KATYA

She isn't very pleasant—is she?

ALEKSEI

She poses, puts on airs and imagines herself to be very special.

KATYA

And Afanasy has decided you like her.

ALEKSEI

Afanasy? How does he know?

KATYA

(Trying to laugh it off) Says he read it in your eyes. What a psychologist! But you don't like her, do you? You don't. . .

ALEKSEI

I like her.

KATYA

You do? A lot?

ALEKSEI

A lot.

KATYA

What about me, Alyosha?

ALEKSEI

What about you?

KATYA

But I've loved you. . .for a long, long time. . .

ALEKSEI

(Taken aback) You have?—for how long?

KATYA

Since I was five.

ALEKSEI

You mustn't. . .

KATYA

W-why? *(She can't hold back her tears)*

ALEKSEI

That's why. . . Stop crying. . . You are nice. . . You are very nice. . . But, you understand. . . *(Lost for words)* Oh, what a melodrama! Why are you crying? What have I done? Don't. . .

KATYA

I'm homesick. I want to go home.

ALEKSEI

Stop it. One more exam and you are in. Get hold of yourself! We— are friends. Yes—good friends. Oh!. . . *(Holds his head in both hands, can't find the words that would console KATYA)*

AFANASY

(Entering, to ALEKSEI) She asked me for your life history. Should I tell her? *(Notices the strained situation between ALEKSEI and KATYA)* Alyosha, you look as if you could use a bit of soap and water—after the exam—you have ink all over your hands.

ALEKSEI

Right.
He goes off.

AFANASY

He didn't know?

KATYA

(Resentful) No, that's not true. He knew. . . It's impossible that a person wouldn't see. . .

AFANASY

It's possible.

KATYA

No, no, it isn't.

AFANASY

I tell you—it happens.

KATYA

How do you know?

AFANASY

You can take my word for it—I've been the victim. . .

KATYA

Not noticing what he's hinting at. Wiping her tears.
I shouldn't carry on like this. How stupid. . .

AFANASY

Never mind, have a cry. . . That's the way to say good-bye—to your childhood.
ALEKSEI returns.

KATYA

Trying to make casual talk
Alyosha, why didn't you tell Anastasia Efremovna you only got a B?

ALEKSEI

It would have made her too happy.
Enter ANDREI, in an exuberant mood.

ANDREI

Who else is home?
Enter ANASTASIA EFREMOVNA.

ANASTASIA EFREMOVNA

So, Andriusha. . .?

ANDREI

I flunked. But good! Didn't answer a single question. Zero.
The end!

ANASTASIA EFREMOVNA

What did I tell you! That's terrible!
ALEKSEI, KATYA, AFANASY all speak at the same time.

ALEKSEI

But you knew your stuff pretty well.

KATYA

Ay-ay-ay!

AFANASY

Eh! What a disgusting business!

ANDREI

Pointing to his room, speaks like an undertaker's assistant.
All the funeral wreaths and flowers go into that room over there.

ANASTASIA EFREMOVNA

What will happen now?

ALEKSEI

I'll hang myself.

ANASTASIA EFREMOVNA

(Calling) Petya! Petya!
Enter PYTOR IVANOVICH.
Of course, he failed.

PYTOR IVANOVICH

(To ANDREI) What do you intend to do now?

ANDREI

I don't know.

PYTOR IVANOVICH

Still?. . . *(ANDREI spreads his arms in a gesture of perplexity)*
Aren't you embarrassed before your friends? *(Pointing to ALEKSEI,
KATYA, AFANASY, working himself up)* They travelled hundreds
of miles to try for the best schools, they subsist here on meager
funds—at times not having enough to eat, or a comfortable place
to sleep. . . And you—what do you lack?

ANASTASIA EFREMOVNA

Good sense.

PYTOR IVANOVICH

Your mother says there is a possibility for you at the Fishing
Institute—you'll enroll there.

ANDREI

Why the Fishing?

ANASTASIA EFREMOVNA

That's the last resort—I've been everywhere.

ANDREI

I'm not interested in the creatures of the sea.

PYTOR IVANOVICH

We are not asking you whether you are interested—you'll go there
whether you want to or not.

ANASTASIA EFREMOVNA

We are thinking of your happiness, Andriusha, we want you to be
somebody—so we don't intend to pay any attention to your whims.
Next year you can transfer to another school—if you get wiser,
that is.

PYTOR IVANOVICH

What's wrong with you?—don't you appreciate the importance of
an education in our times?

ANDREI

(To his father, boldly) When you applied to the Geographic
Institute did you consider a fishing school as an alternative?

ANASTASIA EFREMOVNA

Don't you speak that way to your father!

PYTOR IVANOVICH

Before enrolling anywhere I worked four years with a geological expedition. I began with them as a laborer. I strived for my chosen profession—and succeeded. . .

ANDREI

In the same vein as before.

But imagine—if at that time you had started at a fishing school, or a nutrition institute, a polytechnic—what would you be now? The scholar you are? Not on your life! Besides, you keep saying there are now far too many people in the sciences—that lots of them don't care about knowledge, all they care about is creature comforts—good earnings through their professions. So, where do such people come from? And all of them have a higher education. I think they are all Vadim types—careerists. . .

ANASTASIA EFREMOVNA

(Snapping at ANDREI) You're an idealist, you're stupid, and you don't understand a thing about life.

ANDREI

(Shouting) I don't want to understand life the way you do.

ANASTASIA EFREMOVNA

Petya, he's drunk.

ANDREI

(To his mother) I'm as sober as you are. I don't drink and don't intend to—ever. But were I to become what you call a "somebody"— I'd take to the bottle for sure. I'm warning you!

VADIM

(Entering, to ANDREI) Let me have my physics notes.

ANDREI

Aha! Now you need the exact sciences.

VADIM

It's you and your damn Alyosha who scared my father. . . The old man has lost his courage. . .

ANDREI

So the door to the Foreign Trade Institute is not that open for you after all—not even a chink.

VADIM

It's too soon for you to gloat—I am doing well in the exams so far.

ANDREI

(Sarcastically) Good for you. Honest labor will be rewarded!

VADIM

TO ANASTASIA EFREMOVNA, insolently.
Did you *have* to beg my father for a note—and even shed a tear while you were at it?!

ANASTASIA EFREMOVNA

(Shocked) Vadya!

ANDREI

Don't you dare talk that way to my mother. Get out of here!

VADIM

Give me my notes.

ANDREI

Pushing VADIM roughly into the hall and out the door.
Out, out! You wait down below—I'll throw them down to you through the window.
He returns and goes through living-dining room to his own room to get the notes.

ANASTASIA EFREMOVNA

(To KATYA and AFANASY) You'd better go now—come back another time. . .tomorrow. . .

AFANASY

(Picking up his baggage) Yes, they are waiting for me. . .Uncle Lyova. . .
He and KATYA leave. ANDREI rushes from his room to the balcony with the notes. Shouts down.

ANDREI

Vadya, here—accept my assurances of my deepest respect, signed, Andrei Petrovich Averin. *(Throws down the notes)* Hope you flunk! *(Turns around and notices that there is no one in the room now except his father, mother, and ALEKSEI. Sees that the confrontation will continue.)*

ANASTASIA EFREMOVNA

Now what?

PYTOR IVANOVICH

Andrei, you are free to do what you want. Make up your own mind.

ANDREI

(Incredulous) What?!
PYTOR IVANOVICH goes off to his study.

ANDREI

To ALEKSEI, not daring to believe that he's finally been liberated
How am I to interpret that? What did he mean?
Enter MASHA and ARKADY. He is covered with mud. Both look very happy. She carries a bouquet of flowers.

ANASTASIA EFREMOVNA

Arkasha, what in the world happened to you?

MASHA

(Laughs) He's not hurt, just muddy. We got caught in a downpour, started to run. . .there was mud all around. . .he carried me over the puddles, slipped. . .and look at him.

ARKADY

Yes and you know, she kept hiding from me in the subway—that's the thanks I got. *(Laughs)*

MASHA

I was ashamed to be seen with such a disgraceful-looking character.

ANASTASIA EFREMOVNA

Arkasha, I'm amazed at your cheerfulness: you go off on boat rides. . . You'd do better to think about the future.

ARKADY

I do. I think about it all the time.

ANASTASIA EFREMOVNA

I haven't noticed it. Today a boat ride, yesterday a dog show. . .

ARKADY

An amazing show—dogs as large as hippopotami!

MASHA

Arkady is tired, Anastasia Efremovna. He should take a rest.

ANASTASIA EFREMOVNA

I doubt that it's from overwork at the theatre.

MASHA

I mean he's tired of thinking about the same thing over and over. He'd like to look around, see what else is going on.

ANASTASIA EFREMOVNA

(Crossly) All right—do what you want—even fly to the moon—
but look out!. . .
She goes off, almost in tears.

ARKADY

Mama! Mama! *(To MASHA)* I'm going to change.
He goes to his room.

ANDREI

Mother is upset about me.

MASHA

What happened?

ANDREI

I failed the exams.

MASHA

Serves you right.

ANDREI

Straight from the shoulder and to my midriff! *(To ALEKSEI)*
Did you hear her? *(To MASHA)* Suppose I got into a school,
finished my studies—and then ended up like Arkasha. . .

MASHA

(Exploding) What do you want of him? To be a genius? To play
only leading roles? Aren't you all ashamed to keep hitting him
where it hurts most! *You* can at least show some sympathy!

ANDREI

(Taken aback) Masha, I don't care what size acting star he is, if only
he didn't belittle himself that way. Why does he do it?

MASHA

Because you and the rest of the family already take him for a
failure. If a person isn't a genius, isn't famous—does he have
no right to live?. . . Do you know, the Chief Director called
him yesterday—and asked him to withdraw his resignation.
Begged him! Arkady is talented, yes! Only he is a slow developer,
it's more difficult for him. . . But all of you with your impatience
bear down on him. So he decided to take a broad jump before
he was ready, and failed—didn't get that important part. So,
he had a tantrum and decided to give it all up. He felt mean about
it. And meanness can kill everything in a person, even talent.

ANDREI

You, too, got mean once.

MASHA

Who told you?

ANDREI

You hoped to become a concert pianist—and didn't make it.

MASHA

You're wrong—it all happened altogether differently.

ANDREI

How?

MASHA

In a most prosaic way—I was skating, fell, and broke two fingers—never could bend them fully again.

ANDREI

Rotten luck! And you can't play at all?

MASHA

I don't know. I haven't tried since it happened. At the time, I too, felt: either world fame or nothing. I later learned to settle for something else. I tell you—art is cruel! It lures, then puts every aspiring artist in his place—without mercy.
Enter ARKADY, in clean clothes.

ANDREI

Arkasha, why haven't you married Masha yet?

ARKADY

What?!

MASHA

Andrushka!

ANDREI

If I were a little older, I swear I'd marry you myself.

MASHA

Isn't he fresh! What makes you think I'd marry you? *(Handing half of her flowers to ANDREI)* Here, please put these on Arkady's table.
MASHA and ARKADY leave.

ANDREI

Maybe I shouldn't have babbled about them getting married.

ALEKSEI

Everyone usually forgives you for your idiocies.

ANDREI

Alyosha—I didn't take the exams today.

ALEKSEI

Did you reschedule them?

ANDREI

No. I just walked out.

ALEKSEI

Why?

ANDREI

I come to the school. There's a mob of "aspirants"—as usual.
Everyone's eyes are bleary from cramming and tense with worry.
And me? I couldn't care less. Next I see a pitiful looking girl
standing in a corner. Too thin, with wispy blond hair in little
braids the width of my finger. Dressed so-so, no frills whatever.
She stands there, pale and frightened hugging her books and
mumbling something to herself—maybe still memorizing something,
or praying. . . I couldn't tell. I tell you, the sight of her depressed
me, and I thought to myself, what business have I to be here—
maybe I'd do her out of a place. I don't give a damn—but it
means everything to her. . .and to so many others, too. So I
turned around and left. That was dumb, wasn't it?

ALEKSEI

What do you plan to do instead?

ANDREI

There you go—you, too—asking the same idiotic question! You
see, I don't know, but this is what I believe—everyone has his
particular aptitude.

ALEKSEI

So?

ANDREI

Well, I mean his proper niche—the only thing that's right for
him. You find it, and all your energies well up to the surface. You
give it all you've got. You are satisfied with life, others like
you and value you. It's most important to find that special niche.
Take you—you feel where yours is, and so do others. But me—I

ANDREI (Cont.)

have no idea. None. But it's somewhere. I want to find it. A
desired vocation, a calling is probably a magnet to that niche.
What do you think?

ALEKSEI

It's something like that.

ANDREI

Almost shouting and pacing nervously, desperately.
And I will find mine! I will! I will!

Curtain

The Young Graduates   *Scene Three*

> *Living-dining room. Late evening. The table is set for tea. Only
> ANASTASIA EFREMOVNA is in the room.*

Enter PYOTR IVANOVICH.

ANASTASIA EFREMOVNA

Alyosha has disappeared. He left this morning to take an exam;
and hasn't been back. Andriusha went to the school—he wasn't
there. Then he and Galya went out to look for him. They kept
coming back here to see if he had returned. Now they are out
searching for him again. Where could he be?

PYOTR IVANOVICH

Perhaps he ran into some people from his home-town.

ANASTASIA EFREMOVNA

Shouldn't we at least call the police?. . . Tea is ready.
PYOTR IVANOVICH sits down at the table. His wife pours him some tea.

PYOTR IVANOVICH

Nastya, Andrei must go to work. He can't just sit around a
whole year.

ANASTASIA EFREMOVNA

Work?! What work can he do? You don't expect him to take a
job at a plant?

PYOTR IVANOVICH

Nothing so terrible about that. Others do.

ANASTASIA EFREMOVNA

He's not strong, Petya.

PYOTR IVANOVICH

I haven't noticed it. You baby him. What are you protecting
him from? You still wash the floors—you don't seem to mind
manual work. . . *(A pause)* There's a letter from Alyosha's
mother. She thanks us for our hospitality to her son, especially
you. Sends her love. The money that we usually send them she
wants us to give to Aleksei.

ANASTASIA EFREMOVNA

Of course, he'll need it for his expenses. Petya, couldn't you
find a spot for Andriusha in some laboratory?
Enter GALYA and ANDREI.

ANDREI

Not back yet?

ANASTASIA EFREMOVNA

No.

GALYA

We went to Katya's—she's passed all her exams, went to the theatre to celebrate. We wanted to find Afanasy but don't know his address.

ANDREI

I keep telling her—calm down, don't go out of your mind, but she keeps insisting—call the missing persons bureau.

GALYA

After all, he's a person.

PYOTR IVANOVICH

She's right.
He rises, goes off to his study.

ANASTASIA EFREMOVNA

Sit down and have some tea.

GALYA

(To ANDREI) In the first place, I'm not going out of my mind. . .

ANDREI

(Seeming to concentrate on pouring tea) And secondly?. . . *(GALYA doesn't answer. He pours tea for her)* Do you like your tea strong, or is it bad for your complexion?

GALYA

Secondly, it's possible that he flunked.

ANDREI

And thirdly, you don't have enough control over your feelings—a weakness of your sex. Here—*(Hands her a glass of tea)*—it will give you some strength.
GALYA is upset and absent-mindedly is about to drink, giving no thought to the tea's temperature.
Let it cool, you'll burn your pretty tongue.

GALYA

(Jumping up) Oh, leave me alone! I'm worried about him as a person—but you wouldn't understand that.

ANDREI

I get it—civic duty—concern for a fellow citizen. . .

GALYA

(Heatedly) All right—if you want me to be frank—first. . .

ANDREI

(With sarcasm) Listen, could you make it short and start with "tenthly"!

GALYA

(Angrily) All right! Twenty-fifthly!. . .

ANDREI

Now you're talking.

GALYA

He doesn't only not care for me, at times he's downright rude, even coarse.

ANDREI

You just imagine it.

GALYA

No, I don't. When you began to like me, I knew it—right away.

ANDREI

I'm a fool—that's why you knew.

GALYA

Oh, can't you ever be serious?

ANDREI

I try.

GALYA

When we discuss important things—generally he's patient, but as soon as we get on personal topics—he goes wild. No, he's less than indifferent about me.

ANDREI

Galochka, would you like me to bring relative calm to your disturbed soul?

GALYA

Again your little jokes?

ANDREI

Unfortunately, this time I'm serious.

GALYA

Go ahead.

ANDREI

Remember the time you asked me what he and I had said about you?

GALYA

(Eagerly) Go on!!

ANDREI

If you keep coaxing that way—I'll start kidding again. *(Suddenly divining what he was going to say, GALYA impulsively kisses ANDREI hard. He pulls away sharply, almost violently)* Don't you dare!

GALYA

What's got into you?

ANDREI

Don't you dare, I tell you! *(Wiping his cheek)* Don't use me as a lightning-rod!—to deflect your fiery passion for another man.

GALYA

Dear Andriusha, don't be so upset.

ANDREI

Upset? Who's upset? You take yourself too seriously—you can't upset me! People like you two are beneath me. The hell with the likes of you—all of you!

GALYA

Andriusha, listen. . .

ANDREI

Don't want to.

GALYA

I just want to say. . . *(ANDREI goes quickly to the piano, sits down and plays Chopsticks loudly enough to drown out GALYA'S voice. GALYA pulls his hands away from the keyboard)* Andrei, let me say a few words. . .

ANDREI

(Calling) Mama!

ANASTASIA EFREMOVNA

(Entering) What is it, Andriusha?

ANDREI

Mom, stay with us a while—we're sort of bored with each other.
(To GALYA) What were you saying?

GALYA

Mischievously, with a straight face, gets on ANASTASIA EFREMOVNA'S favorite topic.

I was suggesting that you enroll next year at a Medical Institute—they accept young men with open arms.*

ANASTASIA EFREMOVNA

(With spontaneous enthusiasm) Of course, medicine—its' a noble profession. You can become a surgeon, an ophthalmologist, a cardiologist. . .or pathologist.

ANDREI

See—you came into the room and right away things are perking.

ANASTASIA EFREMOVNA

Your father says that in the meantime you will have to go to work.

ANDREI

Where?

ANASTASIA EFREMOVNA

We'll find you something, something easy. Petya says there's a possibility of a job at the Botanical Garden.

ANDREI

Where, where?

ANASTASIA EFREMOVNA

In the Botanical Garden, in a laboratory.

ANDREI

(Feigning delight) Oh! That I'd like! I'll cultivate palm trees, orchids—bananas! But, Mom, why in a lab? I want to be a gardener. Ah—that's romantic! A gardener! Tiller of the soil.

ANASTASIA EFREMOVNA

(Laughs at the absurdity of it) And carry water, dig. . .

*The great majority of medical students in the U.S.S.R. are women.

ANDREI

You're an incurable pragmatist, Mom. Maybe I should become
a "pragmatherapist".

From the hall comes the sound of someone entering. GALYA jumps up.

GALYA

Alyoshka?! *(Enter ALEKSEI)* Thank God, you're alive! Where were you?

ALEKSEI

I walked all over Moscow—making up stories—but couldn't
think of a good one.

GALYA

How was the exam?

ALEKSEI

I passed.

ANASTASIA EFREMOVNA

Congratulations! But, please Alyosha, don't disappear that way
again—it's very upsetting. *(Calling)* Petya! Petya! *(She goes off
to tell ALEKSEI'S good news to her husband)*

*ANDREI goes off to his room in a huff, still smarting about
GALYA'S interest in ALEKSEI.*

ALEKSEI

What's eating him?

GALYA

What do you think? You could have gotten run over. . .and generally,
there are plenty of accidents. We went to meet you at the Academy,
looked for you at Katya's. . .

ALEKSEI

Why did you go out with him?

GALYA

I didn't go out with him—he went with me. *(A pause)* It was
crowded in the busses and street cars. . . *(Straightening her dress)*
They messed up my dress.

ALEKSEI

It's attractive.

GALYA

At last you're appreciating something I wear. Do you know—I
make all my dresses. . . My mother is a seamstress in a clothing
factory—she taught me.

ALEKSEI

But you said she was an opera singer.

GALYA

Well, when I met Andrei and Vadim recently—at the prom—they seemed so elite that I invented a different mother—fortunately my real one has the same name as the soprano. I know that was silly! But I do like to sew. Sometimes I stay up half the night—thinking up a style. I feel like an artist. Then I meet you guys and I get nothing but teasing. It even hurts sometimes. But I should remember how narrow you boys are. . .

ALEKSEI

(Going over to GALYA) Galya. . .

GALYA

What?

ALEKSEI

(Standing close to her) Strange—I just met you. . . How I hate to leave now!

GALYA

Where are you going?

ALEKSEI

All right—one confession deserves another—I failed today's exam.

GALYA

It's not true!

ALEKSEI

I wouldn't kid about something like that.

GALYA

But you said. . .

ALEKSEI

I didn't want to admit it in front of you—when they were around. I feel terrible about it—you can see it in my face, can't you? I'm just going to leave without saying anything to the others.

GALYA

You're talking nonsense—you ought to be ashamed. To leave that way. . . *(Calls)* Andriusha!. . . Andrei!. . . *(Enter ANDREI)* Alyosha flunked!

ANDREI

You're kidding.

ALEKSEI

I did well with the first two questions, then I stumbled. Lost all my nerve. Began to hem and haw—and it got worse all the time. So I clammed up. They keep on asking questions—I can't get a word out. They ask me more questions, easier ones—right now I'd be able to answer them like a shot, but there—I'm tongued-tied. Finally, I started to answer in two-three words.

ANDREI

What did they give you?

ALEKSEI

I don't know. Didn't wait to find out.

GALYA

Maybe a B?

ALEKSEI

Then what? Certainly not an A—that's for sure. And with two B's they won't take me—that's also a fact.

ANDREI

Wait a minute, not so fast. . .

ALEKSEI

Don't try to reassure me. I walked and walked for hours, nearly bawling, cursing myself. . .for everything—and thinking. . .

GALYA

It's disgraceful—to accept people only on the basis of entrance exams, on grade points. Maybe the one they take is a grind, but actually, a dunce. . .

ALEKSEI

Of course, there's something to that. . . But I couldn't very well wait until they changed the system.

GALYA

(To ANDREI) He wants to leave. . .

ANDREI

What for?

ALEKSEI

Why hang around here? No, I'll go home. Work at the foundry again. I don't mind—it's useful work. I have thought things through. Don't worry, I'll reach my goal yet!

GALYA

When are you planning to go?

ALEKSEI

In four days.

GALYA

So soon!

ANDREI

Wait a while longer—they'll post the marks—maybe you squeaked through.

ALEKSEI

Wait for what—miracles? No, I came here on the off-chance, but why stay on, on another off-chance?. . . Listen, Andrei, leave us alone for about ten minutes, would you?

ANDREI

(Taken aback, and after a pause) That I can do.
He exits.

GALYA

Why did you do that?

ALEKSEI

He won't be offended. The two of us will have a frank talk about things later. *(A pause)*

GALYA

Maybe it was my fault you flunked—you couldn't concentrate— with me around.

ALEKSEI

What are you talking about? You helped, you only helped. I'm crazy about you. I never felt anything like this. And don't you go and forget me. I'll go back, but don't you forget. . . I'll see you again. You can't even imagine how I feel about you! *(A pause)*

GALYA

(To avoid the temptation to respond the way she feels) I have to go now.

ALEKSEI

Can I walk with you?

GALYA

You needn't.

ALEKSEI

It's late.

GALYA

I want—*(She is emotionally overwhelmed)*—I want to be alone, alone. . . *(She is about to go)*

ALEKSEI

Wait—say something.

GALYA

(Fervently) I promise you: I'll reform! I'll be a better woman!
She runs out.

ALEKSEI

(Calls out) Andrei!. . . *(Enter ANDREI)* I apologize. Normally, I have control. . .but about this, about her—I just couldn't. I haven't been fair about it. I'm guilty. . .

ANDREI

(Pretending indifference) How people love to babble. They go on, and on—just to hear themselves talk. You, too. Just count your blessings—and leave me out of it!
ALEKSEI puts his arm around ANDREI'S shoulder. ANDREI shakes it off.
We can dispense with your show off affection. *(A pause)* About your leaving—you ought to give it more thought.

ALEKSEI

There's nothing to think about—I've already bought my ticket.
(He takes the ticket from his pocket and throws it on the table)
My Moscow song is finished.

PYOTR IVANOVICH

(Entering) You're still up? *(To ALEKSEI)* May I congratulate you? Well done, my boy! Your mother said we should give you the money we've been sending. Here, take it—it'll be some time yet before you get a stipend.
He takes some bills from his wallet and gives them to ALEKSEI.

Curtain

ANDREI and ARKADY'S room. Four days later. Afternoon.

ARKADY and MASHA are kissing. ANDREI and ALEKSEI enter.
ANDREI stops short, pretending to be shocked.

ANDREI

Shame!

MASHA

Andriusha—we're married!

ANDREI

At last! *(To MASHA)* You see, I scared him. . .he knew I meant
it when I said I'd marry you.

ARKADY

(To ALEKSEI) At what time does your train leave?

ALEKSEI

I have to push off in forty minutes.

ARKADY

Are you sorry to be going?

ALEKSEI

I'm disappointed, of course. However—I'll wait for a while. . .
it won't hurt me.

ARKADY

Andrei will be going to work, too.

ANDREI

(To ALEKSEI) Come on, let's pack.

MASHA

(To ARKADY) We should be going. *(To ANDREI)* Arkasha is
staying on at the theatre. He really loves it there.
ANDREI and ALEKSEI start to pack. MASHA and ARKADY leave.

ANDREI

You and I will take a different road. Vadim, that louse, managed
to pass. The likes of him, you know—they're resourceful.

ALEKSEI

But sooner or later he'll break his neck—they'll catch up
with him.

ANDREI

Definitely. *(Handing a box to ALEKSEI)* Here, put these pastries on top. You'll need them.

ALEKSEI

I told you not to buy me anything. I won't take it.

ANDREI

Stop it, there isn't much time left. . . Now listen, I'm going with you. I bought my ticket long ago, the day after you showed me yours. I'm in coach 7, too.

ALEKSEI

What are you up to now?

ANDREI

I'll be off, too. Wanted to surprise you—just appear and sit down next to you in the train. But couldn't keep it to myself. So now you know. I hope you have no objections.

ALEKSEI

No. But did you ask your parents?

ANDREI

No, and I'm not going to. They'd raise a row. I'll go to work out there. . .in some machine shop. . .doing something or other. I want to work for a while. Do they post job vacancies out your way?

ALEKSEI

I haven't noticed.

ANDREI

Never mind. We'll think of something. Not all of my classmates made it, some are going to take jobs—most of them unwillingly. But I want to work. I want to find my niche. My own! I find life interesting—but real life—not just acquiring a career, earning a salary, going to the movies, going to bed. You and I will keep exploring—come up with something. Is it a deal?

ALEKSEI

You've got to tell your mother and father.

ANDREI

No, I can't. I'll send them a note from the station.

ALEKSEI

Are you scared?

ANDREI

I'm not scared, but, you know. . .they'll start in. . . Tra-ta-ta! Tra-ta-ta!

ALEKSEI

You really mean you are afraid. Either you tell them or you're
not coming with me. Or let me tell them.
He goes to the door.

ANDREI

Wait! All right. *(Finishes the packing quickly)* I'm not taking
anything useless—nothing in high fashion. Here, keep this
money for me—dole it out.

ALEKSEI

Where did you get all that?

ANDREI

Been saving for a car—a Moskvich. Here, take it.

ALEKSEI

Forget it.

ANDREI

It's my own—Mama and Papa gave it to me—I saved it a penny at
a time. I haven't touched any of it for three years—it was sacred.
(Continuing to pack) We have enough food. I even wanted to leave
without any baggage, but I suppose it would've been childish.
*Enter ANASTASIA EFREMOVNA. ANDREI jumps away
from his suitcase.*

ANASTASIA EFREMOVNA

Alyosha, you must eat something before leaving. *(To ANDREI)*
You, too, have been running around without food since morning.

ANDREI

Mother, I'm going away.

ANASTASIA EFREMOVNA

Where?

ANDREI

With Aleksei.

ANASTASIA EFREMOVNA

Well, eat before taking him to the train, there is still time.

ANDREI

I'm not just going with him to the station—I'm taking the trip with him—to Aunt Olya's.

ANASTASIA EFREMOVNA

You're out of your mind!

ANDREI

Don't try to stop me. I wasn't even going to talk about it, just hop on the train. *(Pointing to ALEKSEI)* He made me tell you.

ANASTASIA EFREMOVNA

(Calls out hysterically) Petya!. . . PETYA!

ANDREI

There, it's starting.

ANASTASIA EFREMOVNA

To her husband as he enters. She can hardly get the words out. He. . .going away. . .he. . .oh, Petya!. . .

PYOTR IVANOVICH

Who's going away?

ANDREI

I am.

PYOTR IVANOVICH

Where?

ANDREI

With Aleksei, to Aunt Olya's—I want to live there.

PYOTR IVANOVICH

What's the idea? *(ANASTASIA EFREMOVNA bursts into tears)*

ANDREI

Oh, stop! Mom, take it easy! I'm not about to die, am I? How about skipping the panic?

ANASTASIA EFREMOVNA

Petya, Petya! Lock him up—with a key! Don't let him out!

ANDREI

What's the matter with you, Mom? Come on, take it easy. *(Walks over it his mother, takes her in his arms and kisses her)* There, calm down, relax. . .don't feel so bad. I said—I'm not going just anywhere, I'll be with our folks. . .

ANASTASIA EFREMOVNA

I won't let you, I won't! *(She holds ANDREI tightly)* Andriushenka! *(She sobs)*

ANDREI

Embracing her again.

Papa, tell me, why can't I go? Why? *(To his mother)* All right. I'm not leaving, I'm not! *(To his father)* Am I a child or something? Aleksei here left home to study—that wasn't so strange—was it? What about me—will the bears eat me up out there? *(To his mother)* If I were leaving to study in Leningrad, you'd let me —wouldn't you? So. . . *(His mother weeps more loudly)* I'm staying, I told you—I'm not going! Stop crying. Look, I'm unpacking the suitcase. *(Her crying subsides)* See I'm a practical person—I took along everything necessary, even warm underwear— remember, you tried to make me wear it and I wouldn't. Out there I would wear it. *(She cries hard again)* Now why are you crying? I told you I'm staying! Here, look, woolen-socks. . . I just can't remain here—I can't. Papa, what is she afraid of, is there only a single road for me—to an institute? Fedka Kuskov didn't get accepted anywhere—and at home they are holding a wake, and making his life so miserable that he's ready to hang himself. And why? They've scared him. He's afraid to go to work. But I'm not afraid. I want to! Mom, is that really so important—who I'll be? What kind of person—that's important! And there are many roads to take. And if something has gotten tangled up inside me, time will unravel it—I promise you. I'll learn—I'll be learning all the time. Papa, do you understand me?

PYOTR IVANOVICH

I understand. .

ANASTASIA EFREMOVNA

(Outraged) Petya!!

ALEKSEI

Don't worry about him, Aunt Nastya. It's nice where we live— safe, and peaceful.

ANDREI

There, you hear! Alyoshka, promise her that you won't let me out of your sight. . . I'll do everything he tells me, Mom. . .

ANASTASIA EFREMOVNA

Don't you dare even talk about it! All right, if you don't want to work at the Botanical Garden—go work wherever you please!

ANASTASIA EFREMOVNA (Cont.)

Only here. In Moscow there are all kinds of·plants, factories, "The Hammer and Sickle," "Ballbearing,". . . What technology! Everything new! Or don't work at all, wait out the year, make plans. . .dreams. . .

ANDREI

No, no. I'm tired of doing nothing—that's what I've done all year— I goofed off. . .at school. . .

PYOTR IVANOVICH

Nasten'ka, listen—if he doesn't like it, he can come back. And you can take a trip out there and look things over. . .

ANASTASIA EFREMOVNA

(Weeping more quietly) Andriushenka, my boy, aren't you comfortable here, at home? If you wish, Aleksei will stay with you here, for good—you'll be together.

ANDREI

Mom, why do you try to bribe me with him as if he were a toy? It's not Aleksei I need.

ANASTASIA EFREMOVNA

But what? What? *(ANDREI doesn't answer)* Oh, my head is splitting. . .

PYOTR IVANOVICH

Take a tranquilizer. Come, take some. Come on. . . *(Trying to get her out of the room)* Nasten'ka. . .

ANASTASIA EFREMOVNA

To ANDREI as PYOTR IVANOVICH starts to lead her off.
I won't let you go, do you hear? I won't let you!
ANASTASIA EFREMOVNA and PYOTR IVANOVICH exit.

ANDREI

Do you think she's about to give in?

ALEKSEI

I think so.

ANDREI

Let's hurry. *(Puts his things back in the suitcase)* I think I have a snapshot of Galya. *(Goes to his desk, rummages in the drawers, finds the photo)* Should I give it to you? Here. . .

ALEKSEI

You needn't.

ANDREI

She didn't give it to me. I stole it from her purse. *(Looks at the picture, quoting a line of poetry in an undertone)* "You, as his first love, the heart of Andrei will not forget!" *(Hides the pciture deep inside the drawer and, waving his hand at the drawer)* Farewell, hope!. . . *(Then casually)* I forgot the handkerchiefs. *(This is a pretext—he doesn't want ALEKSEI to realize how moved he is)* I'll go get them. . .

He goes to another room, leaving just as GALYA enters.

GALYA

I made it in time!. . . Hello! *(She hugs ALEKSEI)*

ALEKSEI

I was beginning to worry. . .

GALYA

I went to your Academy.

ALEKSEI

What for?

GALYA

They posted the results today. I thought maybe they'd accepted you. . . But no.

ALEKSEI

I went down this morning myself—weakened, took a look. So be it. Anyway I didn't come here in vain—I met you. . .

GALYA

They say feelings don't stand the test of time. . .and distance. . .

ALEKSEI

No use exaggerating—it's only a six-day train ride. . . Besides, they are opening a teachers' institute there this year.

GALYA

But my mother would never let me go.

ALEKSEI

I just happened to think of it.

GALYA

Offering him the package she brought.
Here, take it—it's something to remember me by.

ALEKSEI

What is it?

GALYA

Nothing much. A couple of shirts I sewed for you. And this is—
a letter.

ALEKSEI

From whom?

GALYA

From me. Read it on the train. Don't you dare open it here!
Enter AFANASY and KATYA.

AFANASY

We almost missed you! *(To ALEKSEI)* How are things? How do you feel?

ALEKSEI

I'm ashamed to go back. So what—I'll blush a little. It's all
my fault. . . Mother will of course be glad to see me, in spite of
everything. *(Pointing to ANDREI, who has just entered, of
course without the handkerchiefs)* He's coming with me.

KATYA

To us?—To Irkutsk?

ANDREI

Yes, I suddenly felt like it—so I packed my stuff and off I go.
It was as simple as that.

ALEKSEI

(To AFANASY) Where will you be living?

AFANASY

In communal student housing.

KATYA

Do you think he's been living with relatives?. . .

AFANASY

Quit it! It was only at the beginning that I was a "tramp". All
that is over—it's forgotten. Now I'm sharing a room with three
other guys—from now on it's easy living for me.

KATYA

Give Aleksei the package. It's for my mother. And this letter.
And this is for my little brother—a football—he's wanted one
for a long time.

AFANASY

A good idea. I'll scribble one, too.
*He squats down and writes. ANDREI carefully fastens his
suitcase. GALYA stands aside.*

KATYA

(To ALEKSEI, in an undertone) You're not angry with me?

ALEKSEI

I? What for?

KATYA

For some reason I feel guilty. . . I embarrassed you. . . Just forget what I said.

ALEKSEI

It's already forgotten.

KATYA

(Sadly) So soon?

ALEKSEI

I mean. . .I sort of forgot. . .

KATYA

I don't like it here, in Moscow. Where we live, it's better—true?

ALEKSEI

You said it!

KATYA

I wish the next five years were over already!

PYOTR IVANOVICH

Entering, to ANDREI.
Mother says you are to take your felt boots and the thermos.

ANDREI

(Overjoyed) She's letting me go—I'm a free man!!. . . Why the
felt boots—I never wear them.

ALEKSEI

Be sure to take them—you'll need them out there.

PYOTR IVANOVICH

She also says you must take the heavy quilt.

ANDREI

The shiny green one? No way!

ALEKSEI

Take it if she wants you to.

ANDREI

Next she'll load me down with a featherbed.

ALEKSEI

Then you'll take the featherbed, too. Don't upset her. We have a big attic—we can chuck things up there.

ANDREI

Good. *(To his father)* O.K.—I'll take it. Papa, talk her out of seeing me off at the train. Both of you stay home. The kids will see us off.

PYOTR IVANOVICH

I had no intention of doing it.
He exits.

ALEKSEI

What would it cost if your mother did come?

ANDREI

Do you think my heart is made of stone? I've had enough. . . *(he looks around)* I think we have everything.

AFANASY

Handing ALEKSEI his letter.
Give it to my old man—tell him that, in general, everything is fine, and that I said he's to give his pipe a rest now and then. Without me at home he's probably lost in a cloud of smoke. Eh, guess I'll spend my last few cents on his favorite tobacco—"The Golden Fleece"—let him enjoy a good smoke before he cuts down.
Enter ARKADY and MASHA.

ARKADY

(To ANDREI) Another of your pranks?

ANDREI

(Sharply) It's not a prank!

ARKADY

You ought to think of Mother.

ANDREI

I did, I did! How about thinking of myself for a change?
Enter ANASTASIA EFREMOVNA and PYOTR IVANOVICH.
They carry a large suitcase and a huge package.

ANASTASIA EFREMOVNA

To ANDREI.
Your father and I decided to let you go. I won't say anything
else now. I'll write you a letter instead—today. *(Starts to cry, but
soon checks her tears)* Here, take this. *(She picks up the heavy
package and gives it to him)*

ANDREI

Mama—what's in it?

ALEKSEI

(Warningly) Andrei!. . .

ANDREI

I mean—why didn't you let me carry it in—it's too heavy for you.
Thank you, Mom.

ANASTASIA EFREMOVNA

Alyosha, I beg you, keep an eye on him. I'll write to Olya, too.

ANDREI

Taking leave of his mother.

Well, Mama, forgive me. . .

ANASTASIA EFREMOVNA

Don't say anything. *(Hugs him hard and long, holding his head
against her chest)* My little boy—if you get sick let me know right
away. I'll come, I'll come at once.

PYOTR IVANOVICH

(Taking leave of his son) Be a man. Grow up. Grow up! *(Kisses him)*

ARKADY

(To ANDREI) How about a parting embrace?

ANDREI

None of your sentimentality. *(Shakes his brother's hand)*

Liubka and other young guards in the Moscow Central Children's Theatre production.

Gestapo General Kler, his lieutenant Kurt, and Oleg, in the Moscow Central Children's Theatre production.

THE YOUNG GUARD

A Play in Two Acts
by Anatoly Aleksin

Lyrics by Robert Rozhdestvensky   Music by Oscar Feltzman

CHARACTERS:

Óleg Koshevóy
Ványa Zemnúkhov
Ulýana Grómova
Sergéi Tiulénin
Liúbka Shevtsóva
Iván Turkévich
Válya Borts
Seriózha Levashóv   16 and 17-year-old boys and girls, most of
Volódya Osmúkhin   them active in the underground partisan
Nína Ivantsóva   "Young Guard" during the Nazi occupation
Stépa Safónov   of their town.
Rádik Yúrkin
Nína Zemnúkhova
Liúsya Osmúkhina
Válya Filátova
Léna Posdníkhiva
Nádya Tiulénina
Zhóra Arútianiants
Anatóly Pópov
Victor Pétrov

Filíp Liútikov   adult leaders in the underground partisan
Vál'ko ("Uncle Andrei")   resistance movement.
Matvéi Shúl'ga

Oleg's mother
Grandmother Véra, Oleg's grandmother
Alexander Semnúkhov, Vanya's father
Liubka's mother, posing as her housekeeper
Volodya's and Liusya's mother

Kler, a Gestapo General
Kurt, his subordinant officer
Solikóvsky, a collaborator, police officer
Ignát Fómin, an informer working for the Nazis
Several German soldiers, officers and police officers

A boy, about 10
Zén'ka Móskhov, a war prisoner
Several other war prisoners

It is early fall, 1942.

THE SET, in which the color black all but dominates, symbolizing the misery, the violence, the gloom and gore brought into the land by the Nazi invader, as well as the present mining locale, remains on stage throughout the performance.

This set is a stylized representation of the area near the entrance to a mine shaft. All about, there are high black metal super-structures for lifting and lowering mining machinery. The walls of the surrounding buildings are blind, and blackened with coal dust. The mine is not operating. There are two or three German motor-cycles on stage, with headlights glaring. Several Nazi soldiers in dark green uniforms hover around them.

The scenes between KLER and the YOUTHS and YOUNG GIRL whom he interrogates in turn always take place on the stage apron, with KLER sitting stage left in something resembling a captain's chair and the one being interrogated standing at some distance from him to the right. From time to time, especially in moments of rage and exasperation, or when he tries to "ingratiate" himself with the young prisoner, he leaves his chair to go through the appropriate action. During the scenes in which OLEG, the leader of the Young Guard who is interrogated at great lengths does not appear, he sits on a low stool (on the dimmed stage apron) at the extreme right, his posture showing his fatigue and despair and his face turned to the wall. At such times KLER usually remains seated in his chair at the extreme left in a relaxed pose.

In the various scenes which illumine and concretize the information sought by KLER in the interrogations but not obtained, minimal props are used to suggest the setting required for the dramatic action. For these scenes various small sections of the stage are lit while the rest of the stage and the apron go dark. At the end of such scenes the lights go down, the props are quickly removed, and the interrogation is resumed on the lighted apron, continuing until the next dramatic scene. From time to time there is more than one dramatic scene before the interrogation is resumed.

The curtain is up all of the time—even as the audience is being seated. The stage and the auditorium are lit. We see the several Germans on stage at their motorcycles and otherwise making themselves at home in this part of the small mining town they have occupied—Krasnodon, in the Donets Coal Basin, not far from Stalingrad.

The lights are now dimmed in the auditorium. As the play is about to begin, there is a tense, somewhat protracted silence. Then we hear the song (sung by a mixed chorus off-stage or by a baritone voice on tape and amplified) "Where Are You Flying, Bird So Free?" This mood song voices the sadness, yearnings, and hopes of the young boys and girls caught up in the dangerous underground activity against the Nazi invaders whose presence in their beseiged land has so blighted their young lives with its inhumanity:

WHERE ARE YOU FLYING BIRD SO FREE

Complete music for the songs is available from the publisher.

Where Are You Flying, Bird So Free?. . .

Where are you rushing, little river,
So proud of your waters undefiled?
Far, far away, beyond murky mists
The blue sea awaits me, its cherished child.

Why don't you slumber, little seed
In the depth and stillness of earth?
I am wakeful for I sense the sun.
Soon spring will come, and new birth.

Where are you flying, bird so free?
Maybe I shall fly along with you. . .
Beyond the clouds the sky is so clear,
I yearn once more to glimpse its blue!. . .

I want to fathom its purity,
Its lofty depth once more to behold
I shall soar and there up high my strong wings,
Wings of compassion I shall unfold. . .

*The stage lights go up. Slowly, looking about with jaded curiosity,
like a tired tourist in a museum, a middle-aged, somewhat pudgy
German officer walks onto the stage with a moderately military
gait. He is MAJOR GENERAL KLER of the Gestapo. Several
Gestapo officers and a few soldiers enter with him keeping at a
reasonable distance. KLER and the other Gestapo men are of
course in the black Gestapo uniforms. Low-toned German speech is
heard from KLER's entourage.*

KLER

*Speaking correctly and articulating carefully, with Prussian
precision but with a marked German accent*

In Russian, men! Nothing but Russian!. . . A nation's language
expresses its spiritual mechanism. It is impossible to operate a
machine without understanding how it is constructed. It can become
very dangerous to its operator and land him in the sewer. . .

*His retinue comes to attention, and they all begin to demonstrate
their knowledge of Russian. This chatter gradually mounts to a
cacophonous din and then suddenly stops, with a clicking of heels.
KLER sits down at a table near the front of the proscenium. KURT
comes up to him, salutes, and places a stack of dossiers on the table*

Furthermore, by talking Russian we show him that we feel at home
here. That we came to stay. . .forever.

KURT

In German

There'll come a time when we'll make everyone. . .

KLER

Interrupting him

You speak German?. . . I repeat once more: a machine must not penetrate into the soul of the master. It must obey him blindly. But the master must understand the workings of his machine. Is that clear?

KURT

In Russian

I understand.

KLER

Kurt, are you observant?. . .

KURT

I try.

KLER

It's impossible to try to be observant. It is a gift. Is it possible that you haven't noticed that a man who speaks in a language that he knows badly, is ridiculous?

KURT

I have noticed.

KLER

And a master must not appear ridiculous. And must not look frightening. In a state of terror, everything freezes. Even a machine. . . But a machine must function. And it must know that if it behaves itself well, all will be well. But if it functions badly, all will go badly. This isn't a complicated philosophy, Kurt. Is it?

KURT

You explain things like a good schoolteacher. Everything becomes clear.

KLER

Of course. After all, I'm about to deal with youngsters. I'll call them to the "blackboard" one at a time. Who's first?

KURT

Oleg Koshevoy.

He picks up OLEG'S record from the pile of dossiers.

KLER

Without looking at the folder
Does he have a mother? A grandmother?

KURT

He has. . . It's written down there.

KLER

I'm more interested in what is not written down. Is he an only
son? An only grandson?

KURT

Excuse me. . .(He *starts to scan the file but stops as KLER resumes.*)

KLER

You wonder why I don't ask about his father?

KURT

There is no father. Did you guess that?

KLER

The father is not important. Childhood is more closely bound
up with the mother and grandmother. And does he love anyone
else? Besides his mother and grandmother?

KURT

I don't know at what age that sort of thing begins with them, here.

KLER

At the same age as with us. At his age were you in love?

KURT

Even earlier.

KLER

You see! (*A pause*) Every person, especially a young one, has
his Achilles' heel. Who is this one's Achilles' heel? Mother?
Girl friend? Grandmother? Or all three?

KURT

Excuse me. . . (He *tries to read the record rapidly.*)

KLER

I expected that the first one to flunk the oral exam today would
be this. . .Oleg Koshevoy. But it is you.

KURT

One usually studies for an examination. . . .

KLER

But that's where a member of the Gestapo differs from a schoolboy. He must pass examinations at any moment. And without any cramming.

KURT

Flustered

Maybe I'll pass my test yet. . . *(Hands folder to KLER)* There, in his file, you'll find a school composition. We didn't find any letters. . . But this one composition—it's in the form of a letter. . .

KLER

Opens the folder

What's important is to whom he wrote. . . *(He reads)*

VOICE OF OLEG

Mother, Mother! I remember your hands—I remember them from the time I was first aware of existing in this world. In the summertime they were always suntanned—so evenly bronzed, only a little darker over the little veins. They were somewhat rough—your hands—they had done so much work in your lifetime. . . But most of all I'll always remember how gently they stroked my hair and neck when I lay half-conscious in bed. And no matter when I'd open my eyes—in daytime or at night—you were always near me. I remember your hands, firm, reddened by the freezing water at the rocky shore, where you rinsed the wash. At that time we lived alone, and we seemed to be all alone in this world. And I remember how painlessly you could pull a splinter from my finger, how quickly you coud thread a needle, how you sang as you sewed. . .
The stage lights are dimmed, leaving only the apron lit. We see OLEG and KLER on the apron. The interrogation has begun. OLEG looks like an average boy of seventeen. He exercises strict control over himself with great effort.

KLER

You're lucky. . . You have a mother, you have a grandmother. We appreciate them fully only after we lose them. I now have grandchildren. . . Would you like to see what they look like?
OLEG looks at KLER with surprise.

Yes, yes. I understand. You're astonished. . . I suppose for two reasons. First because I address you so politely. Secondly, you can't imagine that I, too. . .perhaps I should say that we, too. . .have children and grandchildren. Believe me, we do. . . Here, take a look! *(He takes some snapshots from his wallet, offers*

them to OLEG who ignores this) So that all remains well with your
mother, with your grandmother, and with my grandchildren, you and
I must find a common language. Do you understand? I mean we
must be frank with each other. And frankness is helped by
reminiscences. *(He pauses)* Tell me, do you respect adults?

OLEG

It depends. . .whom do you have in mind?

KLER

I understand you. And even agree that age does not determine all.
But just the same, one of your popular songs goes: "Everywhere
our elders we honor!" Does that not mean that before undertaking
something important. . .for example, starting your underground
organization, you would consult certain "elders"? Or, more
exactly, certain adults?

OLEG

I didn't consult with any elders. I just talked things over with
one old woman.

KLER

Sharply
With which one?

OLEG

With Grandmother Vera.

KLER

With whose grandmother?

OLEG

With mine. . .my own. As soon as I returned. . . I went home
at once. But there was no longer room for me in my house. I had
to live in the shed. When the General went out, I'd visit Mother. . .

KLER

He was in your way?

OLEG

I simply wanted to see Mother, and not him. . .
*The apron lights are dimmed. Lights go up on a section of the stage.
We see the home of the Koshevoys. The General's orderly lies
sprawled on a divan, with his shoes and fatigue-cap on. He is
smoking. He looks bored. He looks up as OLEG enters.*

ORDERLY

Halt! It seems to me you are putting on airs. Yes, yes, I've noticed it more and more! Hands at your sides! Heels together! You are addressing a grownup! *(After a pause)* Do as you are told! Do you hear—you squirt!

OLEG suddenly puts on a frightened look, quickly squats down, strikes his knees with his palm, and says loudly:

OLEG

The General is coming!

The ORDERLY jumps up, quickly removes the burning cigarette from his mouth, and crushes it in his palm. His face instantly takes on a stupidly servile expression.

Shame! Flopping on the divan while the Master is away. . . Now keep on standing that way!

OLEG'S MOTHER enters hurriedly.

OLEG'S MOTHER

Is that the way to act, Son?

OLEG

Mama, don't pay any attention to this idiot!. . .

ORDERLY

You swine! *(He throws himself at OLEG and begins to shake him)*

OLEG'S MOTHER

To the ORDERLY

Don't! Don't!. . . *(To OLEG)* Olezhek, give in to him. Why start something?. . .

She tries to separate them. OLEG grabs the ORDERLY by his belt, with both hands.

OLEG

Let go of me! Do you hear?

The ORDERLY unexpectedly releases him.

OLEG'S MOTHER

Go away, my boy, go. . .hurry!. . .

ORDERLY

Spluttering

A wild beast! The worst of the lot! We should train you all like dogs—demand obedience!

OLEG

You are the ones who are the worst of wild beasts. All you know is how to steal chickens, ransack people's trunks, take the boots off people's feet.
The ORDERLY strikes OLEG so hard that he nearly falls. Recovering, he throws himself on the ORDERLY, pounding him with heavy blows.
OLEG'S MOTHER pulls at her son's shoulders.

OLEG'S MOTHER

Oleg! Control yourself. He'll kill you!
GRANDMOTHER VERA runs in. She shouts at the ORDERLY.

GRANDMOTHER

What are you doing? How dare you?!
The ORDERLY roars with rage as the old woman starts pushing him out of the room, still shouting at him.

OLEG'S MOTHER

Olezhek, my boy, I beg you. . .the window is open. Run, run!

OLEG

I'm not about to crawl through the window, out of my own home!
(After a pause) Don't worry, Mama, I'll leave. . .
The stage is darkened. The apron is lit as the interrogation continues.

OLEG

And you say that we must respect those older than ourselves. . .
All of them, without exception.

KLER

Yes, of course. . . "Older" doesn't always mean "better." But allow me to ask you a question.

OLEG

Of course you will ask it anyway.

KLER

Was it precisely at that moment. . .after that fight, that the idea first came into your head that the Germans could be defeated? That one could attack them?

OLEG

I don't remember. . .when that came into my mind.

KLER

But come it did?

OLEG doesn't answer.

And where, if it isn't a secret, did you go after your moral
victory over the orderly?

*The apron goes dark. Lights go up on a section of the stage
We see OLEG standing outside the gate to his house. STEPA
SAFONOV appears. OLEG is rubbing his bleeding cheek*

OLEG

We'll see yet who conquers whom!

STEPA

Where are you off to? I want to talk to you. What's with your face?. . .

OLEG

I had a fight with a fascist.

STEPA

Did I hear you right? That's great! *(Looking at OLEG with
respect)* Let's get away from here. I'll go with you—wherever
you were going—in case a Fritz starts something. . .

OLEG

No, I'd better see you home safely. It's on my way.

STEPA

Being practical

Maybe you ought to postpone your business and come with me. To Valya's.

OLEG

To Valya's?. . . *(After a pause)* Have they had to put up some
fascists, too?

STEPA

No. That's why I want to take you there. In fact I was coming
to see you with a message from Valya.

OLEG

You're sure there are no Fritzes there?!

STEPA

Not a one!

OLEG

Then let's go to Valya's.

STEPA

As they walk off

You know, when she and I were returning in the truck, from our work in the fields. . .

The stage is darkened and the apron is lit, as the interrogation continues.

KLER

Your revolutionary theory honors individual heroes but prefers collective heroism. Then who joined in your. . .precisely what collective?

The apron goes dark. Lights go up on a section of the stage. VALYA, a teenage girl, sits at the wheel in the cab of a battered truck. A thin, very pale youth stands on the running-board, hanging on to the door handle. He is SERGEI TIULENIN. He quickly crawls through the open window and sits down beside VALYA.

SERGEI TIULENIN

What a truck!

VALYA

Sarcastically

Didn't they give me the one you expected?

SERGEI TIULENIN

That one is in perfect condition. But I'm so beat that. . . *(He waves his hand as if to say, "It's all the same to me!")*

VALYA

My apologies—but all the sleeping space is taken.

SERGEI TIULENIN

I haven't closed my eyes in six days. So I guess I can stand it another hour. *(Motioning with his head toward the inside of the truck)* Who's asleep in there? Oh, I know— it's Stepa Safonov.

VALYA

How do you know Stepa Safonov?

SERGEI TIULENIN

We met at the stream, in the gully.

VALYA

What were you doing there?

SERGEI TIULENIN

Catching frogs.

VALYA

Frogs? What for?

SERGEI TIULENIN

I thought he needed them to catch catfish. But he wanted them
for vivisection—for scientific purposes.

VALYA

Then what?

SERGEI TIULENIN

I convinced him that he ought to concentrate on catching catfish,
and we fished all night. I caught two—a smallish one, about a pound,
and another—quite a large specimen. Stepa didn't catch any.

VALYA

And then what happened?

SERGEI TIULENIN

I talked him into taking a swim at dawn—skin-diving. He came
out of the water blue as a jay. So I gave him a lesson in how to
warm up instantly and get rid of the water in his ears.

VALYA

With a penetrating look
Now I understand how you carry on your friendship. . .*

SERGEI TIULENIN

Seriously, staring into space
You're a bit late in catching on. . .

VALYA

What do you mean?

SERGEI TIULENIN

I think the Germans will occupy Krasnodon tomorrow.

VALYA

So they'll come—damn them!

SERGEI TIULENIN

Then there'll be no way to escape.

VALYA

Why escape? . . .

*Valya realizes that Sergei's story is symbolic—that he and Stepa are engaged in dangerous
sabotage against the Germans.

SERGEI TIULENIN

Quietly

You're right. *(Suddenly, abruptly)* I'll walk the rest of the way. Thank you for your kindness. I don't want to disturb Stepa. When he wakes up tell him that Sergei Tiulenin would like him to come and see him. *(He jumps off the truck)*

VALYA

First I'm your chauffeur, now you want me to be your post office!
This part of the stage is darkened and another section is lit, showing SERGEI'S home. It is night. The windows in the very partial interiors have no panes—this is symbolic of the war's destructiveness. The frames are charred. SERGEI approaches the house, opens a window, climbs in, and squats down near the bed of his sleeping sister NADYA. Calls to her softly

SERGEI TIULENIN

Nadiusha. . .

NADYA

Frightened, as she wakes
Oh! Who is it?

SERGEI TIULENIN

Sh-h-h! You'll wake Mother.

NADYA

Sergei! You're alive! My dear little brother. . .you're alive!. . .

SERGEI TIULENIN

Softly

I haven't stretched out or slept since the 13th. Since the 13th—from that morning to this evening I've been fighting.

NADYA

Oh! My God! In what battle? Where?

SERGEI TIULENIN

Many of our men were killed. I was spared. . . There were only about fifteen of us left. The Lieutenant says to me: "Go—why waste your life here?!" He was wounded all over—his face, hands, legs, back—he was all bandages and still bleeding. "We're done for, but why should you perish?" I left. . . I don't think any of them are still alive.

NADYA

Thank God you're here—you're alive!. . .

330 The Young Guard

SERGEI TIULENIN

The Lieutenant kissed me. He said, "Try to remember my name. Somov—Nikolai Pavlovich Somov." And he said, "When the fascists are driven out and you are among our people again, go to the Gorky Military Center and ask them to inform my family that I died. . .honorably. . ." I said that. . . *(He chokes on his tears and cannot continue)*

NADYA

Sobbing
How did you fall into their hands?

SERGEI TIULENIN

Our troops had to retreat. They took up a new position. Had to abandon the work on the fortifications, which they had started. All the non-military personnel from Krasnodon who had been helping returned to their homes—all except me. I went back to the trenches. I took a machine gun from a dead soldier and started blasting away with the others. We held off their attack for several days. Then another lieutenant says to me: "If we weren't fated to die here, we'd enlist you in our outfit. But you're a youngster. You must live on—for a long time. . ." I retreated with them nearly to Verkhneduvanna. I saw the Fritzes almost this near— *(He holds his hand in front of his face)*

NADYA

Shocked and terrified
That near?!

SERGEI TIULENIN

I finished off two of them myself. Maybe more—but two for sure. Now I'll keep on wiping out those vermin wherever they appear. I swear it!

NADYA

One against all of them? You'll get killed.

SERGEI TIULENIN

It's better to die than lick their boots. Or just hang around doing nothing. And I met a girl. . .

NADYA

In the trench?

SERGEI TIULENIN

Of course not—in a truck. She gave me a lift. I didn't tell her anything—where I was coming from or what had happened to me. But I'll find her. . .

NADYA

What for?

SERGEI TIULENIN

Go to sleep. . . You wouldn't understand it anyway.
The stage goes dark and the apron is lit, as the interrogation resumes.

KLER

You call your collective a "Guard." This name, as far as I
know, is used to indicate a high function. Your group calls
itself "The Young Guard". . . A guardsman—is one who, in
wartime, is especially active and daring. Am I wrong in this?

OLEG

You're not wrong.

KLER

Then tell me, what specifically was your. . .activity?

OLEG

In these hard times we wanted friends to stand by each other,
to stand together. All together.

KLER

And why do you call today's times "hard"? Because there's a war?
But you could avoid taking part in it. By occupying Krasnodon
we gave you the chance to abandon this cruel and dangerous game.

OLEG

Did you say—"cruel"?

KLER

Yes, I admit it. Sometimes. . .certain individuals wearing our
uniform allow themselves. . . But believe me—such types merely
happen to wear our uniform, but in substance. . . In your country
much is written about the conflict between *form* and *substance*,
that is, form and content. . .

OLEG

In a low, tense voice

Can you imagine the feelings of a mother who fears for the life
of her son—for the danger to her daughter from the lust of those
"certain individuals"? And if her son is ill. . .

KLER

Going back to the table with the stack of dossiers

If he is ill. . .? *(He leafs through a dossier)* Whom do you have
in mind? Volodya Osmukhin?

The apron goes dark. Lights go up on a section of the stage.
We see part of the home of the Osmukhins. Volodya, who has recently
undergone surgery, lies in bed, covered with a sheet. Near him
hovers his MOTHER and his sister LIUSYA. From the other side
side of the wall we hear the noise of mugs being heavily pounded
on the table, glasses clinking, cutlery rattling, and the sound of
drunken voices singing a coarse drinking song.

VOLODYA

To his sister
Liusya. . .what does he call you, that beefy-faced Corporal?

LIUSYA

Louisa.

VOLODYA

I swear, Liusya—if he barges in here once more to bother you,
I'll kill him!

THE MOTHER

Not so loud. . . You mustn't move yet. The stitches might come apart.

LIUSYA

They've turned the hospital into a Storm Troopers headquarters.
You were discharged just in time. The next day they chased out
all the patients. I saw them dragging themselves along the road
in their gray hospital robes. Some were on crutches. Only a
few were carried on stretchers.

VOLODYA

There were wounded soldiers there, too. What happened to them?
In the next room, the drunken song dies down, drowned in
raucous laughter. There is a knock on the door. The CORPORAL
appears in the doorway. LIUSYA hides behind the wardrobe.

CORPORAL

Louisa! Me and my fellow soldiers invite you to come and have a bite with us.

THE MOTHER

We've already had our meal. We aren't hungry.

CORPORAL

Louisa! I see you. . . Me and my fellow soldiers. . .

LIUSYA

My brother isn't well. I can't leave him.

THE MOTHER

Maybe you'd like someone to clear the table. Come, I'll help you. Come. . . *(She pulls the CORPORAL by the sleeve and leads him out of the room. Again we hear the drinking song burst out.)*

VOLODYA

If he comes in here once more. . .!

LIUSYA

Not so loud. You mustn't excit yourself so after the operation.

VOLODYA

"Operation!" "Post-operative complications!" All that was important before, in peacetime! Now none of it has any significance.

THE MOTHER

Returning, to LIUSYA

Maybe you'd be better off going to bed.

LIUSYA

Whispering

I'm afraid to lie down.

VOLODYA

I mean it—if that dog shows his face in here again, I'll murder him! Yes, I'll kill him, no matter what!

Again there's a knock on the door. The CORPORAL again appears.

CORPORAL

With gloating anticipation

Louisa! You mustn't neglect soldiers who, any day, any hour, could be killed. We won't do anything to you. Nothing bad. Our soldiers are honorable men—they are real knights. . .

VOLODYA

Through his teeth

Get out of here!

THE MOTHER

To VOLODYA

Be still. . .be still. . . I beg you!. . .

CORPORAL

In a drunken attempt at dignity

Louisa! The soldiers of the Führer's Army await your answer!

THE MOTHER

All right—very good. She'll come soon. She'll change her dress—and come.

LIUSYA

Terrified

Mama!!

THE MOTHER

She'll just change. . .

CORPORAL

We're waiting, Louisa!

He exits. The MOTHER goes quickly to the wardrobe, opens the door

THE MOTHER

Get in!

LIUSYA hides inside the wardrobe. The MOTHER locks it. She sits on VOLODYA'S bed. The CORPORAL is again in the doorway.

CORPORAL

Louisa!

THE MOTHER

She went out into the yard. . .the yard. . .

She points outside the window.

CORPORAL

I'll go find her. *(He walks off unsteadily.)*

VOLODYA

Half-whispering

Mama. . .she'll suffocate in there.

THE MOTHER

Maybe they'll leave soon.

Again the CORPORAL enters, now very drunk. She turns to him

You didn't find her?

There's a rustling noise from the wardrobe. The CORPORAL listens.

That came from outside the window. She's out there—on the street, in the yard. . . Didn't you find her?

The CORPORAL goes to the window, looks out, then turns toward the wardrobe. The MOTHER stands in his way.

CORPORAL

Phy-oo!. . .

He pushes her in the face with his huge hand, forcing her aside. VOLODYA raises himself in his bed.

THE MOTHER

To VOLODYA

I beg you. . .

*The CORPORAL, in a drunken daze, walks unsteadily into the
other room. The noise in the room subsides suddenly, and there
is a hubbub outside as the drunken soldiers pour out in the
street. The MOTHER runs to the wardrobe, opens the door.
LIUSYA does not come out.*

What's wrong? Liusen'ka, what's the matter with you?
*VOLODYA, barely able to walk, moves toward the wardrobe.
They manage to pull LIUSYA out. They hold her up as
she gasps for air.*

LIUSYA

I—lost—my—breath. . .

*Suddenly flames can be seen through the window not far from
the house. LIUSYA points*

A fire! Look. . .fire!

THE MOTHER

Frightened

Close it! Close the window!

VOLODYA

That must be why they left. They have other things to worry
about now. *(He goes back to bed.)*

LIUSYA goes to the window. Suddenly there is a loud whisper.

SERGEI TIULENIN

Liusya. . . Liusya. . . Don't be frightened. . . It's me—Tiulenin, Sergei.

He appears in the window.

Are there any Fritzes at your place?

LIUSYA

Whispers

Yes.

THE MOTHER

In terror

Who is it? *(The light from the fire shines on SERGEI'S face,
and she recognizes him)* You, Sergei?

SERGEI TIULENIN

Volodya—where is he?

VOLODYA

I'm here.

SERGEI TIULENIN

Who else is still in town?

VOLODYA

Victor Petrov. I don't know about the rest. I haven't been out.
He tries to get out of bed. SERGEI immediately appears in the room.

SERGEI TIULENIN

Don't get up!. . . I don't know either. I think Vit'ka Lukyachenko is still here, and Liuba Shevtsova. And I saw Stepa Safonov. . .

VOLODYA

Whispering
How did you get back? In the night?

SERGEI TIULENIN

I saw the fire. I made my way from the park, house by house— then I noticed that your window was open.

VOLODYA

What's burning?

SERGEI TIULENIN

Their headquarters. They had to escape in their underwear!

VOLODYA

Do you think it's arson?

SERGEI TIULENIN

The place didn't set itself on fire. *(He laughs softly. Then, after a pause)* What are you planning to do?

VOLODYA

What about you?

SERGEI TIULENIN

As if you didn't know!

VOLODYA

I'll be doing the same. . . I'm so glad you're here! You don't know how glad!

SERGEI TIULENIN

The Fritzes you've got staying here—are they the vicious kind?

VOLODYA

They drank all night. Wolfed all of our chickens. Broke into our room. . .

SERGEI TIULENIN

They sound vicious all right—but it could be worse. . . When the Storm Troopers installed themselves in the hospital there were forty of our wounded soldiers there. They drove them all into the Vekhneduvannaya meadow and used an automatic gun on them. The surgeon Fedor Fedorovich had tried to save them. He explained that they were all badly wounded and would never be able to fight again. But the so-and-so's kept dragging them out of bed and piling them in trucks, pell mell. And then. . .

VOLODYA

Shocked, incredulously
Fedor Fedorovich, he's the doctor who operated on me—for appendicitis. . .

SERGEI TIULENIN

They shot him right there in the hospital.

THE MOTHER

What's going to become of all of us?! My God!!
The fire rages outside the window.

SERGEI TIULENIN

Laughing softly, as he looks out
It's burning pretty good—no? *(He starts to leave.)*

VOLODYA

Raising himself, speaks with consternation
Wait, Sergei. . . It was you?! It was. . .

SERGEI TIULENIN

Auf Wiedersehen. I have to go see someone tomorrow morning.

VOLODYA

Whom?

SERGEI TIULENIN

Meaningfully
Her. Auf Wiedersehen! *(He leaves)*
The stage goes dark. Lights go up on the apron. KLER continues his interrogation of OLEG.

KLER

So, after your combat with the orderly put you in the mood for fighting you went to see Valya Bortz.

OLEG

I don't remember.

KLER

It is only the insignificant events that vanish from a person's memory. Did that meeting with Valya. . .mean nothing to you?
The apron goes dark. A section of the stage is lit. We see the outside of Valya's house. It's evening. SERGEI has walked VALYA home

SERGEI TIULENIN

Now it will be easier to die. . .

VALYA

What makes you say that?

SERGEI TIULENIN

I've just spent three whole hours with you! Together we looked down on our town, from a high roof. Together. . . After this. . .what will be will be.

VALYA

You're a strange one. . .

SERGEI TIULENIN

We studied the whole layout from up there, we saw the former central warehouse where the fascists have settled in. The two of us—from such a height. What a sight!. . .
OLEG and STEPA appear, walking toward them

STEPA

Excitedly, gesturing toward OLEG
You know, he had a run-in with a Fritz!

VALYA

He did?! *(To OLEG)* Oleg, you must help. . . You simply must help us!

OLEG

How?

VALYA

We have to establish contact with the underground organization. You probably know how that is done. There were always many comrades where you lived. And I know that most of your friends are grown-ups—more grown-ups than young people.

OLEG

Unfortunately my former connections are gone.

VALYA

Tell that to other people—we are friends. . . Maybe you are in doubt about him? *(Gestures toward SERGEI)* This is Sergei Tiulenin.

OLEG

To SERGEI, in a low voice

I know that the organization exists. First of all, there were leaflets. Secondly, I have no doubt that the burning of the storehouse and bathhouse were its work.

VALYA

I'll leave the two of you to yourselves. . .for a short while. I have to help my mother. Stepa, you come with me.

STEPA

Gladly.

VALYA and STEPA go into the house.

SERGEI TIULENIN

Valya has told me a lot about you. . . I trust you. But I want you to know this, and I'll never mention it again! It wasn't any underground organization that set those fires—I did it. . .

OLEG

You, yourself?!

SERGEI TIULENIN

I, myself. . .

OLEG

That's not good—to take it on yourself. It was nervy, but a bad idea—to do it on your own.

SERGEI TIULENIN

So there is an organization! I came across its tracks, yes. . .but I didn't hook up with it.

OLEG

You—?! How?

SERGEI TIULENIN

A certain person was hiding at Ignat Fonin's. I talked to him.

This section of the stage goes dark. Another section is lit. We see the interior of IGNAT FOMIN'S apartment. He is alone. SERGEI TIULENIN enters.

FOMIN

Startled
What do you want?

SERGEI TIULENIN

Wrought up and pleading
Citizens! Citizens! Save a wounded fighter!

FOMIN

You mean yourself?

SERGEI TIULENIN

No, I'm not hurt. But our soldiers had to retreat fast, and they
left this wounded man right on the street. Near the marketplace. . .
The other kids and I saw him—and we ran straight here for help.

FOMIN

Why, exactly, straight here, to me?

SERGEI TIULENIN

To whom else, if not you, Ignat Semyonovich? The whole town
knows that you were our first Stakhanovite.*

FOMIN

And who are you?

SERGEI TIULENIN

I'm the son of someone you know well—Prokhora Liubeznova,
also a Stakhanovite.

FOMIN

Prokhora?. . .*(After a pause)* I don't know any Prokhora. But I
must tell you, brother, that I have no room for your soldier. My
wife is ill. . .

SERGEI TIULENIN

You are acting strangely, Citizen. Everyone knows you have
a spare room.
*He tries to get past FOMIN, moving toward the other room. In
the doorway of the room appears MATVEI SHUL'GA, who has
overheard the conversation*

---

*Stakhanov was a worker famous for his remarkable productivity. He then served as a model
for other industrious workers, termed *Stakhavnovites*.

SHUL'GA

To FOMIN

Just a minute, friend. . .*(To SERGEI)* And why didn't you take this wounded man, let's say, to your own house? *(SERGEI is silent)* Is your father still in town, or has he left?

SERGEI TIULENIN

He left.

SHUL'GA

And your mother?

SERGEI TIULENIN

Mother is home.

SHUL'GA

Then why didn't you go to her? Is she the kind who would refuse to take in a wounded fighter? *(SERGEI is silent)* Ignat Semyonovich told you the truth—he cannot take in the wounded man. But you will find someone who will, and who will conceal him. It is an act of mercy. Keep looking—and you will find someone. But it has to be kept secret. Don't approach just anyone. . . If no one will shelter him—come back to me. But if someone does—don't come back here. You'd better give me your address right now, so that I can find you if necessary.

This section of the stage now goes dark, and the lights go up on the section where the preceding scene took place. OLEG and SERGEI continue their conversation.

OLEG

And you gave him your address?

SERGEI TIULENIN

No. . . I gave him a false one. I made one up.

OLEG

Why?

SERGEI TIULENIN

·I didn't trust Fomin.

OLEG

But since you had that kind of conversation with this man Shul'ga, you might want to turn to him again.

SERGEI TIULENIN

That's not likely. *(After a pause)* Fomin has since betrayed him to
the S.S. He didn't do it right away but on the fifth or sixth day after
the fascists occupied us. . . He hoped to destroy the entire underground
organization through this man—to get him to confide about it—but
Shul'ga must have been very careful. Fomin waited and waited and
finally exposed him. Then he went to offer his services to the
German police.

OLEG

Thoughtfully

I wonder what they did with that man. . .with Shul'ga. Killed him?

SERGEI TIULENIN

I think they are still holding him. They want to find out everything
from him, but he's not the kind who would tell them. He's probably
still in the stockade. There are other prisoners there. But I haven't
been able to find anyone who could tell me who they are.

OLEG

*Excitedly, and stammering slightly, which he tends to do when
excited. (However, he never stammers during the interrogations since
he always keeps himself under strict control when facing KLER)*

Thank you!. . . Thank you for telling me all this. We must be
on the alert. Sign up the most loyal, the most capable of our
friends for this kind of work, but no one must know about it. . .
Friendship is friendship, but this is a bl-bloody business. You,
Vanya Zemnukhov, and myself—that's all! We'll establish
contact and they'll tell us what we must do. We'll maintain
contact only through Valya.

SERGEI TIULENIN

With obvious satisfaction

Exactly! Through no one but her! Auf Wiedersehen!
*The stage goes dark. The apron is lit. The interrogation of
OLEG continues.*

KLER

I have made a study of all the famous interrogations that have taken
place in the history of mankind. I came to the conclusion that
one of the most brilliant cross-examiners was your Czar Nicholas I,
but he interrogated people who, in all circumstances, told the
truth. They were incapable of lying. To anyone. Even to an enemy.
That was a unique phenomenon. They were your countrymen. And,
perhaps, it would pay you to take an example from them?

OLEG

In my opinion, a person can confide only in a friend.

KLER

The least hostile enemy among enemies—is almost a friend. Especially in the kind of situation in which you find yourself at present. Tell me then, why did you go specifically to Valya? Did you have a crush on her?

OLEG

You know, as to personal things like that—even the Decembrists* remained silent.

KLER

All my life I have tried not to interfere in people's personal affairs. Especially in the case of young people. This wounds them. . . But evidence in this investigation began to accumulate even before my arrival here. And this evidence shows that it wasn't Valya whom you made your conquest. . .but Lena Pozdnysheva. Isn't that true? *(After a pause)* Forgive me. . . Knights do not answer such questions. Although here, in this report, it is stated clearly: "Lena Pozdnysheva". Yes, Lena. . .

The lights on the apron go down slowly. We hear the sound of piano music as they dim. A high feminine voice begins to sing. The accompanist stumbles and the girl singer laughs. Then she repeats the musical phrase which the accompanist stumbled over. The apron is now dark, and a section of the stage is lit. We see the outside of Lena's home. Oleg is standing near the doorway listening to the music. A voice is heard over the music.

FIRST MALE VOICE

There's someone out there.

The music stops.

LENA

(Offstage) You probably imagined it.

SECOND MALE VOICE

An officer cannot fail to hear a sound. Or he might mistake an automatic rifle for a machine gun.

The men laugh boisterously.

---

*The *Decembrists* were young intellectuals, officers, and young members of the Russian aristocracy who staged a rebellion in 1825, during the despotic reign of Nicholas I. It was the interrogation of these rebels that Kler referred to.

LENA

(Offstage) I'll go see. . .and at the same time I'll take your gifts to the kitchen.

After a pause, LENA appears on the doorstep carrying canned food. OLEG fixes her with a stare.

Oleg! And we were. . . *(She is embarrassed)*

FIRST MALE VOICE

Who is it?

LENA

A boy—from my school.

SECOND MALE VOICE

Men are not jealous of boys!

The two men again laugh boisterously.

LENA

To OLEG

Do you remember that love song?. . . For a whole hour I've been trying to teach it to them. *(Loudly)* We'll go over it once more, gentlemen! *(To OLEG)* Stay with us a while, please. . .

OLEG

As though he didn't hear her—musingly

Before, when Valya used to accompany you, she never stumbled. Do you remember. . .those times?

LENA

Of course I do! *(Uneasy)* Come in, stay with us a while. . .

OLEG

What's that in your hands?

LENA mechanically, and innocently, holds out the cans to him.

(Drily) Is this the stuff they pay you with? *(He looks accusingly at the cans)* Margarine, isn't it? You sell youself cheap!

This section of the stage goes dark. The whole stage is dimly lit now, and we hear "The Song of Faith," as the teenage boys and girls, members of the Young Guard, stroll about the stage, mostly in couples, as though for a romantic evening walk. Most of them have already appeared in the play.

The Song of Faith

On long, hard and murderous roads,
Far from the dreamed-of goal,
Have faith in people, near you and far,
Then faith in yourself will fill your soul.

Again you must face a violent day,
Your nerves groan with the strains.
Faith in people,
Faith in people!
That's the weapon to break our chains!

Hurricane winds howl round about us,
Blizzards wail, but you—hold on!
Believe in people as they believe in light!
Believe in people as they believe in life!

Refrain

Again we must face a violent day,
Your nerves groan with the strains.
Faith in people,
Faith in people!
That's the weapon to break our chains!

*The stage goes dark. There is a pause. Then lights go up on a
section of the stage. We see a GUARD with an automatic rifle
standing near the home of the KOSHEVOYS. Two girls approach.
They are LIUBKA SHEVTSOVA and her friend NINA IVANTSOVA.*

LIUBKA

To NINA

Come along, Ninochka. He'll let us pass. *(She jostles the GUARD'S
arm and goes up the steps to the entrance. She turns around and
calls to the hesitating NINA)* Come on!. . .
*NINA still hesitates. The GUARD rushes up to the entrance and
spreads his arms, blocking the door. LIUBKA addresses him.*
Blockhead, does Oleg Koshevoy live here?

OLEG

Coming out of his house
I'm—Koshevoy.

LIUBKA

As though to herself, checking him out and then convinced
That's right—you are Oleg. . . *(After a pause)* We'd better have
a talk—privately.

OLEG

Go ahead, talk.

LIUBKA

No, we have something *romantic* to talk about. . . Right, Ninochka? *(Lowering her voice)* I come from Uncle Andrei. . .

OLEG

You're pretty bold. . . I s-saw how you bumped the guard.

LIUBKA

Never mind that, a flunky likes to be pushed around.

OLEG

And w-who are you?

LIUBKA

Liubka—I'm Liubka Shevtsova.

This section of the stage goes dark. The apron is lit. We see KLER interrogating LIUBKA.

KLER

What is your name?

LIUBKA

Brashly, throughout this scene
Liubka.

KLER

Isn't that an unusual and coarse version of your name? Isn't your real name Liuba, short for Liubov? Which means "love"?

LIUBKA

You may consider it my pseudonym—my stage name!

KLER

Sit down, please.

LIUBKA

Please. . .?

KLER

You may remain standing. I never give orders to women. *(LIUBKA sits down)* What kind of an actress are you? Last time, you weren't able to remember a thing. Yet you must have an excellent memory. You will have to memorize the lines for your roles.

LIUBKA

Do you think I'll still have a chance to do that?

KLER

I will not conceal the fact that your future artistic career depends
a good deal on our chat.

LIUBKA

And on my talent.

KLER

You do have acting talent.

LIUBKA

You're already convinced of that?

KLER

With precision
Yes. I am convinced.

LIUBKA

Will you give me a reference?

KLER

They say talent must be treasured, and I want to save your talent. . .
together with your life. But you must help me do this.

LIUBKA

Are you asking that I, a defenseless girl, help a General?

KLER

The "defenselessness" of women—is their power. By means of their
so-called "defenselessness", they have captivated leaders of
armies. Their "defenselessness" has at times conquered entire
countries. It has made men of great wisdom—and great
psychologists—gullible and stupid. . . And I am also inclined to
be influenced by all that you are going to tell me.

LIUBKA

Let me sing for you instead.

KLER

No, you'd better stage for me what you people call a documentary
play, based on facts. Only on facts! I should like the characters
in this performance to be. . . *(He looks into the dossier)* Well,
for example, Seriozha Levashov, Nina Ivantsova, and—by all
means—Oleg Koshevoy. You may rehearse it all in your mind.
I shall not hurry you.

LIUBKA

I've never really been a dramatic actress. Maybe I'd better dance for you.

KLER

No! I would like to see the documentary play. Think about it—rehearse. . . I'll not disturb you.

The apron goes dark. A section of the stage is lit. We see the interior of LIUBKA'S home. She is alone. There is a knock at the door.

LIUBKA

Loudly
What do you want?

VOICE AT DOOR

Open up, Liuba. *(Liubka opens the door. In the doorway stands SERIOZHA LEVASHOV)*

LIUBKA

Come in! Quickly, quickly!

SERIOZHA LEVASHOV

Do you know whether there are Fritzes quartered in our house?
He walks into the room.

LIUBKA

There were—and here, too. But this morning they went away. Some go, others come.

SERIOZHA LEVASHOV

Noticing a large portrait of Hitler hanging on the wall, over Liubka's bed
I see you've hung up Hitler.

LIUBKA

I'd *like* to hang him! But so far I have not been able to.

SERIOZHA LEVASHOV

Don't joke about it. Did you put him there for protection, or what?

LIUBKA

Oh, let him hang. . . Do you want to wash up?

SERIOZHA LEVASHOV

Okay.

LIUBKA

Take off your things. Don't be shy. *(She brings a pail of water and a basin)* Where have you been?

LEVASHOV splashes water on his face and blows it out of his nose. But he does not answer.

Listen, you came here. That means you trust me. So why do you hesitate now? You and I are leaves from the same tree. . .

SERIOZHA LEVASHOV

Give me a towel. . . I didn't expect to find you at home. I dropped in, just in case—and here you are. I don't understand it. You took the radio operator's course along with the rest of us, but now you're here at home, not working at it. How come?

LIUBKA

You didn't answer my question, so I will be silent, too.

SERIOZHA LEVASHOV

After a pause

They parachuted us radio operators. . . So many people have been lost in this occupied territory that we were even surprised that our advance instructions had not been totally lost. The mine pits are full of corpses. . . We operated singly. But for a while we were able to maintain contact. Then it became impossible. They caught one of our men—broke his arms and cut out his tongue. I probably would not have fared better if I hadn't received orders to leave. . . It's lucky I met Nina Ivantsova—on the street, here. I passed on my report through her to the regional center. Later we decided to come home, together. We walked. . . *(After a pause)* I kept thinking: what if you had been left, like us, with the enemy. . .and you are alone?. . .

LIUBKA

Overcome with emotion

Oh, Seriozha!. . .Seriozha! *(Glancing cautiously through the window)* They did leave me here. . . You understand why. . . Told me to wait for orders. And now it's been almost a month and I have seen no one and heard nothing. The officers keep crawling around me like flies on honey. It's disgusting! *(After a pause)* Seriozha, you must get away! . . . What do you plan to do?

SERIOZHA LEVASHOV

You, yourself just said: We're leaves from the same tree. . .

LIUBKA

Goodbye, Seriozha. . . I hope we see each other soon.

She sees him out and returns at once. Again there is a light knock at the door. LIUBKA'S mother, looks in anxiously from the next room, then enters.

THE MOTHER

Is it fascists?

LIUBKA

Do they ever knock that quietly? Seriozha probably forgot something. *(She goes and opens the door, then, startled, backs away)* Come in, Comrade Val'ko.

VAL'KO

Correcting her, as he enters
"Uncle Andrei!". . . Remember—"Uncle Andrei!". . .

THE MOTHER

But isn't this. . .you? *(After a pause)* And where is. . .?

VAL'KO

I am Uncle Andrei—remember this! *(He sees Hitler's portrait)* I see you honor the Führer.

LIUBKA

Don't suspect anything bad.

THE MOTHER

One of the officers hung him there. Two officers were quartered here with us, and you can imagine, Comrade Val'ko—

VAL'KO

Interrupting
Uncle Andrei!

THE MOTHER

Imagine. . .she forbade me to say that I'm her mother. Told them I was her housekeeper and that she was—an actress. "And my parents," she said, "are business people. They were owners of mines and the Soviet authorities sent them to Siberia." See what she's thought up?

VAL'KO

Yes, she's thought it up all right.

THE MOTHER

The officer who slept on this bed got hold of the portrait and hung it on this wall. And she—she goes at him screaming, "Get that picture down! I don't want Hitler to hang in my room!" But when they left, she wouldn't let me take Hitler down. "Let him hang," she says.

VAL'KO

To THE MOTHER

Maybe you happen to have some men's clothes—something simpler than I have on. It's not safe for me to appear the way I am.

THE MOTHER

And what happened to him?. . . What happened to my husband?

VAL'KO

Dear neighbor—and you, Liuba—I never thought that fate would bring me to you with tragic news. Your husband—and your father, Liuba, and my best friend—the best friend I ever had—Grigory Ilich. . .perished. Was killed by a bomb during the evacuation. They drop bombs on peaceful people, the accursed vermin! *THE MOTHER weeps quietly. LIUBKA rushes over to her.*

LIUBKA

Don't cry, Mama—my little dove. . . What can we do? There are just the two of us now. . . (*She sobs, then checks herself*) Now I am a qualified victim. We'll drive out the fascists. The war will end. I'll beome a good radio operator and I'll go to work at the radio station—I'll even get to be in charge of the station. . . I know how much you like peace and quiet. I'll find you a place near the station. It's always very, very quiet there. Everything is soundproof. No noise penetrates. The little apartment will be clean and cozy. . . (*She starts to cry again*) and we'll live together, you and I. . . (*VAL'KO turns away, wiping his eyes on his sleeve*) Isn't that the way it's going to be, Uncle Andrei?

VAL'KO

I think you're right.

LIUBKA

You see, Mommy! Come, let's go to your room, lie down—I'll cover you. (*She leads THE MOTHER to the next room and then returns*) I'll get you something to eat right away, Uncle Andrei.

VAL'KO

Wait. . . (*He looks at her fixedly*) Our people left you here for
certain work. Who did it and for what work, I will not ask you.
But I ask that you help me—hide me for at least a day—put me
in touch with Kondratovich. Do you remember him? And do you
know Oleg Koshevoy? Do you know Oleg?. . .
*This section of the stage goes dark. Another section is lit. We
see LIUBKA, NINA, and OLEG near the home of the Koshevoys.
They are continuing their conversation.*

OLEG

C-can I personally see Uncle Andrei?

LIUBKA

No—personally you cannot. But first let's take care of the romantic
business. Ninochka, come on over. Meet this young man. (*NINA
approaches. She and OLEG shake hands awkwardly*) Relax. You
will soon get used to each other. I will leave you now, and the two
of you go for a walk, arm in arm, and have a heart-to-heart talk.
I with you happy times together.
She leaves.

NINA

We mustn't stay around here. We'd better go somewhere else. And
it would be better for you to take my arm, or hold my hand.
They start to walk off, holding hands.
You must not see Uncle Andrei. Maintain contact through me. . .
Don't take this personally, I've never seen him, either. Uncle
Andrei wants us to find out whether there are some kids among us
who could get the lowdown on which of our people have been arrested.

OLEG

One of our boys is very active, absolutely fearless—he took
this on himself. There are many of us who can take part in the
struggle. I am sure. . . Here, let me write down the address of
Zhora Arutinants. (*He writes it down then continues*) A-as I
was talking to you, those few moments, I counted three ack-ack
guns to the right of the school, and right next to them there's
a dugout shelter. I looked but didn't see any machine guns.

NINA

Testing him
And what about the machine guns and the two Fritzes on the school roof?

OLEG

Darn it! Those I didn't notice. *(After a self-conscious pause)* Say,
I hope the two of us won't be meeting only for. . .business. . .

NINA

Aware of his attraction to her

No, why should we? We can meet whenever we have free time. . .

OLEG

Where do you live?

NINA

Softly

Why don't you walk me home?. . .

*They hold hands and walk along to the accompaniment of a
popular ballad about budding love.*

A Love Song

> The sun hovers over glade and slope,
> And when its work has been done,
> A flower suddenly has grown
> Even from a cold grey stone.
>
> But how, how comes into being,
> Whence comes the miraculous feeling?
> Mysterious, so very beautiful!
> Most defenseless yet all powerful!
> From the whirl of swift passing time
> Is singled out one day sublime
> When two are destined to meet
> In a world where countless hearts beat!

Refrain

> But how, how comes into being,
> Whence comes the miraculous feeling?
> Mysterious, so very beautiful!
> Most defenseless yet all powerful!

*The stage goes dark. The apron is lit. The interrogation
of LIUBKA continues.*

KLER

So. . . I see that you don't want to act out that play with the
characters I have mentioned.

LIUBKA

I feel embarrassed. After all, I'm not that experienced an actress.

KLER

Inexperienced players are not sent out on the road, yet you, to my knowledge, have already done "roadshows." Isn't that true? Not in Paris, of course. Not in Milan. But in a certain large city not far from here.

LIUBKA

In Lugansk?*

KLER

I understand. . . For the daughter of a mine owner—the character that you have taken on—Lugansk* sounds better than Voroshilovgrad, as I believe the Soviets call it. I mean, from the point of view of the class you allegedly belong to. *(After a pause)* Was it a pleasant trip?

The apron goes dark. A section of the stage is lit. We see LIUBKA, the COMMISSARY COLONEL, and his accompanying LIEUTENANT having a meal out of doors. It is a bright, sunny day. On a tablecloth spread on the grass there are bottles, canned food and other viands.

COLONEL

He is tipsy
And what do you do, Beautiful?

LIUBKA

I am an actress. I haven't appeared in the theatre but I've had some success in revues. I sing and dance. My father is a well-known businessman, a mine owner. Of course the Soviets robbed him of everything and he, poor thing, died in Siberia leaving a wife and four daughters. We're all pretty.

COLONEL

Are you the youngest?

LIUBKA

How did you guess?

COLONEL

I invite you to stay with me. . .

LIUBKA

I decline, with regret. It could cast a shadow on my image, and an actress's reputation must be. . . You understand.

*Lugansk was the pre-Revolutionary name for the city now called Voroshilovgrad.

COLONEL

Then will you make me a present of your address?

LIUBKA

But of course. As soon as I know where I'll be staying, I will let your Lieutenant know where we can meet.

COLONEL

To LIEUTENANT

Oh, Rudolf, it seems that you have a better chance than I.

LIEUTENANT

If that is so, I will use it for your benefit, my Colonel.

LIUBKA

Are we far from the front?

COLONEL

Such things should not interest a pretty girl like you. Any day now we will take Stalingrad. We have already penetrated into the Caucasus.

LIUBKA

But the front is not so far from the upper Don. . .

COLONEL

Who told you that? They say that attractive Russian girls—are spies. Is that true?

LIUBKA

Except those whose mines were taken away by the Soviet government. But really, I would so much like to know—can I relax here or should I go somewhere further away with my troupe? What if they should suddenly break through here?

COLONEL

Oh, how can you offend me that way with your lack of confidence in our armed forces? To reassure you. . .(*He whispers something in LIUBKA'S ear*)

From the side of the road we now hear a growing din of running feet. We hear cries and voices. The COLONEL and the LIEUTENANT stand up and LIUBKA jumps to her feet.

COLONEL

What dust! (*He takes out a handkerchief and sneezes*)

LIUBKA

Prisoners of war. . . Half naked. . .barefoot. . . Let's give them some of this food.

COLONEL

Why should *you* want to feed them?

LIUBKA

Men like those worked in the mines for my poor father. *(She looks toward the road)* They're gone now—it's too late. . .

COLONEL

Come, sit down. There's still some wine left. Tell me when we can get together again.

LIUBKA

I told you that I'll give you my Lugansk address through your Lieutenant. *(She remains standing)*

COLONEL

Ah, Rudolf, were I as young as you!

LIEUTENANT

My youth will be of service to you, my Colonel.

LIUBKA

I must leave. I mustn't be late for the performance.

They leave. We hear the sound of a departing car. This section of the stage goes dark. The apron is lit. The interrogation continues.

KLER

Every traveller, were he Christopher Columbus, Miklukho-Maklai, or this actress—has a definite purpose in mind. Search—discovery. . . What did she seek there in Lugansk? Wht did she discover?. . . She received instructions from the underground. *Obkom*—didn't she? If only my children and grandchildren had the kind of faith in me that these youngsters have in their *Obkoms* and *Raikoms*!*

The apron goes dark. A section of the stage is lit. We see a room with a small window which is covered with a blanket for blackout purposes. The room is dimly lit by an oil lamp. Two people are sitting at a table. They are OLEG and FILIP LIUTIKOV.

*Obkom is the abbreviation for the two words meaning Regional Committee; *Raikom* is the abbreviation for the two words meaning District Committee.

LIUTIKOV

Remember—vigilance is the mother of the underground. Did you see the film *Chapayev?*

OLEG

Yes.

LIUTIKOV

Why did he perish? He perished because his guards were not watchful enough and allowed the enemy to get too close. His patrols were asleep at the switch. Always be on the alert! Night and day. Be exact. Keep in touch with me through Volodya Osmukhin. The two of us must not meet again.

OLEG

Thank you.

LIUTIKOV

What for?

OLEG

You, Filip Petrovich, permitted me to come. . .to you. . .and during curfew time. That means—

LIUTIKOV

It means that I trust you as I trust myself.

OLEG

Thank you!
The stage goes dark. The apron is lit. We see KLER, alone.

KLER

Shouts

Bring me Koshevoy!
Two soldiers drag OLEG in, fling him to the ground. He is haggard from torture, and one of his arms has been broken. He raises himself to a standing position with great difficulty, determined to face Kler on his feet.

KLER

As though shocked
Is that you?!

OLEG

Don't you recognize me?

KLER

Unctuously

The hardest thing in the world to deal with are touchy and stubborn people. *You* would add: "people of conviction." But when a conviction is fanatical, lacking in logic, it becomes just ordinary obstinacy. And here is the result. I interrogate your acquaintance Liutikov, your famous actress Liubka Shevtsova, and during that time. . . You will agree that even a mother can't always watch over her children and they at times come home with scratches and bruises. Other boys have beaten them up.

OLEG

He speaks slowly and with difficulty

Boys, you can fight back—that's number one. And it's seldom that a gang of them jumps on one.

KLER

But there are times when a father and mother punish their child. They try to put some sense into him. They, too, are older than he is and there are two of them against one. This comparison isn't very exact. I admit it. But fanaticism and stubbornness can bring one to. . . Although, of course, I don't justify such methods. And I guarantee you that, should our present talk succeed, they will not be repeated. Don't think, by the way, that all of your friends are as true to their pledge as you are. I tell you this not to play a banal trick of cross-examination. It is a fact. Not all are true to their vow.

OLEG

What vow are you referring to?

KLER

Continues, as if he had not heard the question

A vow—is generally a kind of hysteria. It serves to express feelings of the moment, but not at all to guide one's behavior. Is there anyone who in his youth did not pledge eternal love? And for whom has love ever been eternal? So don't ascribe any special significance to—

OLEG

To what?

The apron goes dark. A section of the stage is lit. We see a gathering of members of the Young Guard. OLEG steps forward and faces them.

OLEG (Cont.)

I, Oleg Koshevoy, as I join the ranks of the Young Guard, in.
the presence of my friends in battle, before my native, deeply
suffering land, before all my people, I solemnly pledge to
unquestioningly carry out any and all assignments of the
Organization, to hold in deepest secrecy everything that concerns
my work in the Young Guard. And I vow to avenge without mercy
the burnt and ravaged cities and villages, the blood of my people,
the torture unto death of the hero-miners! And if, for this cause,
my life must be given, I will give it without a moment's hesitation.
If I should violate this sacred pledge under torture or out of
cowardice, let my name be forever accursed and may I, myself,
be punished at the stern hand of my comrades! Blood for blood!
Death for death!

ULYANA

Comes forward and stands beside OLEG

I, Ulyana Gromova, as I join the ranks of the Young Guard, in the
presence of my friends in battle, before my native, deeply
suffering land, before all my people, I solemnly pledge. . .

IVAN

I, Ivan Turkevich, solemnly pledge. . .

VANYA

I, Vanya Zemnukhov, solemnly pledge. . .

SERGEI TIULENIN

I, Sergei Tiulenin, solemnly pledge. . .

LIUBKA

I, Liubov Shevtsova, solemnly pledge. . .

All the Young Guards, one after another, repeat the word "pledge"

VOICES

Pledge! . . . Pledge! . . . Pledge! . . .

End of Act I

It is mid-winter, 1943.

The set is the same as for ACT I, and the action follows the same pattern, with the interrogation taking place on the apron and the rest of the action in various sections of the main stage which are lighted for this purpose as required.

The apron is lit, and we see KLER in the process of interrogating LIUTIKOV.

KLER

You, Liutikov, accuse us of heartlessness. I agree: it happens. Unfortunately. . . You accuse us of lifting our hand even against your children. This also happens—in the smoke of battle it is hard to tell who is an adult and who is a youngster. But what about you people—didn't you lead your own boys and girls to ruin? The whole of your so-called Young Guard?

LIUTIKOV

This is a total war. Therefore everyone has risen to resist it—the young as well as the old. But this—what you call "guard", I am hearing about it for the first time.

KLER

Today—or generally?

LIUTIKOV

I'll continue to say, no matter how I'm tortured, that these youngsters are not involved!

KLER

We'd like to avoid the torture. *(After a pause)* It is your conscience that should torture you. . .above all. . .

The apron goes dark. A section of the stage is lit. We see a room in the home of the OSMUKHINS. The whole family is present: THE MOTHER, VOLODYA (now recovered from the appendectomy), and LIUSYA. LIUTIKOV enters.

THE MOTHER

Astonished

Filip Petrovich! You? You've come to us?. . .

LIUTIKOV

I came to drag your son off to work. You and Liusya leave us, as though you were going on an errand, and he and I will have a talk.

While they speak we hear from the next room the voices of the German soldiers who have been billeted here.

VOLODYA

Work? Did you say—you have work for me? *(After a pause)* It's all the same to me—work or no work. My only goal in life now is to help destroy the fascists.
THE MOTHER and LIUSYA leave.

LIUTIKOV

With sarcasm

Splendid!. . . Be sure to say this to everyone. No matter who comes here. Like me, for instance. . . But better still—why don't you run out into the street and announce your goal to every passerby: "Listen, I'm off to do relentless battle. I want to disguise myself. Help me!"

VOLODYA

Heatedly

But you are not just a chance passerby!

LIUTIKOV

Me—maybe, and maybe not. . . But in times like these you don't take anyone for granted. *(After a pause)* Well, luckily for you, I'm well known around here and I've been assigned to bring everyone back to work in the machine shops. That's why I came And that is what you tell your mother and sister. And to them, too. *(He motions with his head to the adjoining room where the German voices are coming from)* We'll put in a little work for them! I'll now give you a certain assignment. . .

VOLODYA

Eagerly

Oh, great!

LIUTIKOV

Some printer's type is buried in the park. We could start a secret press. Do you understand? *(He takes a piece of paper from his pocket)* Here's where it is—approximately. . . Get in touch with those you think you can trust. But not with all of them at the same time. One at a time. When you are convinced in each case that the person is with us. . .

VOLODYA

They're with us, Filip Petrovich. . .

LIUTIKOV

Ignoring VOLODYA'S words.

When you are convinced that the person is with us, carefully hint that there might be a possibility. . . Ask if they are willing.

VOLODYA

I'll do exactly as you say. But I have to tell them on whose authority I'm talking. Of course if I spoke to them simply as myself, Osmukhin, they'd probably believe me anyway. But it's better to tell the kids that I'm not acting on my own, but on instructions from the Organization—do you understand what I mean? And to carry out the assignment about the printing press, I'll need several of them. Then I'd certainly need to explain. . .

LIUTIKOV

All right, tell them. . . But without naming names, of course.

VOLODYA

I understand.

LIUTIKOV

Now that we've had this talk, I want to give you a piece of advice, not an order: do nothing without consulting me! You could bring disaster on yourself and on the rest of us. . . I don't act on my own, either, but consult with others. Be sure to explain this to your circle of friends. That's all for now. *(He stands up, smiles)* Tomorrow—get to work!

LIUTIKOV leaves. THE MOTHER and LIUSYA return

LIUSYA

What were you whispering about for so long?

VOLODYA

"What about?" "What about?" You know perfectly well what about.

LIUSYA

Indignant

So you, too, will be going to work for the Fritzes?

VOLODYA

In an undertone

We'll give them the works!. . .

The stage goes dark. The apron is lit. KLER'S interrogation of LIUTIKOV continues.

KLER

Somehow I expected from you—an engineer, an intelligent person—more sensible behavior.

LIUTIKOV

Do you think I acted senselessly? I went to serve in your machine shop. I did honest work there.

KLER

You and I probably ascribe to the words "honest work" different meanings.

The apron goes dark. A section of the stage is lit. We see the machine shop where FILIP PETROVICH LIUTIKOV and NIKOLAI PETROVICH BARAKOV "work". There's the buzzing of machines, the clank of iron. . . Then, suddenly, frantic cries:

VOICES

(Offstage) "The pipes have burst! They've cracked! We'll have to start from the beginning!"

LIUTIKOV

To BARAKOV

Who would have thought it could happen! But we've had such frosts! Let's not get discouraged. We'll have to change the pipes. . . There aren't any spare ones—that's true— but we'll keep looking!

BARAKOV comes over to LIUTIKOV. The two remain alone

BARAKOV

You came for the water-pump yesterday evening—didn't you?

LIUTIKOV

I did.

BARAKOV

But you didn't take it with you.

LIUTIKOV

No, I didn't. I thought it would be all right to wait till morning— but the frost hit during the night. All the pipes have burst. No one could have foreseen it.

BARAKOV

Aren't you taking too great risks, Filip Petrovich?

LIUTIKOV

And what about you? Your forges are manned by leaders of partisan cadres.

BARAKOV

How could I be suspected of knowing that? This way, if the frontline moves closer and the Fritzes put us to work mending captured munitions, then. . .

LIUTIKOV

If the front gets closer, we'll leave the damn place and go underground—join the partisans.

The stage goes dark. the apron is lit. KLER is now interrogating both LIUTIKOV and OLEG

KLER

The adult underground people we have gradually uncovered. . . And you, Liutikov, were probably planning to substitute for the "old guard" *(He points to OLEG)* the young.

LIUTIKOV

Youth always replaces age—it's a law of nature.

KLER

I'm not talking about laws of nature, but about a war which has no rules or laws!

LIUTIKOV

And who is it that leads such a war?

KLER

People who do not wear a uniform! Only soldiers should fight against other soldiers!

LIUTIKOV

Pointing to OLEG
Is that why you are fighting him?

KLER

As they say in detective novels, "*I am asking the questions!*"

LIUTIKOV

Once in a while you should answer some!

KLER

Barely holding his temper
Take him away!

The soldiers haul LIUTIKOV off. The apron goes dark. A section of the stage is lit. We see a room in which the members of the Young Guard are in session.

IVAN TURKEVICH

Speaking in a low voice, but emphatically
First: Uncle Andrei and Matvei Kostievich have been arrested. . . That is the most significant news.

LIUBKA

Exclaiming

Uncle Andrei? And Shul'ga?

IVAN TURKEVICH

Next: we don't know what's happened to our "polizei"*—Tolya
Kovalov and Vasya Pirozhkov. They left home yesterday evening
and haven't come back. This means that now we don't have "eyes"
and "ears" in the stockade. How can we undertake any action
blindfolded?. . . I'll never allow myself to say anything bad about
our members, but what if the thing failed? How can we do
anything without a link to the prisoners?

OLEG

I-I'll take care of this. Some of the prisoners' relatives will
probably pass on our messages to them. Also, we might be able
to pass a note—in a loaf of bread, inside a dish of food I'll
organize this through my mother.

IVAN TURKEVICH

That won't be easy. The fascists, you know. . .are thorough. . . .

OLEG

Interrupting

We mustn't adapt ourselves to the fascists—we must make them
adapt themselves to us.

*Enter VASYA PIROZHKOV. His face is bruised and bleeding.
His hand is bandaged.*

LIUBKA

Vanya!! What happened to you?

IVAN TURKEVICH

Who did this?

VASYA

The Fritzes at the police station.

IVAN TURKEVICH

And where is Tolya?

OLEG

Did you see any of our people there?

*This is the German word for "police." It was used by the Russians to designate
collaborators who worked with the German military police. Some took on these jobs
as covers for their underground resistance work.

VASYA

We didn't see anybody. They beat us up in the office of their chief.

IVAN TURKEVICH

Don't babble like a child. Tell us everything in proper order.
Where is Tolya?

VASYA

At home. Lying down. What is there to say? The police called us
in during the day. Ignat Fomin had told us to report, armed, that
evening—to come to the place where they keep the prisoners—that
they'd be sending us along as guards with the ones who were
arrested—but where, he didn't say. . . Tolya and I went home. We
kept thinking: "How could we manage to help some of those
prisoners to escape?" But if the thing went wrong, we'd never
forgive ourselves! So I said to Tolya: "Let's go to the saloon and get
stinking drunk and not report to the police this evening." We worried
and worried about what they'd do to us and decided that the
worst that could happen was that they'd smack us around and
then let us go. And that's how it was—they questioned us, beat
us up, and threw us out.

OLEG

Were you able to get to Matvei Kostievich's cell—the day
before yesterday. . .when I sent you?

VASYA

I was there with the chief of police, Solikovsky.*
*This section of the stage goes dark. Another section is lit.
We see a cell in the stockade. On the floor sits SHUL'GA. The
door to the cell opens with a loud squeak. In the doorway are
SOLIKOVSKY and VASYA PIROZHKOV, who is also in the
uniform of a "polizei."*

SOLIKOVSKY

Now you are in the beast's cage! I'll lock the door and we'll see
how you make out here. The scum!
SOLIKOVSKY leaves, banging the door shut behind him.

VASYA

Bending over SHUL'GA and speaking in a low voice
Your friends aren't yawning. Be on the alert next week—I'll let you
know in advance which night. . . (*He turns toward to door, speaks
very loudly*) You can't scare me! You've got the wrong guy! I'm not
scared of your pals, the Bolsheviks, either. . . I'm not scared!
The door is thrown open. SOLIKOVSKY appears.

*Solikovsky is a collaborator working with the Gestapo.

SOLIKOVSKY

Guffawing, to VASYA

I see—you're shaking—probably wetting your pants with fear!

VASYA

Swaggering

Who—me? *(To SHUL'GA)* So you thought you could bang me around? You're damn lucky that I'm a decent person, you—! *(He gives SHUL'GA a rough push, then leaves with SOLIKOVSKY.)*

SHUL'GA

Now alone in the cell

Of course all this might be a put-on—a provocation. But why bother doing that when they can kill me any time they want to? No, this means that Val'ko is alive and is active. This means they haven't forgotten about me.

The door again swings open. A man is thrown into the cell. It is VAL'KO. SHUL'GA raises himself. They look at each other intently in the semi-darkness. SHUL'GA speaks softly

Andrei?. . .

VAL'KO

Matvei? That's fate for you! *(He puts his arm around SHUL'GA)* We did everything we could to get you out, but fate decided that instead I, myself, would join you here. . . Come, let's take a look at you. . . What have they done to you?

SHUL'GA

And you, I see, got plenty too! You must have had a real brawl with the swine. . . Tell me, how are things out there?

VAL'KO

What can I tell you? Things are as is to be expected under the circumstances. Normal. But I. . .

VAL'KO waves his hand in hopelessness and covers his face with his hands.

This section of the stage goes dark. Another section is lit. We see the interior of the military police station. VAL'KO and SHUL'GA have been brought in from the stockade for interrogation by police officers BRUCKNER and BALDER. To the side stand SOLIKOVSKY and several policemen

BRUCKNER

To VAL'KO, pointing to SHUL'GA.

Have you known this man a long time?

VAL'KO

We met in the stockade.

BRUCKNER

Who is he?

VAL'KO

All I know about this citizen is what he told me himself.

BRUCKNER

If you expect to be treated according to your status, name the persons who were left in the rear, along with you, for demolition sabotage work.

VAL'KO

I don't know any such people. And I doubt that there was time to select them and leave them in the rear. I came back here from Donets. I got there too late for evacuation. Every person out there can testify to this.

BRUCKNER

Offering VAL'KO a cigar
You are an engineer?

VAL'KO

Takes no notice of the cigar
Yes.

BRUCKNER

A man with your training and experience could occupy a higher and materially more lucrative position in the new order.
If you wish. . .

SOLIKOVSKY

Take the cigar. . .take it!

VAL'KO

Ignoring him
What offer are you making me?

BRUCKNER

The Donets coal basin, with all its mines, has been put under the management of the Eastern Society for the Exploitation of Coal and Metallurgical Enterprises. It has delegated me to offer you the post of Chief Engineer for the local branch.

VAL'KO

I would accept this offer—if I were given good conditions for the work.

BRUCKNER

Conditions? The conditions are the usual ones: you will disclose to me your whole organization—all of it! All! You will do this at once! *(Looks at his wristwatch)* Within fifteen minutes you could be a free man and within an hour—you could be sitting in your own office. . .

VAL'KO

I don't know of any organization. I came to these parts entirely by accident.

BRUCKNER

Oh, you—bastard! You are its chief! We know everything!
He pushes his burning cigar into VAL'KO'S face. VAL'KO swings hard and knocks BRUCKNER down.
He roars
Haul him away!
The policemen throw themselves at VAL'KO. SHUL'GA rushes in to help him.

SHUL'GA

Oh, you Siberia of our damned Czar! *(With one blow he sends BALDER flying into the farthest corner of the room, and then turns on the policemen.*

VAL'KO

Ah, give it to them, Matvei! *(He goes at another officer)*

THE OFFICER

Jumping back
Don't shoot! Grab them—grab them—the devils!
SHUL'GA strikes out with his fists, feet and head, scattering the policemen. VAL'KO, freed for the moment by SHUL'GA'S attach on the Germans, sweeps up from the desk everything on it— desk-set, inkwell, paperweight, and hurls them at his attackers

BRUCKNER

Grab them! Take them away!

SOLIKOVSKY

Grab them!

Two policemen rush into the room. They all jump on VAL'KO and SHUL'GA, swarm over them and begin to beat them and stomp on them

This section of the stage goes dark. Another section is lit. We again see the interior of the cell. SHUL'GA and VAL'KO, their faces and arms bleeding, their clothes in tatters, lie limp on the floor.

VAL'KO

Raising himself painfully

You are a mighty powerful cossack, Matvei—may God give you strength!

SHUL'GA

Also raising himself with difficulty

Andrei, you're not bad yourself, Brother Cossack! Not bad!

Then suddenly break into lusty laughter, occasionally sighing from the pain brought on by the laughter

Andrei, I haven't told you yet how I got caught. I didn't trust Kondratovich because his son is a criminal—while I did trust Ignat Fomin. His family record is clean. . .

VAL'KO

Sitting up in consternation

You trusted a piece of paper more than a man! We keep filling out and filing these forms without noticing how gradually they begin to control us.

SHUL'GA

Aren't there cases of decent fathers who have degenerate sons? This time, in doubting Kondratovich. I didn't trust a good man.

VAL'KO

In a low, ominous voice

Too bad you didn't! . . . *(After a pause)* The fascists may kill you and me. . .but just the same, they're the ones who will in the end perish—not our people! Right, Matvei?

SHUL'GA

That's the holy truth, my friend!

VAL'KO

May the Lord grant happiness to our people, who will live on after us!

*Enter German soldiers, military policemen. They push SHUL'GA
and VAL'KO roughly out of the cell, prodding them with bayonets
and rifles. They take them off to be executed.*

*The stage goes dark. The apron is lit. KLER is now continuing
his interrogation of the badly beaten OLEG.*

KLER

Unable to contain his furious exasperation

Is it possible that your elders didn't teach you that you must draw
your own conclusions from the experience of others?. . . Not to
repeat their mistakes. Didn't the story of Val'ko and Shul'ga
convince you of the uselessness of resistance? Didn't it teach
you anything?!

*The apron goes dark. A section of the stage is lit. We see the
interior of the home of the KOSHEVOYS, where a meeting of
the Young Guards is in session. They look overcome with sorrow.*

OLEG

Winding up his report

. . .All the prisoners were murdered. They buried them. Alive.
And the earth that covered them stirred for quite a while, as though
breathing *their* last breath. . .

SERIOZHA LEVASHOV

Rising

I have an announcement. I want to talk about Ignat Fomin. How
long will we put up with this beast? This Judas betrayed Shul'ga,
Val'ko—and we don't know how many of our miners lie buried
in his black conscience! I propose that we kill him! Delegate
me to do it—I'm going to kill him anyway.

IVAN TURKEVICH

He's right. Ignat Fomin is an informer! He should be hung!
This is my opinion as the Commander of the Young Guard.

OLEG

I-I ag-gree. . .

IVAN TURKEVICH

We've got to string him up. In a place where everyone can see him.
We'll hang a sign on him telling why he was executed. Make an
example of him. We know the fascists will show us no mercy, so
what can we lose? Assign the job to me and Sergei Tiulenin.

OLEG

We must get permission to do this from our older comrades. But first we must know the majority view on this. I'll put to a vote the question about Fomin—then we'll vote on whom to assign.

IVAN TURKEVICH

There's no argument. The case is clear.

OLEG

Yes, it's clear, but just the same we'll take a vote. Who is for the hanging?
All slowly raise their hands.

IVAN TURKEVICH

We'll need some help. . . Are you willing, Zhora Arutinants?

ZHORA

This will be a useful lesson to other scum. Of course I'm willing. But we haven't yet chosen a panel of judges. It needn't drag out the trial. But it is important for the traitor to be tried.

IVAN TURKEVICH

We'll appoint a tribunal.

ZHORA

Let's try him in the name of the people! Under present circumstances, we now represent the people. . .

IVAN TURKEVICH

We'll need one more person.

ZHORA

In my group of five* there's Radik Yurkin. Do you know him? He is from our school. I think he'd do well.

IVAN TURKEVICH

But he's just a boy. He'll get too shook up.

ZHORA

Never mind about that. Our boys don't get shook up that easily. It is we, the older ones, who are always in an emotionally tizzy about something or other. But the younger boys can take it. This one is quite cool, and daring!

*Each Young Guard member works with five (or less) youngsters who are not yet members of the organization.

IVAN TURKEVICH

All right. I agree.

ZHORA

Another thing. Everything is okay with the printer's type.
Instead of printer's ink, my father mixed an original concoction.
It is a perfect substitute.

VOLODYA

And I have already composed the first sentence. It is dedicated
to Zhora. It goes: "Don't be so secretive about Liusya, don't be
so nervous about it—we know the secret of your heart. Yes, yes,
yes." I tried to choose words with the letter "e"—we seem to
have more "e's" than any other letter.

OLEG

That's pretty clever! By the way, do you know that a couple of
more girls have asked to be taken into the Guard.

ZHORA

Among my incomplete "five", there's a youngster who wants to
join. It's the same Radik Yurkin. So far my group of "five"
consists of only one—Radik.

OLEG

We can use our press to print temporary membership cards. We
have the right to accept new members. Our organization is
officially recognized.
Enter VERA, OLEG'S GRANDMOTHER

GRANDMOTHER VERA

How about some tea? I happen to have some ready. I'll call
Valya and Nina—they've had enough guard duty outside. Let
them come in and warm up. And here is some candy for all of
you—five pieces.
*She goes to call the two outside guards. VALYA BORTS and
NINA IVANTSOVA enter*

OLEG

How would you like to hear Moscow?

LIUBKA

What do you mean—Moscow?

OLEG

On one condition—no questions asked! Just have a little patience.

He exits to the adjoining room. From there we hear light static, the sounds of music. Someone speaks in German—fast, frenzied. Then suddenly, a familiar newscaster's voice in Russian.

NEWCASTER'S VOICE

From the Soviet Informburo. News summary for September 7th. . . Evening report. . .

IVAN TURKEVICH

Write it down! Write it down!

ULYANA

We'll issue it tomorrow!

VOLODYA

We'll use our printing press!

NEWCASTER'S VOICE

During September 7th our armies fought fiercely against the enemy forces to the west and southwest of Stalingrad and in the area of Novorossisk and Mozdok. . . There have been no substantial changes on other fronts.

The Young Guards are deeply moved as they listen to this voice from the unoccupied part of their country. In the doorway, unnoticed by anyone, stands GRANDMOTHER VERA.

GRANDMOTHER VERA

Whispering, her voice shaking with emotion
This is our Moscow. . . The heart of our Motherhood. . . Moscow!

This section of the stage goes dark. Another section is dimly lit. It is night. In the semi-darkness we see the figures of three YOUNG GUARDS moving cautiously—the ones who were selected to render the verdict on Ignat Fomin.

IVAN TURKEVICH

He's on duty tonight at the plant—here, near the Gorky School.

ZHORA

There he is! . . . He moves like a cur on a chain.

SERIOZHA LEVASHOV

The bastard!

FOMIN, in a long black coat, the collar raised, walks back and forth, now and then pausing under the wooden arch at the gate to the plant.

THE FATHER

Why did Tiulenin come here yesterday? During curfew time?

VANYA

Who pays any attention to the curfew? Doesn't Nina go out on dates during those hours?

THE FATHER

Smacking the table with his palm

Don't lie! For this—prison! If you don't care to save your own skin, spare your parents grief!

VANYA

I first heard about Fomin just now—from Nina. He deserved what he got—the skunk! You think so, too. I'm not going to lie: I do everything I can to help our people. I haven't told you about it so that you wouldn't worry.

THE FATHER

You forget how we once lived in a barracks, with twelve other families? How we slept on the floor? Your mother and I worked ourselves to the bone for you children. Have you given a thought to her?

VANYA

What am I supposed to do—according to you?

THE FATHER

Go to work. Nina works—you do the same. She's a clerk, does unskilled work. And what do you do?

VANYA

But for whom—for whom am I to work? For the Fritzes? Your other son, my brother, is in the Red Army—and are you telling me to go and help the enemy, so that they can kill him sooner?

THE FATHER

Shouting

But how will you fill your stomach? Will you be better off if the first person you make sacrifices for sells you down the river? You don't know people. But I know them! Everyone has his price. It's every man for himself.

VANYA

That's not true. Did you "have your price" when you helped pack and ship government property to the rear?. . .

IVAN TURKEVICH

Forward!

Before FOMIN has time to scream, SERIOZHA LEVASHOV jumps him and throws him to the ground. The other YOUNG GUARDS run in, and they all surround FOMIN in a tight ring, push a gag into his mouth, and tie his hands and feet with ropes. Looking up at the arch

This would be a good spot.

RADIK YURKIN climbs up to the top of the arch, with a rope

SERIOZHA LEVASHOV

From below

Tie it with a double sailor's knot!

IVAN TURKEVICH

It was a lot easier for him to kill others than it will be to die himself!

SERIOZHA LEVASHOV

To FOMIN

Do you understand what he means, *polizei?* Do you understand!

ZHORA

In the name of the Union of Soviet Socialist Republics, the informer Ignat Fomin is sentenced by this tribunal to die by hanging!

IVAN TURKEVICH

To SERIOZHA

Let me have a pin.

SERIOZHA LEVASHOV

What did you write?

IVAN TURKEVICH

One word—"Traitor!"

We see in the depth of the stage the shadow of the hanged FOMIN. The young people scatter.

ZHORA

Putting his arm around RADIK

How do you feel, Radik?

RADIK

Visibly shaken, but trying to show bravado

RADIK (Cont.)

I want to go to bed. I'm dying of sleep. After all, I'm not used to such late hours. . . (*There's pathos in his words nevertheless*)
The stage goes dark. The apron is lit. KLER'S interrogation of the battered OLEG continues.

KLER

You, just like myself, are an active opponent of cruelty. You, that means, believe that we should treat our enemies like friends. Right? But don't you agree—that what is honorable in this world must occur according to the rules of reciprocity?. . . Why did you hang Ignat Fomin? Why do your partisans kill our soldiers— not in open battle, but at night, sneaking from around corners? I am sure that Ignat Fomin was not killed by one person, but by a whole group. Yet you, it seems, are against such an uneven contest of strength?

OLEG

He speaks slowly, with difficulty. He is in great pain.
I don't know who killed Fomin. And I don't believe that enemies should treat each other as friends. Each side has the right to defend its righteousness. But anyone who begins to kill must face trial. That's the way it has always been. I am sure that's the way it happened with Fomin. And our partisans, although they attack, are in reality defending themselves. More exactly—they are defending their country and their people. Everyone has the right of self-defense.

KLER

Then grant us the same right! We are defending ourselves from the Young Guard, from your partisans. We can put it that way—right?

OLEG

No, we can't. Because you invaded—overran—our homeland, and not we yours.

KLER

With nostalgia and in maudlin tones
Home! . . . It is the most beautiful word in the world! I'd give anything to find myself at home—among my children, among my grandchildren.

OLEG

Casually
Then do go back to them. The sooner the better.. . .

KLER

One of the great sages said that the most ruthless conflict is the conflict between duty and happiness!

OLEG

Matter-of-factly
And who has decided. . .what your duty is?

KLER

Oh, if only we ourselves could determine this! Alas, it is always ordained from on high. But—you and I have now wandered in our conversation into a philosophic maze from which we won't be able to extricate ourselves. Answer me one question—you have created an organization. You began, as you say, to "defend" yourselves from us. But what about your parents? Is it possible that they calmly look on as you risk your lives, as you go to meet death?

OLEG

Different parents react differently to everything.
The apron goes dark. A section of the stage is lit. We are at the home of the ZEMNUKHOVS. The father, ALEXANDER FEDOROVICH, and his son VANYA are sitting at the table. VANYA'S sister NINA rushes in.

NINA

Do you know what happened?—Ignat Fomin is hanging from the arch!!

THE FATHER

What do you mean—hanging?

NINA

They hung him. So he's hanging. A piece of paper is pinned to his coat. There is only one word on it. The people seem to approve.

THE FATHER

What word?

NINA

I didn't read it. Some say, "polizei"—others, "traitor."

THE FATHER

But which is it? Well, we can probably get exact information right here, in our own home. (*Turns to VANYA*) Why do you keep quiet? You are, so to speak, close to that sort of thing.

VANYA

You mean to the police?

THE FATHER

Gruffly

I'm not talking about myself.

VANYA

No, let's talk about *you*! "Every man for himself," you say. What kind of selfishness was it when, while you were sick, you went out there just the same to help load the trucks—worked night after night? Are you the only unselfish exception on earth? That's even against the law of probability.

THE FATHER

Again shouting

I am not trying to prove things scientifically—but according to life itself!

VANYA

Then prove that I'm not right. You won't convince me by shouting. I can shut up. But I'll go on doing what I think is right!
The stage goes dark. The apron is lit. VANYA ZEMNUKHOV is now being interrogated along with OLEG.

KLER

I don't like to use judicial terms. Why say "interrogation" and not just "a talk"? Why call this a "confrontation" and not "a meeting of friends"? Are you two friends?

OLEG

We used to live in the same town. But far from each other. That's all.

KLER

And you had nothing in common?

VANYA

We used to go to the same school. But I'm older than he is. At our ages every year makes a big difference.

KLER

Oh yes, in one's youth and especially in one's boyhood, every year—is an eternity. Just the same, did you have nothing in common? At least, didn't both of you write poetry?

VANYA

I like poetry. Especially Pushkin.

KLER

And Oleg even wrote some? *(To VANYA)* I believe you,
too, composed verse?

VANYA

I did. . . How do you know?

KLER

There was a time when I never entered anyone's room without
knocking, without some warning. Never opened another person's
letters. Even when my wife received them. Now, I am forced to pry into
kids' notebooks and diaries. War dictates its own laws. And makes one
change his habits. *(Loudly, as though losing control over himself)* But
I do it with only one purpose. I want to explain this to you: to
continue to read poetry, and to write it, to love and be loved, one
has to *remain alive*!! Do you hear?! Remain alive! I want to give
you this chance—*to live.* Then help me! *(Calms down)* So, you
composed verses? At least you admit that much.

OLEG

It's hard to find a youth, or a young woman, who doesn't write poetry.

KLER

I agree. Everyone has written at least four lines in his lifetime.
But I'd rather talk about prose. Because I am convinced that
when you planned the escapes of the Russian prisoners you
didn't talk in rhymes. . .

VANYA

We didn't discuss it at all.

KLER

Such an operation could not have come off spontaneously.

OLEG

There are partisans who. . .

KLER

Interrupting, speaks waspishly
I know there are partisans. They don't let us forget about them!
But in this specific case. . .

*The apron goes dark. A section of the stage is lit. We see the back
yard of the Popov house. ANATOLY POPOV and VICTOR PETROV
are standing close together while ANATOLY studies a piece of paper
in his hand—it is the layout of the P.O.W. barracks. ULYANA
joins them, climbing through the fence*

ANATOLY

To VICTOR

Here is Ulyana. Probably with instructions from headquarters. She doesn't come here these days unless. . .

VICTOR

To ULYANA

We've missed you. Thought of going to the housing settlement to look you up.

ULYANA

You mustn't go there. They're rounding people up. Sending them off to Germany. . . *(Noticing the plan)* We need that. Headquarters want you to. . .

ANATOLY

To VICTOR

I told you. . .

ULYANA

You are to be in charge of the operation—to free the war prisoners. . . The ones who work in the forest.
ANATOLY and VICTOR exchange looks.

ANATOLY

Is the guardhouse far from here?

ULYANA

To the right of the road, near the farm.

ANATOLY

And the P.O.W. barracks, I think, is very close—near that grove. . . Do you remember? *(He is referring to a trysting place.)*

ULYANA

Embarrassed

What has it got to do with the grove? We're talking about prisoner barracks.

VICTOR

There used to be a storehouse there. They broke it up into cells and put barbed wire around it.

ULYANA

There's only one guard. I think it's better not to tackle the guardhouse, but only dispose of the guard.

VICTOR

We can take along some tools to cut the wire and do the whole thing quickly, without any sound.

ANATOLY

To ULYANA
What's your opinion?

ULYANA

To ANATOLY, anxiously—she cares for him a lot
Please be careful!. . . *(Embarrassed, she turns to VICTOR)* And you, too, Vitya. And all of the other kids—don't let them take risks—unnecessary ones. At headquarters they beg you not to.
ANATOLY and VICTOR go off. Enter VALYA FILATOVA. She runs to ULYANA and drops to the ground near her. ULYANA is startled. After a pause, softly.
What's wrong, Valiuka?

VALYA FILATOVA

Lifting her head
Ulyana! They're going to drive me off to Germany!

ULYANA

You must escape. . . Yes—you must!

VALYA FILATOVA

But where? My God, where? I have no identity papers.

ULYANA

Valiuchka, my darling, I understand—there are Germans all around us, but this is *our* country. . . It is huge! Everywhere there are the same kind of people as those among whom we grew up. You can find a way out! I'll help you, too. All of us boys and girls will help!

VALYA FILATOVA

And Mama? What are you saying, Ulechka? They'll torture her!

ULYANA

And if they take you off to Germany—do you think that'll be easier on her? Do you think she'll be able to stand that?

VALYA FILATOVA

Ulechka. . . Ulechka. . . Why do you torment me even more?

ULYANA

With anger, and despair

I despise you! Yes, I despise your helplessness, your tears.
There is so much grief all around us—so many healthy, strong,
wonderful people are dying at the front, in torture chambers—
imagine how their wives, their mothers suffer. But everyone
works, struggles! And you. . .you are offered help and you whine,
and even want to be pitied. I don't pity you. No, I don't! *(After
a pause)* Valya! Valiuchka, what good friends we were! My
little heart! *(VALYA sobs)* Think back—did I ever give you
bad advice? Valiuchka! I implore you!

VALYA FILATOVA

No, no. . .you've forsaken me! You lost your affection for me
when you went away—to work for the underground. And
after that there was never again any friendship between us. Do
you think I haven't felt this? And now—now I'm all alone
in the world. . .

ULYANA

Quietly and with calm

Valya, I'll say it to you for the last time. Either you listen
to me. . .then we'll call Anatoly right away and he'll take you
to Victor, to the farm, or. . .

VALYA FILATOVA

Goodbye, Ulechka! Goodbye forever! *(She holds back her sobs
with difficulty and runs off)*

*This section of the stage goes dark. Another section is lit, dimly.
We see ANATOLY and VICTOR lying on the ground near the P.O.W.
barracks. They are concealed from the GUARD, who is pacing
back and forth along the barbed wire fence, at some distance
from their hiding place. They speak to each other in low tones.
It is night.*

ANATOLY

Victor, do you remember this place? You know, it's the same. . .

VICTOR

No, that one was further down. Over there, where the shorefront
gave way. Crumbled right under your feet. I had to swim across
to you, and I kept worrying that the current would pull you
down and carry you right into the whirlpool.

ANATOLY

I was scared to death. I almost lost my breath and choked.

VICTOR

Zhenka Moshkov and I had just come out of the forest and we
saw you struggling. If he hadn't dived in from the cliff, in all
his clothes. . . I would never have been able to drag you to
the shore by myself.

ANATOLY

I know. . . And what has become of Zhenka Moshkov?

VICTOR

He's a second lieutenant in the infantry—and you know how
few of them survive!

ANATOLY

He's quite a guy! He saved my life!—that's for sure!

VICTOR

Looking toward the fence
Well, I'd better get started.

ANATOLY

Yes, the others should be just about ready to cut a passage
through the barbed wire on the other side.

VICTOR

Look, the Guard has turned around. He's standing still. This is
the right moment.
*The GUARD, with his rifle dangling from the shoulder strap,
his hands in his pockets, stands perfectly still, with his back to
the barracks.*

ANATOLY

Shouldn't we both crawl over to him?

VICTOR

Certainly not! I'll get him from behind.
*VICTOR crawls silently over to the GUARD. ANATOLY, his
head raised, watches his comrade. VICTOR leaps up and hits the
GUARD on the head. The GUARD falls to the ground. VICTOR
throws himself on top of him. ANATOLY runs over to help.
From the other side of the building comes the sound of wire
snapping as it is cut.*

ANATOLY

To VICTOR

They've cut open the fence! I'll go inside the barracks. You and the others spread out along the road. Keep close watch! *(He goes to the barracks and kicks open the door)* Comardes!. . . You are free! Escape through the woods to the river. Then spread out along the shore!

A number of ragged and bandaged P.O.W.'s rush out. They thank the Young Guardsmen on the run. One of them hastily embraces ANATOLY

ANATOLY

Shaking him off

Who are you?

ZHEN'KA

In a feeble voice

It's me Anatoly. . . Tolen'ka, don't you recognize me?

ANATOLY

Who—*(Astounded)* You!? Zhen'ka Moshkov!

ZHEN'KA

I recognized your voice. . .

ANATOLY

Zhen'ka! The guy who saved my life! Victor and I were just talking about you. And suddenly. . . It's like in a fairy tale!

ZHEN'KA

Sorrowfully

Fairy tales are nothing like life. . . Life can deal you some rotten hand!

Suddenly there's an explosive burst of fire lighting up the whole sky. The last of the escaping P.O.W.'s can be seen disappearing into the woods.

ANATOLY

It's Sergei Tiulenin—he's set their hayricks on fire. He does this every night now.

ZHEN'KA

Am I really free? Friends. . . *(He covers his face with his hands and sinks to the ground from weakness and emotion)*

ANATOLY

Lifting him

Get up! Hurry! Hurry!

*They run toward the town, ANATOLY supporting him. The
conflagration continues to light up the sky. At a safe distance,
they stop. They are joined by OLEG and NINA IVANTSOVA*

OLEG

Looking at the conflagration

Well done, Sergei! *(To NINA)* If we could only get hold of some
cloth of the same color—scarlet, like those flames!. . .

NINA

What for?

OLEG

Have you forgotten?. . . In a week it'll be the twenty-fifth
anniversary. . . A quarter of a century of Soviet power! We've
got to have banners. . .hang them all over! But where can we
get them now?

NINA

It's simple. We can dye some cloth red. That's a woman's job.
Valya, Olya, Ulya, Liuba and I will take care of it. . .

OLEG

That's a wonderful idea! You deserve a kiss for that. . . *(Elatedly)*
W-would you like me to recite some poems to you?

NINA

Your own?

OLEG

Just listen!. . . No—you'd better read them yourself. . . *(He takes
a few sheets of paper out of his pocket and hands them to her.)*

NINA

Reading, softly

> "Sing, my sweatheart, a battle song,
> Don't lose heart, don't sorrow. . ."

OLEG

N-not out loud. . .to yourself. . .

NINA

And you dedicated this to me? To me—yes!. . . Why didn't you
tell me before that you write—that you are a poet?

OLEG

I was too shy. . . I've been writing for a long time. But I've never shown anything to anyone. Most of all I'm self-conscious because of Vanya. You know how well he writes! But I. . .my rhythm is not steady and I have trouble finding the right words.

NINA

That's not so important. . . Thank you, Oleg!

OLEG

And thank you—for everything. And for the scarlet banners, like that fire. . . *(Points to the conflagration)*
The stage goes dark. The apron is lit. The interrogation of OLEG continues.

KLER

As you people are fond of saying: facts are facts. They are stubborn things. But you are even more stubborn than facts! I know everything without your confessions.

OLEG

Then why are you trying so hard to obtain them?

KLER

You set up not just an action organization—it was a political organization. Membership cards, pledges, dues. You took in new members and dropped others. We want *all* the facts.

OLEG

Whom did we drop? Whom?. . .

KLER

But you did sign some up!
The apron goes dark. A section of the stage is lit. We see a meeting of the Young Guard group.

SERGEI TIULENIN

Pointing to RADIK
He didn't only participate in the execution of the traitor Fomin. Those nights we attacked the fascist truck transport—he behaved like a man!

OLEG

A-are there any questions to be put to Radik Yurkin?

IVAN TURKEVICH

Let him tell us about himself.

OLEG

Give us your biography.

RADIK

I was born in the town of Krasnodon in 1928. I studied at the school named after Gorky. . . That's about all. *(After a pause)* And when the Fritzes came, I stopped studying. . .

IVAN TURKEVICH

Did you fulfill any civic duties?

RADIK

No.

IVAN TURKEVICH

Do you know what the duties of a komsomolets* are?

RADIK

To wipe out the fascist occupiers—until there's not one of them left!

IVAN TURKEVICH

So. . . I consider this fellow fully informed politically.

LIUBKA

We should accept him!

ULYANA

I agree—we must let him join!

OLEG

Who is for accepting Radik Yurkin into the Komsomol?
Everyone raises his hand
It's unanimous. *(To RADIK)* Come here.
RADIK comes over to OLEG
You are joining the Komsomol on the eve of the October anniversary! This is extremely important. . . On instructions from the regional staff-committee, we issue to you a temporary card. And when the Red Army returns, the District Committee will exchange it for a regular one.

RADIK

Exalted

I'll sew it into my jacket. . .and I'll always have it with me. Always!

Komsomolets is a member of the *Komsomol* (The Young Communist League of the Soviet Union), founded in 1918. Members aged 14 to 28 years of age.

OLEG

You may go.

RADIK leaves. OLEG addresses the others

Friends, an announcement. . . To commemorate the Anniversary, we have gathered a sum of money to help the families of front line soldiers. As you know, we earned this money by selling cigarets, matches, and other things like that—and especially gasoline— which we steal from the German trucks. *(After a pause)* And one more announcement. . . This evening we'll have a party to celebrate the great holiday. And tomorrow morning. . . Do you know what will happen tomorrow morning? There will be red banners all over the town! We, we'll hang them up everywhere tonight! Then we'll all gather here. . . And tomorrow. . .

We hear the song "Tomorrow":

> Once more o'er our land the sun has grown dark,
> But it will rise, it will rise once again
> Tomorrow!
>
> Evil the storms that are sweeping the earth,
> But gardens and orchards will flower and bloom
> Tomorrow!
>
> The rule of the world—it eternal shall be,
> Eternal the faith in our fellowmen,
> In tomorrow!
>
> Through all times and all ages always it was hailed
> The word bearing hope for mankind:
> Tomorrow!
>
> I may miss my goal, I may fail, I may fall,
> In the mire I may sink, in the struggle die,
> Tomorrow!
>
> But I know that more than once
> Good people will remember us
> Tomorrow! Tomorrow! Tomorrow! Tomorrow!

While we hear the song, SERIOZHA LEVASHOV and LIUBKA, SERGEI TIULENIN and VALYA BORTS leave to carry out their difficult assignment. The scene of the meeting is darkened.

Soon we see SERIOZHA LEVASHOV and LIUBKA. He helps her climb up to some of the iron posts of the set, then he climbs up too. After putting up a banner and making it secure, they climb down and continue the same procedure. They disappear into the darkness.

On the other side of the stage VALYA is waiting for SERGEI TIULENIN, who now appears.

VALYA

Are you ready? Let's start.

SERGEI TIULENIN

Ready. . . I have some extra ones. Let's put one up on the General Management Building.

VALYA

And how about the Police Headquarters?

SERGEI TIULENIN

By all means. We can use the fire escape ladder.

VALYA

Let's go!

This section of the stage goes dark. Another section is lit. We see the Police Headquarters building. A guard is on duty. VALYA and TIULENIN appear, walking stealthily in the darkness. Right under the nose of the guard, TIULENIN climbs the fire escape ladder. VALYA keeps watch below. TIULENIN hangs up the banner and comes down. They leave. We continue to hear the song "Tomorrow."

This section of the stage goes dark. The apron is lit. We hear LIUBKA'S cries from off-stage. She is being tortured. Now we see German soldiers drag her into KLER'S presence.

KLER

So, you freed the prisoners. . . And you drove away the cattle which we could have used. . . There was some sense in that. But these bits of red cloth? These pieces of pillow cases and sheets? What for?. . .

LIUBKA

She speaks with difficulty, obviously in great pain from the torture
I don't know who hung them up. . . But they are pretty!. . .

KLER

You—are an "actress". You like decorations. But decorations. . . which mean someone's blood? Isn't that a bit too much? It seems to me that these pillow cases are soaked in your blood. Yours. . . personally. . .do you understand? And I feel sorry for you.

LIUBKA

As if she hadn't heard him
I think it was the 7th of November?

KLER

Why don't you say, the eve of your national holiday?

LIUBKA

One can say it that way, too. Because I remember that we danced that day. . . Yes, I remember it all. . .

The apron goes dark. A section of the stage is lit. We see the interior of OLEG'S house, where the Young Guard has gathered to celebrate.

OLEG

Listen, everybody! W-We've just heard the Voice of Moscow! Moscow has sent us greetings on the eve of the Anniversary!

SERIOZHA LEVASHOV strikes the strings of his guitar, then plays a popular foreign fox-trot. Everybody dances. LIUBKA with SERGEI TIURKEVICH, ULYANA with ANATOLY, and OLEG with NINA IVANTSOVA.

GRANDMOTHER VERA

What kind of a dance is this? What kind of dancing did they invent abroad?! *(To LEVASHOV)* Seriozha, let's have a *gopak!*

LEVASHOV strikes up a gopak. OLEG gets hold of his GRANDMOTHER and with surprising agility she dances the Ukranian folk dance with her grandson—the two of them beating out the lively rhythm with their heels.

OLEG

What kind of a grandmother are you—to dance this way?!

GRANDMOTHER VERA

Out of breath
Oh, an old one!

LIUBKA

It's the Ukrainian in her! *(To LEVASHOV)* Seriozha, play our "Pouloshnaya."

Even before LEVASHOV begins to play, LIUBKA is already into this favorite high school dance, and SERGEI TIULENIN comes to join her. They dance dazzlingly.

ULYANA

Bravo, Liubka! She's some dancer!

LIUBKA

Suddenly stopping, speaks sorrowfully
What has become of her, our poor "Pouloshnaya?". . .
LEVASHOV strikes up again, but OLEG stops him.

OLEG

I think it's time to break up. Congratulations to all! And
tomorrow you'll be greeted by our banners. . . And the people
of Krasnodon will say: "This they did for us. . . They remembered
us. We are not forgotten!. . ."
*And all at once the stage is flooded with light, and we see
the red banners waving everyhwere, like tongues of flame. We
hear the frantic blowing of police whistles, the cries of the
maddened Nazis.*
The stage goes dark.
*A small section at the front of the stage is lit. We see OLEG
and LIUTIKOV standing close together, deep in conversation.*

LIUTIKOV

And you burned down the Labor Exchange Center. That's great!

OLEG

With all its files and addresses. . .of those they were going to
herd off to Germany to do slave labor.

LIUTIKOV

But didn't you notify the groups too openly about this
operation? Another thing: the pasting up of leaflets—didn't too
many take part in this?

OLEG

I thought the more, the better!

LIUTIKOV

Quietly, with emphasis
We can say. . .yes, you've grown: the organization has developed. . .
and you with it. This is good. But don't accept a single other
person without my permission. Not one! *(After a pause)* By
the way, how are things now at the Gorky Club?

OLEG

It doesn't exist any more.

LIUTIKOV

Then go to the German authorities and get permission to turn
it into a social club.

OLEG

I don't understand. . .

LIUTIKOV

It's simple—a youth club for the local population. Organize the
boys and girls who are non-political, who think only about fun,
who are bored. . . Tell the Fritzes that you want to help bring
the kind of culture to the people that would be in the spirit of
their new order. And let the youngsters dance and amuse
themselves under our guidance, or else they will drift away
and get rotten ideas into their empty heads.

OLEG

What good will it do?

LIUTIKOV

That's the way I thought you'd feel about it. You don't quite
understand what I'm trying to say. But if you did understand,
you'd do me a great favor—me and the entire organization!
Are you afraid—to dirty yourself? The unsullied will remain clean.
This has to be done so that the club will remain under our control!
And the programs you'll plan for it will be—"neutral."

*The stage goes dark. Another section is lit. We see the interior
of the new club. The lights are bright. We hear applause. There
is a "revue" in full swing. SERGEI TIULENIN is the M.C.*

SERGEI TIULENIN

With feigned enthusiasm

We have been privileged to enjoy the performance of the artist
of the Regional Lugansky Variety Stage. . . Liubov Shevtsova!
Her accompanist is Valya Borts!

*Applause. LIUBKA runs onto the stage to take a curtain call.
Wild applause, developing into an ovation. TIULENIN waits
for the applause to die down, then announces the
next number:*

And now, some gypsy ballads!. . . Vladimir Osmukhin!. . . His
accompanist, guitarist Seriozha Levashov!

VOLÓDYA

Sings a parody of sentimental gypsy ballads, ending:

> "Oh, tell us, dusky vagabond,
>   Where is your birthplace, whence do you come?. . ."

*Stormy applause. Now the sound of hastily revved-up motors and of
exploding bombs drowns out the applause. We hear voices off-stage:
"They are ours!! It's our planes that are bombing—our own planes!"*

*Quick blackout of this section of the stage. Another section
is lit. We see the office of police chief Bruckner. Present are
BRUCKNER, BALDER, SOLIKOVSKY, FENBONG, SOLDIERS.
VANYA ZEMNUKHOV is being interrogated.*

BRUCKNER

Come over here! *(Two SOLDIERS push VANYA forward)*
Are you Vanya Zemnukhov?

VANYA

Yes, that's me.

SOLIKOVSKY

You're finished! *(He drags over to BRUCKNER'S desk a small boy
who was not visible before. He points to VANYA)* Is he the one?

BOY

He. . . Yes. . .

SOLIKOVSKY

To VANYA

Did you hear? Now tell us who helped you. Make it snappy!

VANYA

I don't know what you are talking about.

SOLIKOVSKY

Looking around at the others

Did you hear that? That's the kind of education Soviet power gives
them! *(Pushing the BOY toward VANYA)* Aren't you ashamed?
You should take pity on the boy. He's paying for your sins.
(Pointing to a corner of the room) Take a look—what's lying
there? *(VANYA looks toward the corner and sees an open sack
full of New Year presents)* Our soldiers' New Year's gifts! How
did they get to your club! And to the marketplace?

VANYA

I don't know what that has to do with me. And I've never seen
this boy before.

BALDER

My superior, the Meister *(He gestures toward FENBONG)* orders
you to tell him how many times you attacked our motor transport,
with what purpose in mind, who worked with you, what else you
did. . . You are to tell everything! Everything!

VANYA

Adjusting his glasses

How could I have attacked the car with the presents when I'm so nearsighted that I can't even see you? Everyone knows that!

BALDER

You are to answer the Meister's questions and address yourself to him.

BRUCKNER

Waving his hand

To Fenbong!

FENBONG and the SOLDIERS throw themselves on VANYA and knock him down. This section of the stage goes dark. Another section is lit. We see a meeting of the YOUNG GUARD. The members surround OLEG.

OLEG

No matter how it hurts, no matter how hard it is to do it, we must give up all thought of remaining here until the Red Army recaptures the town—of helping them—of even doing what we had planned for tomorrow. . . Otherwise we're done for, and we'll ruin all of our contacts as well. The fascists have penetrated the center of our organization. Even if they don't find out anything else, besides about the New Year's gift, they'll seize everyone connected with the club. And many who are not involved. . . So what must we do? Leave. Leave town. We fought honorably, and we have the right to disperse with the feeling of having fulfilled our duty. We did all we could. . .

The young people begin to take leave of each other. Someone among the girls can be heard weeping quietly. OLEG and SERGEI TIULENIN are in the forefront of the group.

To SERGEI

Do you understand why?

SERGEI TIULENIN

Nods

Someone might break down under. . . Is that it?

OLEG

Yes. . . It's better not to talk about it. Not to trust when you don't know. . . They are probably torturing them already—and we are still free.

OLEG (Cont.)

NINA IVANTSOVA impulsively embraces and kisses OLEG
Do you remember how I once wanted to kiss you?

NINA

I remember. I remember everything. I remember more than you
think. I'll always remember you!. . . I'll wait for you!. . .
*This section of the stage goes dark. The apron is lit. We again
see KLER and OLEG*

KLER

I have spent many hours on these talks. . .with you. I thought
that you loved your mother, your grandmother, Nina Ivantsova. . .
I thought that you loved life! But I am now concluding. . . How
could you have sewn your Komsomol membership card into your
coat and so stupidly have gotten caught because of it, if you really
loved life?. . . It's better, I would say, to part with the card rather
than with your life!. . . After all, of what value is that piece
of cardboard?

OLEG

Quietly and emotionally
What value. . .this piece of cardboard?!
*We hear again the song, "Tomorrow"—the words: "But I believe
that the sun will rise. . ." And suddenly something baffling
happens to the "cultivated," discursive KLER. He bolts from his
chair and, his face contorted with rage, he shouts:*

KLER

Fanatics! . . . Execute them? Shoot them?. . . No. . . That's too
light a punishment! Into the coal pit with them! Down the
shaft! The coal pit! And the coal trolleys down on top of them!
The coal trolleys!. . .
The stage is lit.
*We see the members of the Young Guard being dragged to the mine
shaft. Some walk with calm pride, others resist desperately.
They are thrown down the shaft. We hear the clang and thud of
the iron trolleys thrown down on top of them. And the song "In
the Name of the Fallen in Battle" soars above the horror*

> Once we were live, like the tides,
> Once we were quick, like the tides.
> Now we are—in legends of gloried days. . .
> Now we are—in granite and bronze,
> Now we are—in stories and verse,
> Now we are—in the silence of tombs. . .

In sketching with the players the psychological line of the interrogation-combat, it is useful to point out the play's major events. The play is shaped as a complex composition with a multiplicity of episodes linked, not by a sequential development, but by the inner rhythm of the narrative. The various scenes are links in the overall chain representing the struggle of the young guardsmen and the underground organization against the fascist invaders. The counteraction is Kler's psychological "counter-attack" with its aim, by means of incontrovertible logic and brilliant demagogy, of undermining in his young enemies their belief in kindness, in the sacredness of such concepts as honor, freedom, love of one's homeland.

It is important to take special note of the opening scene, in which we meet the German officers serving under Gestapo General Kler. It is essential to convey that the invaders are sure of their victory. They make themselves at home. They have come to stay. Kler is sure in advance of the success of the interrogation—after all, he'll be dealing with adolescents.

Apart from the main events, there are numerous episodes in the play directly tied in with the activities of the Young Guard. They help broaden and deepen the inner reality of these events, to round them out, and they help the audience to grasp the play's overall meaning. These less central episodes are important also because, as they expand the play's theme, drawing into the circle of events new characters and situations, they lend the dramatic work a lifelike atmosphere and theatrical effectiveness. According to Stanislavsky, such scenes are the "little bridges" which the playwright erects between one major event and another.

A few words about Kler. Under no circumstances must the character of Kler be simplified, crudely acted, or made to appear stupid. This is a clever, forceful and far-seeing enemy. He is skilled at psychological combat, conducting the interrogation with competence. It is important to select the actor for this role with utmost care, for the theme and rhythm of the performance are largely in his hands.

The players taking the roles of the young guardsmen, whenever it is at all possible, should be the ages of the boys and girls in the Young Guard. This will lend much credibility to everything occuring on the stage.

It is not advisable to use a complicated and cumbersome staging for this play. Its form is simplified: a few steps, and the hero moves before our eyes (that is, in the view of the audience) from Kler's interrogation to Liubka's house, to the Osmukhin apartment, and so forth. The interrogation should be conducted on the stage apron. A wooden armchair for Kler and a stool for Oleg are all that is necessary. On the stage only the most necessary props need to be used—only props that the players use in the course of the scene. It is unnecessary to lower the curtain after each scene.

It is inadvisable to encumber the play with special effects either for dramatic expressiveness or for the super-realistic enactment of roles, or with the physical verisimilitude of props.

two world outlooks. Herein is the thematic and ideational content, the core of the play and what determines the conception of its staging.

In the process of the face-to-face interrogation, Kler strives to understand what these youngsters are made of, what caused them to undertake what was, from his point of view, such a senseless and insane opposition to the fascist war machine. He wants to understand what gives these boys and girls their spiritual strength and convictions, fortitude and faith.

For Kler, the struggle of the young guardsmen is a sort of "model" which he hopes will give him an insight into the nature of the Russian miracle—the nature of the resistance of the Soviet nation, the equal of which the Nazis had nowhere encountered. Youth, he knows, experiences a rage to live such as an individual does not feel at any other stage of life. Kler tempts his victims with the possibility of being spared, of survival. His weapon is logic, the sober and cold logic of an experienced and shrewd demagogue. The choice, as he presents it to them, is, on the one hand, life; on the other, what he cynically regards as meaningless symbols: "But these bits of red cloth? These pieces of pillow-cases and sheets? What purpose did that serve?"

The whole play serves as the answer. It reveals the broad spectrum of the resistance of the Soviet people, including the underground youth, to the fascist invaders. The interrogations cause the young heros to recall, to sort out the recent past in their minds, without revealing anything to Kler.

The play has the structure of a symphony in which two motifs are juxtaposed: the theme of Soviet love of country, youth, and life, and the theme of fascist inhumanity, bearing death.

Herein is the essence of the play's dramatic conflict. The scenes of the cross-examination serve as a springboard for the action scenes throughout the play, and together they must build in the spectator's consciousness as a continuing combat. It is important to make sure that while returning again and again to the face-to-face encounter of Kler and his opponents, the director does not each time begin the action from the beginning. With each ensuing scene the action takes on an ever tenser rhythm, culminating with the execution of the young guardsmen and the defeat of Kler. Yes, his defeat. He believes that his logic has to shatter the hopes of these "reckless" boys and girls. He seeks reasonableness in their actions, not understanding that for Oleg Koshevoy it is more reasonable to die with honor then to betray his friends and his ideals in order to survive.

After using every psychological device on his prisoners, Kler in the end drops his mask, shows his true face and shouts hysterically: "Execute them? Shoot them? No! That would be too easy on them! Throw them down the mine!" And therein is his defeat. The psychological combat with the experienced Kler is won by the young guardsmen. And Kler is forced to admit to himself the failure of his strategy, seeing in it the future defeat of the fascist war machine.

AFTERWORD: A NOTE TO THE DIRECTOR

On the 14th of February, 1943, the Soviet Army in its pursuit of the routed fascist forces after its victory at Stalingrad, liberated Krasnodon, a small coal-mining town in the Donets Basin. It was then that the tragedy which took place there just before the town's recapture became known.

An underground youth organization had been active in Krasnodon. Boys and girls of sixteen and seventeen had set up a wide network of groups which functioned as a single organization. They named it "The Young Guard." Freeing Soviet war prisoners, distributing leaflets urging resistance, destroying enemy supplies, burning down Nazi headquarters and slave-labor recruiting centers—these were only some of the exploits of the Young Guard. Finally the fascists succeeded in tracking them down. More than one hundred persons linked to the organization were arrested.

Then began the interrogation and torture of these young prisoners. In the end, most of them were thrown to their death down a mine shaft, just before the retreat of their executioners under the blows of the Soviet Army. Others were taken to the edge of town and shot. In the Rovenki district they shot Oleg Koshevoy, the head of the youth organization, and Liubov Shevtzova, who had posed as a collaborationist—both seventeen-year-olds.

A special Commission was sent to Krasnodon from Moscow soon after the tragic story became known. For several months it gathered facts on the background and war activities of the boys and girls in the Young Guard.

The title, Hero of the Soviet Union, was conferred posthumously on Oleg Koshevoy, Ivan Zemnukhov, Sergei Tiulenin, Liubov Shevtsova, Ulyana Gromova. Twenty other outstandingly active members of the organization were also awarded posthumously the Order of the Great Patriotic War, and the rest of the young victims were awarded medals as Partisans of the Great Patriotic War.

To memorialize their martyrdom, the Komsomol asked Alexander Fadeev, a major Russian writer, to write a book about the Krasnodon boys and girls in the Young Guard. They passed on to him all the materials and documents relating to the group's work and to its individual members. Fadeev spent a month in Krasnodon, met with relatives and friends of the victims, and with members of the organization who had escaped their fate. Thus was written the famous novel *The Young Guard,* which has become in its own way a monument to the heroism of the youthful partisans.

Many years later, the writer for young people, Anatoly Aleksin, and the Moscow Central Children's Theatre turned back to Fadeev's documentary novel, and resurrected the brief but glorious life of the Krasnodon young guardsmen.

The playwright begins his story about the Young Guard as though from the end. The Gestapo General Kler conducts the interrogation. Many members of the Young Guard have been arrested. The organization has been crushed. But the play represents not so much an interrogation as a clash of ideas, the polarity of

KLER

Slowly and in a tone of utter hopelessness, to Kurt

If you and I, Kurt, had such children, such grandchildren. . .such children and grandchildren. . .we could win this war.

KURT

But we are winning!

KLER

Almost inaudibly

You only imagine it. . .

The song, "In the Name of the Fallen in Battle" continues. It gains in volume and intensity, filling the whole stage, the entire auditorium. And the YOUNG GUARDS reappear in the depth of the stage. They come forward, shoulder to shoulder, walking to the rhythm of the song. Then, facing the audience when they reach the very edge of the apron, they address it with the words:

> We give thanks to you, our heirs,
> For your loyal memory, our heirs,
> We give thanks too for the promise of new dawns!
>
> Not in vain did we scorn and mock death,
> Not in vain our tears and our wrath. . .
> Not in vain our songs. And our vows.
>
> You now have the gift of life,
> Of a long and a splendid life. . .
> You who are—our reincarnation,
> You who are—our consolation,
> You who are our glory! And our hope!

The End

The lyrics by the poet Robert Rozhdestvensky, set to music by the composer Oscar Feltzman, are in the favorite idiom of our contemporary youth, and they add special emotional color to the dramatic action. They can be used as effective "lyrical commentaries," and played on a tape.

Pavel Khomsky

Director of the Young Guard for the Central Children's Theatre of Moscow